by Stuart Schwartz and Craig Conley

Consultant:
Robert J. Miller, Ph.D.
Professor of Special Education
Mankato State University

CAPSTONE
HIGH/LOW BOOKS
an imprint of Capstone Press
Mankato, Minnesota

Capstone High/Low Books are published by Capstone Press
818 North Willow Street • Mankato, MN 56001
http://www.capstone-press.com

Library of Congress Cataloging-in-Publication Data
Schwartz, Stuart, 1945–
    Buying insurance/by Stuart Schwartz and Craig Conley.
    p. cm. — (Life skills)
    Includes bibliographical references and index.
    Summary: Explains the different kinds of insurance, including automobile, health,
disability, life, homeowner's, and renter's, discusses how to choose which type to buy,
and provides advice on choosing an insurance agent.
    ISBN 0-7368-0045-X
    1. Insurance—Juvenile literature. [1. Insurance.] I. Conley, Craig, 1965- .
II. Title. III. Series: Schwartz, Stuart, 1945–   Life skills.
HG8052.5.S39   1999
368—dc21   98-35116
        CIP
        AC

Editorial Credits

Christy Steele, editor; James Franklin, cover designer and illustrator; Michelle L.
  Norstad, photo researcher

Photo credits

All photographs by Barb Stitzer Photography

Table of Contents

Chapter 1 Insurance 5

Chapter 2 Automobile Insurance 7

Chapter 3 Automobile Insurance Coverage 9

Chapter 4 Health Insurance 11

Chapter 5 Disability Insurance 13

Chapter 6 Life Insurance 15

Chapter 7 Homeowner's Insurance 17

Chapter 8 Renter's Insurance 19

Chapter 9 Getting Quotes 21

Chapter 10 Deductibles 23

Chapter 11 Choosing an Insurance Company .. 25

Chapter 12 Meeting Insurance Needs 27

Words to Know 28

To Learn More 29

Useful Addresses 30

Internet Sites 31

Index 32

Chapter 1

Insurance

People buy insurance to protect themselves in case of unexpected expenses. Insurance is a contract between a person and an insurance company. The person pays money to an insurance company. In exchange, the insurance company agrees to pay some or all of the person's unexpected expenses. Unexpected expenses can come from events such as car accidents or floods.

People receive policies when they buy insurance. Policies describe the agreements between people and their insurance companies.

Each policy describes coverage. Coverage is the expenses the insurance company agrees to pay. A policy also lists the requirements for receiving payment for the expenses. People should read their policies carefully. They should ask questions if they do not understand their policies.

People can buy insurance to protect almost anything. Some people even buy insurance for their pets. People should think about which items they would like to protect with insurance.

Some people buy insurance for their pets.

Chapter 2

Automobile Insurance

Automobile insurance provides coverage for unexpected automobile expenses. Automobile insurance policies list information about the insurance people buy.

Every car owner must buy liability insurance. A liability is something a person is responsible for under law. People need liability insurance in case they cause an accident. Their insurance then will pay most of the expenses of any accident victims. Car owners need this protection in case someone sues them for damages they cause.

Some states require people to buy no-fault insurance. No-fault coverage protects the car owner no matter who causes an accident. The insurance company pays the policy holders for any expenses.

Many people buy other types of insurance too. Collision insurance covers car repairs for damage caused by accidents. Comprehensive insurance covers other kinds of damages such as car theft or dents left by hail.

Automobile insurance provides coverage for unexpected automobile expenses.

Chapter 3

Automobile Insurance Coverage

People can choose to buy different types of automobile insurance coverage. People choose the amount of coverage they want to buy. The car owners must pay any expenses over the amount of coverage they have purchased.

Personal injury coverage protects a person from medical expenses due to accidents. The insurance company pays part or all of the hospital costs. It also pays funeral costs if the person dies.

Property damage coverage is automobile insurance that pays for damage to property. For example, the insurance company pays if a driver damages fences, lawns, or houses.

The cost of an automobile insurance policy depends on the kinds of insurance and coverage a person buys. The cost also depends on the value of a person's car. Expensive cars cost more to insure than inexpensive cars. An insurance company must pay more to replace or repair expensive cars.

Expensive cars cost more to insure than inexpensive cars.

Chapter 4

Health Insurance

Health insurance covers part or all of a person's doctor, hospital, and medicine bills. For example, a hospital stay may cost several hundred dollars per day. Insurance helps people pay for the care they need.

Many people have two kinds of health insurance. Basic medical insurance covers doctor bills and hospital bills. It also covers surgical bills when a person needs an operation. It pays for hospital care and treatment such as medical tests and medicine.

Major medical insurance is another type of health insurance. It pays for large expenses that basic medical insurance does not cover. It pays for extended hospital stays and certain treatments.

Some people buy individual health insurance. Others buy health insurance as part of a group. Most large companies offer health insurance for their employees. Workers usually pay part of their medical costs. This is called a co-payment. Companies pay for the insurance policies.

Health insurance covers part or all of people's doctor, hospital, and medicine costs.

Chapter 5

Disability Insurance

Some people buy disability insurance. People with disability insurance have protection if they become disabled and unable to work.

The insurance pays a percentage of their salaries to policy holders who are unable to work. The insurance company pays until the policy holders can return to work again. There usually is a limit on how long the insurance company will pay for disabilities. But some policies guarantee that the insurance company will pay as long as doctors say policy holders cannot do their regular jobs.

Insurance policies list important details about disability insurance. For example, the policy may say that people cannot collect disability benefits until a certain amount of time has passed. People might have to wait 30 days or more to receive benefits.

Some companies offer disability insurance to their employees. Other workers buy their own disability insurance.

Insurance policies list important details about disability insurance.

Chapter 6

Life Insurance

Some people buy life insurance. Life insurance pays money to a beneficiary when a policy holder dies. The policy holder chooses a beneficiary to receive benefits from the life insurance policy.

There are two kinds of life insurance. Term life insurance covers a person for a certain length of time. For example, a term life insurance policy might cover 10 years of a person's lifetime. That person would need to buy a new policy after the 10-year period ends.

Whole life insurance covers a person until the person dies. Whole life insurance is more expensive than term life insurance.

Many people buy life insurance to support their families or friends. Parents may want to leave money to their children. People may want to leave money to help their families pay for funerals.

People buy life insurance to support their families.

Chapter 7

Homeowner's Insurance

People who own houses need homeowner's insurance. Homeowner's insurance policies pay part of the costs for damaged homes.

Homeowner's insurance also covers the contents of a house. The insurance company will pay to replace any stolen items. It also will replace belongings damaged in a fire or a storm.

Homeowner's insurance also covers personal liability. A homeowner is responsible for visitors' safety. The homeowner might be sued if people fall and hurt themselves.

Insurance companies will not pay to replace possessions unless people can prove the value of these items. People should keep records of what they own. They should write down the model numbers and the serial numbers of their possessions. They also should take photographs of each room. They then will be able to ask for the proper amount from their insurance company. People should keep these records in a safe place.

People should take photographs of each room to prove the value of their possessions.

Chapter 8

Renter's Insurance

People who rent houses or apartments can buy renter's insurance. Renter's insurance covers a renter's belongings. The insurance company will pay to repair or replace damaged items.

Renter's insurance does not cover damage to a renter's building or apartment. The renter must take care of walls, carpets, or cabinets. Renters have to pay for any damage they cause to their apartments.

Renters should keep a record of their possessions just as home owners do. They should take photographs of their property. Renters should write down the model and serial numbers of their possessions.

Renters should write down the model and serial numbers of their possessions.

Chapter 9

Getting Quotes

It is important to be a careful shopper for insurance. People will receive better protection if they shop carefully. They also can save money by shopping for the best deal.

People find the best insurance deals by getting quotes from many insurance companies. A quote gives them the estimated price that insurance companies charge for different policies.

People should ask insurance agents for copies of the policies they are interested in purchasing. They should read each policy carefully and compare what each one offers. People should choose the best policy for the least money.

People find the best insurance deals by getting quotes from many insurance companies.

Chapter 10

Deductibles

People should find out how much the deductible is on each policy. A deductible is the amount of expenses a policy holder must pay before the insurance pays anything.

People can choose the amount of their deductibles. For example, a person might choose to have a $500 deductible. That means they must pay the first $500 if they have an accident, become ill, or have property damage. The insurance company pays the remaining costs.

People should compare the deductibles of different policies. They should decide on the amount of deductible they can afford. Policies with high deductibles cost less than policies with low deductibles. People with high deductibles pay less for their insurance because the insurance company's risk is lower. Insurance companies do not have to pay as much in damages to policy holders with high deductibles.

People should decide what deductible they can afford.

Chapter 11

Choosing an Insurance Company

Insurance agents can answer people's questions. Agents can help people decide what kinds of insurance they need. People should choose an insurance company with helpful insurance agents who answer questions honestly.

People need to talk with agents to see which insurance companies meet their needs. People should look for a company that has been in business for a long time. People also can check with the Better Business Bureau to make sure the insurance company is honest.

People should choose insurance companies with helpful agents.

Chapter 12

Meeting Insurance Needs

People should know what kind of coverage they need. They then should make sure insurance policies meet their needs before buying them. They should read policies carefully and know what the insurance covers. People should understand the advantages and disadvantages of each kind of insurance.

People must decide what type of insurance policies they can afford. Their insurance companies will send bills for the insurance. The amounts people pay are called premiums. It is important to pay insurance premiums on time. Insurance companies may cancel policies if payments are late.

People who have a good safety record receive lower insurance premiums than those who do not. For example, safe drivers often receive lower insurance rates than unsafe drivers. An insurance company may raise the insurance rates of people who have had car accidents or speeding tickets.

It is important to pay insurance premiums on time.

Words to Know

beneficiary (ben-uh-FISH-uhr-ee)—a person who receives benefits from a life insurance policy

benefit (BEN-uh-fit)—a service an insurance company provides

coverage (KUHV-rij)—the expenses that an insurance company agrees to pay

deductible (di-DUHK-tuh-buhl)—an expense a policy holder must pay

insurance (in-SHU-ruhnss)—a contract between a person and an insurance company

liability (lye-uh-BI-luh-tee)—something a person is responsible for under law

policy (POL-uh-see)—a written agreement between a person and an insurance company

premium (PREE-mee-uhm)—the amount a person pays for insurance

quote (KWOTE)—an estimated price for insurance

To Learn More

Enteen, Robert. *Health Insurance: How to Get It, Keep It, or Improve What You've Got.* New York: Paragon House, 1992.

Garner, John C. *Health Insurance Answer Book.* New York: Aspen Publishers, 1998.

Humber, Wilson J. *Buying Insurance: Maximum Protection at Minimum Cost.* Chicago: Moody Press, 1994.

Scott, David L. *The Guide to Buying Insurance.* Old Saybrook, Conn.: Globe Pequot Press, 1994.

Useful Addresses

American Insurance Association
1130 Connecticut Avenue NW
Washington, DC 20036

I.C.T. Insurance Consulting
2 Bloor Street West, Suite 100-538
Toronto, Ontario M4W 3E2
Canada

Independent Insurance Agents of America
127 South Peyton Street
Alexandria, VA 22314

Insurance Information Institute
110 William Street
New York, NY 10038

Internet Sites

Better Business Bureau
http://www.bbb.org

Consumer Insurance Guides
http://www.iiaany.com/constips.htm

Health Insurance Terms
http://www.jalden.com/Website/netdef.html

Insurance Canada
http://www.insurance-canada.ca/

Insurance News Network
http://www-002.connix.com/resources.html

Life Insurance Needs Calculator
http://www.1stquote.com/Insurance_Needs.htm

Index

automobile insurance, 7, 9

beneficiary, 15
Better Business Bureau, 25

collision insurance, 7
comprehensive insurance, 7
coverage, 5, 9, 27

deductible, 23
disability insurance, 13

health insurance, 11
homeowner's insurance, 17

insurance agent, 25

liability, 7, 17
life insurance, 15

no-fault insurance, 7

personal injury insurance, 9
policy, 5, 7, 9, 11, 13, 15, 17, 21, 23, 27
premiums, 27

quote, 21

term life insurance, 15

whole life insurance, 15

This LAND

SO-AAB-57

60
WAYS

Farmers Can Protect Surface Water

Michael Hirschi

Robert Frazee

George Czapar

Doug Peterson

Produced by Information Technology and Communication Services
College of Agricultural, Consumer and Environmental Sciences
University of Illinois Extension, University of Illinois at Urbana-Champaign

**Made possible with funding from the Illinois Environmental Protection Agency
through Section 319 of the Clean Water Act**

This publication was coordinated by *IDEA — Information Development for Extension Audiences,* a collaborative effort initiated by the North Central Cooperative Extension Services to increase the efficiency and effectiveness of developing, producing, and/or marketing educational products nationwide. Publications are subject to peer review and prepared as a part of Cooperative Extension Activities in cooperation with the Cooperative State Research Education and Extension Services (CSREES)– US Department of Agriculture, Washington, D.C. The following states cooperated in making this publication available. For additional copies contact the publishing university.

For copies of this and other North Central Regional Extension resources contact the distribution office of the university listed below for your state. If your university is not listed, contact the producing university (marked with an asterisk).

*University of Illinois
Information Technology and
   Communication Services
Taft House
1401 Maryland
Urbana, IL 61801
(217)333-2007

Iowa State University
Extension Distribution Center
119 Printing & Pub. Bldg.
Ames, IA 50011-3171
(515)294-5247

Lincoln University
Cooperative Extension Service
900 Moreau Drive
Jefferson City, MO 65101
(314)681-5557

Michigan State University
Bulletin Office
10B Ag. Hall
East Lansing, MI 48824-1039
(517)355-0240

University of Minnesota
Distribution Center
20 Coffey Hall
1420 Eckles Avenue
St. Paul, MN 55108-6064
(612)625-8173

Ohio State University
Publications Office
385 Kottman Hall
2021 Coffey Road
Columbus, OH 43210-1044
(614)292-1607

University of Wisconsin
Cooperative Extension
   Publications
Room 170
630 West Mifflin Street
Madison, WI 53715-2609
(608)262-3346

*Publishing University

In cooperation with *IDEA (Information Development for Extension Audiences).*

Issued in furtherance of Cooperative Extension work, Acts of Congress of May 8 and June 30, 1914, in cooperation with the U.S. Department of Agriculture and Cooperative Extension Services of Illinois, Indiana, Iowa, Kansas, Michigan, Minnesota, Missouri, Nebraska, North Dakota, Ohio, South Dakota, and Wisconsin. Dennis R. Campion, Interim Director, Cooperative Extension Service, University of Illinois at Urbana-Champaign, Urbana, Illinois 61801.

August 1997

Library of Congress Catalog Card Number:
ISBN 1-883097-15-0

This publication is printed with soybean ink on recycled paper.
    7.5M—8-97—92332—PP

This Land series coordinators: Michael Hirschi, UI Department of Agricultural Engineering; Doug Peterson and Gary Beaumont, Information Technology and Communication Services.

Technical coordinators: Michael Hirschi, UI Department of Agricultural Engineering; Robert Frazee, natural resources management educator, and George Czapar, integrated pest management educator, University of Illinois Extension.

Writer: Doug Peterson

Editor: Phyllis Picklesimer

Designers: Marisa R. Meador, Gerald E. Barrett

Technical illustrator: M.R. Greenberg

Support staff: Irene Miles

Indexer: Barbara E. Cohen

Photo credits:

Page	
1	Information Technology and Communication Services, University of Illinois
16	David Riecks, Information Technology and Communication Services
31-32	Natural Resources Conservation Service–Iowa
33	Natural Resources Conservation Service–Kansas
97	USDA-Natural Resources Conservation Service
105	Kent Mitchell, University of Illinois
106	Michael Hirschi, University of Illinois
117	National Cattlemen's Beef Association, Englewood, Colorado
122	Robert Frazee, University of Illinois
153	David Riecks
165	Michigan Milk Producers Association, Novi, Michigan
196	David Riecks
233	*Sidney Daily News*, Sidney, Ohio
255	University of Illinois
260	Hinze Consulting, Inc., Juniata, Nebraska
265	David Riecks
266	David Riecks
274	Jerry and Diane Nibarger, Chillicothe, Missouri
282	David Riecks

Technical reviewers:

The following people reviewed drafts of the text in its entirety.

University of Illinois at Urbana-Champaign
George Czapar, Extension educator, integrated pest management
Robert Frazee, Extension educator, natural resources management
Michael Hirschi, Extension specialist, soil and water

Illinois Environmental Protection Agency
Christy Trutter, Division of Water Pollution Control

The following people reviewed portions of the text.

University of Illinois at Urbana-Champaign
Ed Ballard, Extension educator, animal systems
Mike Bolin, Extension specialist, forest management
Mel Bromberg, Extension specialist, water and health
Don Bullock, associate professor, crop production
Bill Campbell, Extension educator, farm systems
Rick Farnsworth, Extension specialist, natural resources economics
Ted Funk, Extension specialist, farm structures
Carroll Goering, professor, agricultural engineering
Don Graffis, Extension specialist, forage crops
Michael Gray, Extension specialist, field crops, entomology
Robert Hoeft, Extension specialist, soil fertility
Rob Hornbaker, Extension specialist, farm management
C.J. (Jim) Kaiser, associate professor emeritus, forage crop production and
    pasture management
Ellery Knake, Extension specialist, weed science
David Kovacic, associate professor, landscape architecture, natural resources and
    environmental sciences
Marshal McGlamery, Extension specialist, weed science
Kent Mitchell, professor, agricultural engineering
Emerson Nafziger, Extension specialist, crop production
David Pike, Extension specialist, pesticides
Michael Plumer, Extension educator, natural resources management
John Siemens, Extension specialist, power and machinery
Bill Simmons, Extension specialist, soil and water management
Loyd Wax, USDA/ARS research agronomist
Rick Weinzierl, Extension specialist, entomology
Robert Wolf, Extension specialist, pesticide applicator training

Illini FS, Inc.
Mark Schluter, VRT coordinator/service manager

Illinois Department of Agriculture
Terry Donohue, supervisor, Office of Soil and Water Conservation
Warren Goetsch, chief, Bureau of Environmental Programs

Illinois Environmental Protection Agency
Dale W. Brockamp, agricultural engineer

Illinois Hazardous Waste Research and Information Center
Dan Kraybill, technical assistance engineer

Illinois State Water Survey
Don Roseboom, director of the nonpoint pollution program

Iowa State University
Wendy Wintersteen, interim director, Extension to Agriculture and Natural
    Resources

John Deere
Wayne Smith, project manager

National Soil Tilth Laboratory
Jerry Hatfield, director

Natural Resources Conservation Service
Harry Means, Illinois state conservation engineer
Jerry Misek, district conservationist
Brett Roberts, conservation agronomist
Leon Wendte, district conservationist

The Ohio State University
Clive Edwards, entomologist

University of Nebraska
Leon Higley, associate professor, entomology

Also, thanks to the following people who helped arrange specific farmer profiles: Roger Bender, Extension agent and assistant professor, agriculture and natural resources, The Ohio State University Extension; Larry W. Bledsoe, entomologist, Purdue University Cooperative Extension Service; Ted Louden, Extension specialist, agricultural engineering, Michigan State University; and Mark Loux, Extension specialist, weed science, The Ohio State University Extension.

Contents

Making progress on the waterfront 1

Managing surface cover

1. Distribute residue evenly at harvest 6

   The Great Terrain Robbery: The erosion process 9

2. Avoid fall tillage 11

   No-till boom continues 13

   Dean Sasse: Watching yields go up as tillage goes down 16

3. Determine how your operations will affect residue cover 18

   Conservation tillage reduces pesticide runoff—usually 26

4. Estimate residue cover in the field 28

   Estimating erosion with RUSLE 34

5. Adjust equipment to preserve residue 36

   No-till boosts soil tilth 42

6. Plant a cover crop 46

7. Rotate crops 50

8. Select vigorous perennial pasture species 53

9. Protect the soil with special-use annual forage crops 58

10. Protect the soil with rotational grazing 62

11. Use no-till when renovating pasture 66

12. Manage timberland to protect soil 68

    Harvesting trees: Key best management

    practices in wetland areas 71

Controlling the flow of water

13. Reduce soil compaction and increase infiltration 74

14. Install grassed waterways 78

15. Plant vegetative filter strips or make critical area plantings . . . 85

    Constructed wetlands show promise as filter 89

16. Farm on the contour 91

17. Use contour stripcropping and contour buffer strips 95

18. Install terraces 100

19. Install grade control structures 105

20. Install water and sediment control basins 109

21. Use diversions 112
22. Install a farm pond 114
  Ralph and Joyce Neill:
  Managing land means managing water 117
23. Maintain your drainage system to protect surface water 119
24. Control streambank erosion with the willow-post method ... 122
25. Avoid channelization of streams and creeks 127

Managing nutrients effectively

26. Set realistic yield goals 130
27. Monitor the level of nutrients 132
  Fertilizer philosophies: What's the difference? 137
28. Credit other nitrogen sources 139
29. Select nitrogen fertilizers wisely 141
30. Apply nitrogen in the spring 145
  Broadcast, incorporate, or inject? 147
31. Apply fertilizer with a global positioning system 148
  Arlen Ruestman: Cutting back with variable rates 153

Managing livestock waste effectively

32. Keep livestock out of water 156
  Alternative water for cattle: A tempting option 160
  Microscopic mischief makers reside in livestock waste 161
33. Divert runoff water 163
  Ken Gasper: Composting manure
  reduces odor, phosphorus problems 165
34. Collect and store contaminated runoff 167
  What about semi-solid and solid manure storage? 172
35. Install a vegetative filter—if appropriate 175
36. Determine accurate manure application rates 178
37. Calibrate manure application equipment 182
38. Apply manure wisely 185

Reducing insecticide use

39. Scout fields for insects 190
  Jim Wilkinson: Adding profit through scouting 196
40. Base decisions on the economic thresholds for insects 198
41. Use insect-resistant crop varieties 205

42. Use crop rotation and plant diversity to control insects 210

43. Spot-treat insect infestations when possible 214

44. Conserve beneficial insects 218

Reducing herbicide use

45. Scout for weeds and know their economic thresholds 224

46. Fine-tune your weed control program
to cut back on herbicides 230

Berning family farms: Reduced rates, one step at a time 233

47. Manage crops to compete aggressively with weeds 236

48. Don't assume that no-till requires more herbicide 238

49. Band herbicides and cultivate 243

50. Control weeds with cover crops 245

Selecting pesticides

51. Select the least-toxic pesticide 248

Earthworms and pesticides: Consider toxicity levels 251

52. Determine your soil's potential for runoff 253

53. Determine your pesticide's potential for runoff 255

Mark and Janice Hinze:
Using software to select herbicides 260

Handling pesticides safely and efficiently

54. Calibrate your sprayer 264

How to measure ground speed 268

55. Consider direct injection and closed handling systems 270

Jerry and Diane Nibarger:
Targeting sprays: Just what the doctor ordered 274

56. Observe setback zones 276

57. Rinse and dispose of chemical containers safely 281

58. Dispose of excess chemical safely 285

59. Construct a rinse pad 287

60. Dispose of other farm waste safely 290

For more information 295

Index 305

Making progress on the waterfront

Jerry and Diane Nibarger sat down to do some serious calculations in 1980, and they were astounded to discover just how much they were spending on fuel for tillage operations.

At the time, their farm in central Missouri was 1,500 acres, but they estimated that with all of their equipment passes, they were covering about 5,000 acres each year.

So, like many producers throughout the Midwest, the Nibargers first became attracted to no-till farming because of the economics involved. Not only did no-till eliminate the cost of plowing, it maintained strong yields and freed up time for them to diversify into custom application. Today, the Nibargers custom-apply pesticides on about 10,000 or more acres annually.

In addition to the profits, no-till brought needed protection for the Nibargers' soil and helped to keep eroding sediment out of the Grand River, which adjoins some of their farm.

No-till success stories such as the Nibargers' have been repeated throughout the Midwest, and the result has been an impressive improvement in erosion rates. In Illinois, for instance, erosion has been brought within "tolerable levels" on a steadily increasing percentage of cropland acres—from 59 percent in 1982 to 77 percent in 1995.

This is the good news. The downside is that there remains a lot that agriculture can do to safeguard the nation's surface water—streams, rivers, and lakes. In 1992, the U.S. Environmental Protection Agency reported that 206,179 miles of U.S. rivers and streams had been impaired in some way by nonpoint pollution—pollution that cannot be traced to a specific point such as a pipe discharging industrial wastes. Those miles amounted to about 16 percent of the total miles of rivers and streams in the 40 reporting states.

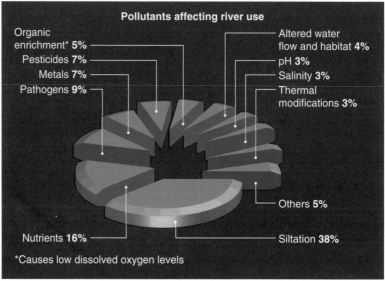

SOURCE: *Managing Nonpoint Pollution*, USEPA, 1992.

The same EPA study said that 20 percent of the nation's *lake* acreage had been affected by nonpoint pollution (excluding the Great Lakes, the Great Salt Lake, and Alaska's lakes).

The leading contributor to nonpoint source pollution remains agriculture. And despite the gains in erosion control, the movement of eroded soil into water (siltation) is still the number one form of nonpoint pollution in U.S. streams and rivers. In lakes, nutrients are the leading form of nonpoint pollution, with siltation a close second.

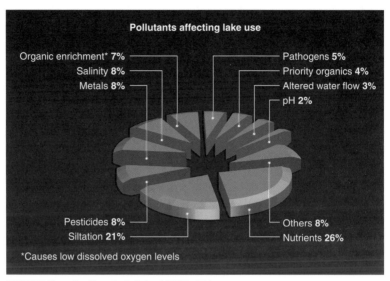

Pollutants affecting lake use

Organic enrichment* 7%
Salinity 8%
Metals 8%

Pathogens 5%
Priority organics 4%
Altered water flow 3%
pH 2%

Pesticides 8%
Siltation 21%

Others 8%
Nutrients 26%

*Causes low dissolved oxygen levels

SOURCE: *Managing Nonpoint Pollution*, USEPA, 1992.

When surface water becomes contaminated, whether it is by nitrogen, siltation, or pesticides, the consequences ripple throughout a region. For those communities that draw their drinking water from a lake or river, the consequences are especially serious. Some cities have been fighting high nitrate levels in their drinking water for over a decade now. But even where a lake or river is not a source of drinking water, problems can multiply: A community can lose recreational opportunities, fish and wildlife may be threatened, and the use of water for industry and agriculture can suffer.

60 Ways Farmers Can Protect Surface Water outlines many of the most practical and effective tools that farmers can use to keep contaminants from entering our streams, rivers, and lakes. And it deals with the most serious contaminants—eroding soil, fertilizers, nutrients and bacteria from livestock wastes, and pesticides. *60 Ways* takes a fresh look at some of the oldest strategies available—such as terraces—but it also stays on the cutting edge by examining new technology—such as global positioning systems that target fertilizer applications with greater accuracy.

In Missouri, the Nibargers have used this mix of old and new strategies to stay ahead of the game in both production and environmental protection. Not only did they switch to no-till, but they planted willows to stabilize the banks of the river running through their land, and they are testing some of the latest technology to reduce the amount of pesticides they apply (see page 274 for more details).

The Nibargers pull no punches when it comes to confronting these problems. As Jerry Nibarger puts it, "I despise erosion. My soil is my bank account. And erosion is like going to my savings account, drawing a little money out every day, and then throwing it away."

It's costly to lose soil, and it's also costly to use excessive amounts of chemicals; that's why a growing number of producers are looking for ways to cut back on fertilizers and pesticides. But saving money is not the only factor driving these trends. For many producers, including Nibarger, the passion to be faithful stewards of the land has led to a unique partnership of economic and environmental incentives.

As Nibarger puts it, "I want not only to protect the land, but to *improve* upon it. And when I quit farming, I hope people will feel that I left my ground in better shape than when I started."

The following are 60 ways to do just that.

Managing surface cover

Controlling soil erosion is an undercover operation. Keeping the land under some form of surface cover is the single most important factor in keeping soil from eroding. Prior land use, crop canopy, surface roughness, soil type, and other factors also play a part, but the key is surface cover, which can be provided by crop residue, a cover crop, or pasture.

Surface cover absorbs the explosive power of rain—a power that can detach soil particles from the soil mass, setting them up for transport by runoff water. Surface cover also slows the flow of water across the soil surface, further reducing the threat of erosion.

The statistics tell the story. In a Purdue University study, for example, researchers measured erosion levels of 12.4 tons per acre annually when the soil surface was left completely bare. With 41 percent surface cover, the annual rate of soil erosion dropped to 3.2 tons per acre annually. And with 71 percent surface cover, the erosion rate was only 1.4 tons per acre annually.

The following chapters offer key management ideas for keeping the land under cover.

1 Distribute residue evenly at harvest

Potential problems

Harvest operations set the stage for your entire conservation tillage system. If you distribute residue evenly on the ground during harvest, you may reduce the need for tillage operations or planter attachments to handle residue. But distribute residue *unevenly*, and the resulting wind rows or bunches can create a number of problems:

- The need for an additional tillage trip to redistribute residue
- Weed problems
- Tillage and planting equipment plugged with residue
- Poor seed placement when planting with a no-till planter that is not equipped with row cleaners. When residue builds up in spots, the planter may not cut completely through the residue and may not get the seed into the soil. Also, residue can be pushed into the soil along with the seed, resulting in poor seed-to-soil contact, germination, and growth.
- Very wet soil under thick deposits of residue when the rest of the field is ready to plant
- Delayed soil warming and seedling emergence in areas where residue is thick
- Deformed plants as plants are forced to grow through and around heavy amounts of residue
- Pest infestations. Piles of residue make welcome habitats for insects, rodents, and soil pathogens (disease-causing organisms).
- Interference with pesticides. A thick layer of residue can intercept herbicides and insecticides meant to be applied to the soil or plants. If weeds have emerged from the soil, but have not yet cleared the residue, they may not be affected by a herbicide application.

Distribute straw and chaff evenly

A large portion of the residue moving through a combine passes over the straw walkers of a conventional combine or out the end of the rotar cage of a rotary combine. This residue can be allowed to simply fall on the ground, but it is preferable to distribute it evenly on the soil surface with either a straw chopper or a straw spreader. For successful conservation tillage, larger combines should be equipped with a straw chopper, especially when harvesting soybeans or small grain crops. A straw chopper distributes the residue from soybeans or small grains much better than a straw spreader.

Also, a significant percentage of the residue passing through the combine is small or broken up into small material, normally called chaff. Chaff passes through the concaves or straw walkers of the combine and then moves to the chaffer sieve. Chaff on the chaffer sieve is either blown out or drops out the back of the combine. This chaff drops directly to the ground, never reaching the straw chopper or straw spreader. As it falls from the rear of the combine, it can form a heavy windrow (especially with large combines).

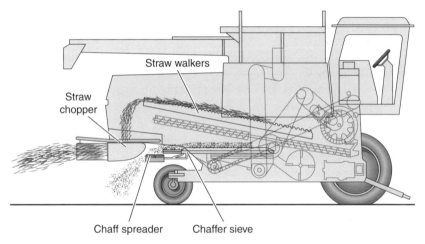

Straw walkers

Straw chopper

Chaff spreader   Chaffer sieve

A straw chopper or straw spreader will evenly spread the residue that passes over the straw walkers of a conventional combine. A chaff spreader will spread the smaller material, or chaff, that passes over the chaffer sieve.

The solution is to install a chaff spreader, which typically uses two spinning disks with rotating batts to throw the chaff in all directions behind the combine. The amount of chaff passing through a combine depends on the type of crop, crop variety, yield, and width of the cut. When harvesting wheat, for example, anywhere from 40 to 70 percent of the residue passing through the combine is chaff. A lot of chaff is also created when harvesting soybeans.

The spread width and uniformity of spreading by different types of straw and chaff spreaders varies. The most basic and least expensive units may not spread residue over as wide an area as the more expensive, more complicated units. Ideally, chaff and residue should be distributed evenly across the *entire* harvested width.

If you alter a combine or spreading attachment, or if you install add-on equipment, provide adequate safety shields to the extent possible. Also, residue can be thrown out of the back of the combine by a chopper or spreader at a high speed; therefore, make sure no individuals are standing close by when the combine passes. A piece of residue could put out an eye.

Finally, make sure that an add-on unit will not adversely affect the combine's performance. If the spreader is hydraulically operated, find out whether the combine has an adequate hydraulic system and engine cooling capacity to handle the extra load.

Prepared with John Siemens, power and machinery specialist, and Robert Frazee, natural resources management educator, UI Extension.

THE GREAT TERRAIN ROBBERY:
THE EROSION PROCESS

To catch a thief

Soil erosion is a thief that leaves no fingerprints. But it still leaves plenty of clues that it has been at work, some of them obvious and some quite subtle. Setting this soil robbery in motion is splash erosion.

Splash erosion

During a rainstorm, millions of raindrops may hit the soil surface at velocities reaching 30 feet per second. Striking the ground like miniature bombs, raindrops can splash soil as high as 3 feet in the air and as far as 5 feet from where they hit.

Splash erosion also sets up the next stage of erosion by dislodging soil particles—freeing them up for easy transport by runoff. In addition, an intense rain will cause the surface to seal, creating ponds in low areas and increasing surface runoff. If water cannot infiltrate down through the soil, it will move across the surface.

Sheet erosion

When runoff water begins to move, it is called sheet erosion. Contrary to its smooth name, sheet erosion usually moves with sluggish irregularity, detouring around clods and spilling out of small depressions.

Sheet erosion is not strong enough to dislodge much soil on its own. But by working in tandem with raindrops, the damage can go deep. Rain dislodges soil particles, and runoff water carries them away. In fact, a raindrop falling on a very thin sheet of water detaches soil particles more readily than one falling on dry soil.

This often invisible destruction can become noticeable when a plow turns up light-colored subsoil on sloping land. Exposed subsoil means much of the topsoil has been scoured away.

Rill erosion

Rill erosion develops when concentrated runoff water begins to cut definite channels. Rills look like miniature rivers and become wider and deeper as the velocity of runoff increases. At this point, raindrops continue to break the soil apart, but runoff also has built up enough momentum to break particles loose. Rills are very efficient at transporting soil particles.

Gully erosion

Rills left unchecked can become large enough to be considered gullies, which means they cannot be obliterated with normal tillage practices. They are large, noticeable scars on the land. In the Midwest, gully erosion has not only removed valuable topsoil; it has divided fields into small parcels that are inefficient to farm.

Sedimentation

Whenever the flow of runoff water is interrupted, ponds develop and soil is deposited—a process known as sedimentation. While most soil may only travel from one part of the field to another before being deposited, a significant amount of soil particles can eventually reach nearby waterways.

Sediment can choke lakes, reduce the capacity of water-supply reservoirs, and carry chemicals into lakes, streams, and rivers, making water uninhabitable for game fish. Everyone, from the farmer and the fisherman to the recreational enthusiast and the taxpayer, pays for the damage.

The irony is that erosion has a greater tendency to carry away the finest soil material, the clay particles, than it does the coarsest material, the sand. Plant nutrients often attach to the finer clay particles, proving that erosion is no different from any other thief. It makes off with the most valuable riches.

Prepared with Michael Hirschi, soil and water specialist, UI Extension, and Kent Mitchell, UI professor of agricultural engineering.

2

Avoid fall tillage

Save soil, save money

The chart on page 23 pretty much tells the story about fall tillage. If you chisel plow in the fall after soybean harvest, you may bury anywhere from 40 to 70 percent of the residue. Soybean residue is considered "fragile," which means that any fall tillage will bury a significant portion of it, greatly increasing the potential for soil erosion. After corn, the residue repercussions are not as great, but chiseling in the fall can still bury from 15 to 50 percent of the surface cover.

Avoiding fall tillage can sometimes make the difference between adequate erosion control and out-of-control erosion. Even if you end up tilling in the spring, you can buy yourself six to eight months of additional soil protection by not tilling in the fall.

Avoiding primary tillage in either the fall or spring means a savings in fuel and equipment wear and tear. For 1995-96, University of Illinois agricultural economists estimated that chisel plowing cost $9 per acre, subsoiling cost $9.50 per acre, and moldboard plowing cost $17.50 per acre.

To cut these costs and reduce soil erosion, producers throughout the Midwest are setting aside their plows, especially after soybean harvest. However, fall tillage continues to be commonly performed after corn. The primary justifications are to combat soil compaction and control weeds.

Fall tillage and weed control

Fall tillage can help control perennial weeds, as well as winter annuals such as shepherdspurse. But it is often more economical and just as effective to rely on a knockdown herbicide in the spring, rather than fall tillage. Some perennials may be difficult to control with herbicides alone; but then again, some perennials (such as hemp dogbane) also are difficult to control with tillage.

Disease and insect control usually do not justify fall tillage.

Deep tillage and soil compaction

Combating soil compaction can sometimes justify deep tillage with a subsoiler or ripper, because compaction can hurt plant growth. In a corn-soybean rotation, however, if you deep till after corn, you shouldn't need to till after soybeans the following fall. The effects of any deep tillage that you did after corn should carry over to the next year.

Before considering deep tillage to solve compaction problems, make sure your soil actually is compacted. Some signs of soil compaction include:

- Reduced soil drainage
- Slow crop growth and root development due to poor soil aeration
- Increased plant injury due to some soil-applied herbicides
- Deformed or flattened roots where they encounter the compacted zone
- Slow plant growth due to reduced uptake of nutrients
- Poor soil structure

Because these signs are not always obvious and they can also have other causes, the most reliable way to check for soil compaction is to measure the soil density. However, soil density is not easy to measure and requires special equipment.

An easier way to measure the compaction level is to use a tile spade to examine soil structure and density or use a soil cone penetrometer, available for as little as $150. Soil penetrometers can help determine how severely your soil is compacted and at what depth.

If you find out that the soil is seriously compacted, make sure the soil is dry before doing any deep tillage work. If you deep till when the soil is wet, you will waste fuel and possibly even *increase* compaction.

CHECK IT OUT

For ideas on how to prevent soil compaction: page 74.

Prepared with John Siemens, power and machinery specialist, and Marshal McGlamery, weed science specialist, UI Extension.

NO-TILL BOOM CONTINUES

When no-till farming began to emerge in the 1960s and 1970s, many people brushed it aside as purely experimental or demonstrational—a passing fad. But no-till is still going strong. Although the yearly increases in no-till acreage are not as dramatic as in the 1980s, no-till continues its steady rise. In 1996, no-till corn rose 3 percent nationwide and no-till soybeans went up 2 percent, according to the Conservation Technology Information Center.

The growth and success of no-till has been due to lower production costs, improved planters and drills, a lower capital investment in equipment, better herbicides, the desire to control erosion, and the need to meet conservation plan goals.

The charts on the following pages tell the picture, depicting the upward trend in no-till, as well as the leading no-till states.

No-till corn
Top 5 states – 1996

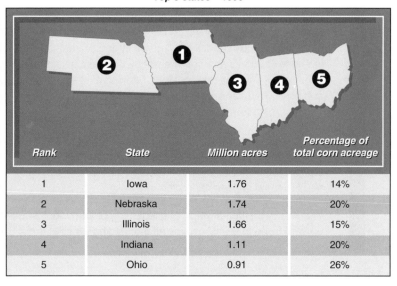

Rank	State	Million acres	Percentage of total corn acreage
1	Iowa	1.76	14%
2	Nebraska	1.74	20%
3	Illinois	1.66	15%
4	Indiana	1.11	20%
5	Ohio	0.91	26%

No-till soybeans
Top 5 states – 1996

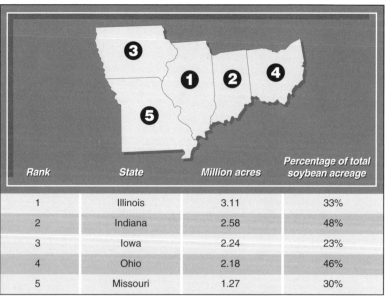

Rank	State	Million acres	Percentage of total soybean acreage
1	Illinois	3.11	33%
2	Indiana	2.58	48%
3	Iowa	2.24	23%
4	Ohio	2.18	46%
5	Missouri	1.27	30%

SOURCE: Conservation Technology Information Service in cooperation with the USDA Natural Resources Conservation Service.

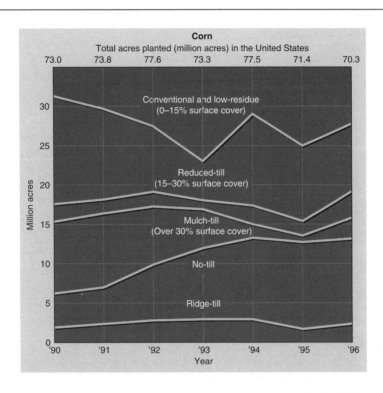

Corn
Total acres planted (million acres) in the United States

| 73.0 | 73.8 | 77.6 | 73.3 | 77.5 | 71.4 | 70.3 |

Conventional and low-residue (0–15% surface cover)

Reduced-till (15–30% surface cover)

Mulch-till (Over 30% surface cover)

No-till

Ridge-till

Million acres

Year: '90 '91 '92 '93 '94 '95 '96

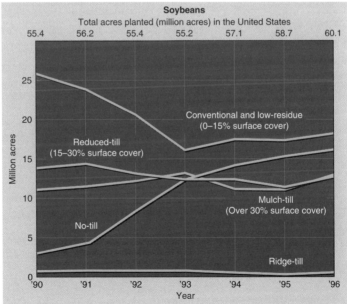

Soybeans
Total acres planted (million acres) in the United States

| 55.4 | 56.2 | 55.4 | 55.2 | 57.1 | 58.7 | 60.1 |

Conventional and low-residue (0–15% surface cover)

Reduced-till (15–30% surface cover)

Mulch-till (Over 30% surface cover)

No-till

Ridge-till

Million acres

Year: '90 '91 '92 '93 '94 '95 '96

Prepared with Robert Frazee, natural resources management educator, and Michael Hirschi, soil and water specialist, UI Extension.

15

Watching yields go up as tillage goes down

Dean Sasse's farms have their share of black, poorly drained soils. But such formidable soils didn't prevent Sasse from making a successful transition to no-till on virtually all of his 1,400 acres in Logan County, Illinois.

"Our yields have done nothing but go up with no-till," says Sasse.

Flat, poorly drained land poses a challenge to many no-till farmers because heavy residue keeps the soil in a wetter condition. But Sasse's poorly drained land did not suffer a yield loss under no-till, as some would have predicted; yields remained generally stable. Meanwhile, Sasse's rolling land underwent a dramatic yield boost when he switched to no-till.

Sasse credits the overall yield improvement on less fertility loss because nutrients had been washing away with eroding soil before he switched to no-till. He also lost yields in areas that had been consistently washing out.

In his pre no-till days, Sasse saw the telltale signs of severe erosion, such as grassed waterways filling with silt after a rain. But since going to no-till, he says the difference in erosion has been "amazing." The result: Less topsoil enters the narrow streams and ditches that meander through his farms, en route to nearby Salt Creek and Kickapoo Creek.

While yields have gone up, fuel costs have gone down without tillage. In 1995, Sasse says his fuel and oil costs were $5.60 per acre—an impressive $2 per acre lower than the state average.

By not tilling, Sasse has freed up time, which he spends scouting. When crops are small, he goes into the cornfields twice a week to check for cutworms. Although insect problems have not been any greater in no-till, he says he has to keep a closer eye on cutworm activity.

Neither has weed control been any more difficult in no-till, Sasse notes. He sprays more often than he did before, but at lower rates.

One of the keys to Sasse's success has been getting good crop stands. To establish a good stand, he says the corn planter "is loaded down" with row cleaners, starter fertilizer, no-till coulters, and cast-iron press wheels.

When he first began no-tilling, Sasse used bubble coulters on the planter, but he found that instead of working the soil, they pried apart the soil into a V shape. "We had trouble getting closure," he says, "and when it was dry, roots of the corn plants couldn't penetrate the sidewalls of the trench."

Sasse solved the problem by switching to a 1-inch wavy coulter, which turns up a 2-inch wide strip.

To keep track of yields throughout each field, Sasse has taken the high-tech approach in recent years, installing a global positioning system (GPS). GPS taps into satellite signals to locate the position of equipment on the field, enabling him to map both yields and soil fertility levels. In turn, he can use the fertility maps to vary phosphorus and potassium application rates on-the-go, according to nutrient needs in different parts of a field. Sasse also uses GPS to keep track of different varieties in the field, as well as the location of tile lines.

With GPS-based yield monitoring, Sasse says he was able to document dramatic yield differences between areas that were drained and those that were not drained. The well-drained areas typically outyielded the poorly drained land by 50 bushels per acre or more of corn.

GPS has been bringing some dramatic changes to farms throughout the Midwest, but change is nothing new to Sasse. He remembers that when he began working his present farms over 20 years ago, he buried all of the residue with a moldboard plow. Next came the chisel plow, and then he eventually retired the plow altogether, except on a small piece of land where he grows seed corn.

"Before we started no-tilling, when things didn't go right, we simply pulled out a tillage tool. But when we made the change, we had to resist the urge to rely on tillage as the problem solver. It's a different way of thinking."

3

Determine how your operations will affect residue cover

The percent surface cover method

Whenever you go into the field with most equipment, it is usually safe to say that there will be less residue on the soil surface when you leave. Production activities—such as primary and secondary tillage, herbicide incorporation, and planting—break up and bury some percentage of crop residue.

The line-point method, described in Chapter 4, is an easy, fast way to find out how much residue cover actually remains on the ground after various field operations. However, for planning purposes, it's important to *predict* what residue levels will be on the soil surface throughout the year. To do this, you can estimate the impact of field operations on residue by using the percent surface cover method. All it takes is a pencil, paper, calculator, and the tables presented on pages 23-25.

The percent surface cover method includes two basic steps:

Step 1. Estimate the percentage of soil surface covered with crop residue immediately after harvesting the previous crop.

Step 2. Estimate the percentage of surface cover remaining after field operations and natural decay.

Step 1: Estimating surface cover after harvest

In general, high-residue crops—such as corn and wheat—provide enough residue to cover between 80 and 95 percent of the soil surface after harvest. Other crops, such as soybeans and most vegetables, produce smaller quantities of residue that cover between 65 and 85 percent of the soil surface after harvest.

The accompanying table, "Residue cover after harvest," shows the percent of surface cover that is typically left after harvest for different crops and yield levels. The estimates are for crop residue that is uniformly distributed over the field.

Keep in mind that the "Residue cover after harvest" table does not include the effects of a fall-planted crop or a cover crop. Fall-planted wheat provides considerable protection of the soil surface through the critical erosion period—April to mid-June. Cover crops such as rye and hairy vetch also provide effective surface cover. For these and similar cases, work with your local conservationist and follow available guidelines for determining erosion-control benefits.

Residue cover after harvest

Corn

Yields per acre	Percent surface cover	Percent surface cover in continuous no-till*
Less than 100 bushels	80	87
100 to 150 bushels	90	97
151 bushels or more	95	100

Soybeans

Less than 30 bushels	65	68
30 to 50 bushels	75	78
51 bushels or more	85	88

*Residue from prior crop years tends to build up under continuous no-till systems. This buildup contributes about 7 percent of added surface cover for crops such as corn and about 3 percent for fragile residue from crops such as soybeans.

SOURCE: Natural Resources Conservation Service

Residue types

Non-fragile residue	Fragile residue
Corn	Soybeans
Sorghum	Canola/rapeseed
Wheat*	Sugar beets
Alfalfa or legume hay	Peanuts
Cotton	Sweet potatoes
Rice	Corn silage
Flaxseed	Dry peas
Oats*	Dry beans
Rye*	Lentils
Sugarcane	Vegetables
Tobacco	Potatoes
Grass hay	Grapes
Forage silage	Guar
Pasture	Mint
Millet	Flower seed
Triticale*	Fall-seeded cover crop
Forage seed	Safflower
Speltz*	Sorghum silage
Popcorn	Sunflowers
Buckwheat	Mustard
Barley*	Green peas

* If a rotary combine is used in harvesting small grain, then the residue should be considered fragile.

Example

John and Jane Smith have just harvested a corn crop that produced 160 bushels per acre. According to the "Residue cover after harvest" table, a corn crop with that yield level produces enough residue to cover 95 percent of the soil surface immediately after harvest.

Step 2: Adjusting percent surface cover

Refer to the "Residue remaining" table to find out the proportion of residue that remains on the soil surface after you complete a field operation. For example, if the "Residue remaining" value is 0.80, then 80 percent of the residue will be left on the surface *after* the operation.

Note that the "Residue remaining" table provides figures for both fragile and non-fragile residues. To find out which crops produce fragile residue and which crops leave non-fragile residue, check the "Residue types" list on page 19.

The values in the "Residue remaining" chart are grouped in three ranges—high, average, and low—because of differences in the condition of residue and the way operators set and use their equipment.

Low range. The low range of values may be more accurate under conditions in which residue is more easily broken up and buried. For example:

- If producers operate equipment at higher speeds or greater depths than is common practice, they will bury more residue.
- If residue is partially decayed, it is more easily broken apart and covered.
- If residue is dry, it becomes brittle and is easily broken up and covered.
- If soil is sandy or dry, equipment is likely to throw more soil and bury more residue.

Average range. Unless you have reason to believe the low or high values are more appropriate for you, it is a good idea to start with the average values.

High range. The high range of values may be more accurate under conditions in which residue is *less* likely to be broken up and buried. For example:

- If producers operate equipment at lower speeds or shallower depths than is common practice, they will bury less residue.
- If residue is moist, it is less likely to be broken apart.
- If soil is high in moisture or clay, equipment is less likely to throw as much soil and bury as much residue.

List all of the operations you plan to use between harvest and closure of the canopy of the next crop. Then, for each operation, look up its value in the "Residue remaining" table. Don't forget to include overwintering—the reduction in crop residue that occurs because of winter weather conditions. You can find the value for overwintering in the "Residue remaining" table under "climatic effects."

When you multiply the percent surface cover by the value for a particular operation, the result is the estimated percentage of soil surface that will remain covered after the field operation is completed. The equation looks like this:

Percent surface cover *before* operation	X	Value for operation	=	Percent surface cover *after* operation

Adjust the percent surface cover for every activity that breaks up and buries residue. If you plan to use a tool that is not listed in the "Residue remaining" table, try to estimate the value. For example, if you are using a combination tool that the table does not list, separate it into its component parts. Treat each part as if it is a separate residue-burying operation.

After you have adjusted the percent surface cover to account for all of your field operations, as well as for overwintering, check your results against the surface cover guidelines listed in your conservation plan. Does your estimate of percent surface cover exceed or match your plan's goals? If not, you may have to reconsider some of your activities, especially if you used the average or high values listed in the "Residue remaining" table.

Example

The Smiths have selected three residue-reducing operations that will be part of their conservation system for soybeans following corn: subsoiling, tandem-disking (finishing), and planting.

First, they need to find out how much of the surface will remain covered with corn residue after they use their "V" ripper/subsoiler in the fall. The value from the "Residue remaining" table is 0.80 for the subsoiler. So they multiply the percent surface cover after harvest (95 percent) by 0.80.

95 Percent surface cover after harvest	X	0.80 Value for subsoiling	=	76 Percent surface cover after subsoiling

Given average conditions, the Smiths can expect 76 percent surface cover after one pass with their subsoiler. Using this new figure, they must find out how much residue will be left after winter. They multiply the new percent surface cover by the value for overwintering.

76		0.88		67
Percent surface cover *before* winter	X	Value for overwintering	=	Percent surface cover *after* winter

In the spring, the Smiths want to use a tandem finishing disk. According to the "Residue remaining" table, one pass with a tandem finishing disk nearly halves the percent surface cover.

67		0.55		37
Percent surface cover *before* disking	X	Value for disking	=	Percent surface cover *after* disking

To plant their soybeans, the Smiths will use a conventional planter mounted with double-disk openers.

37		0.90		33
Percent surface cover *before* planting	X	Value for planter	=	Percent surface cover *after* planting

According to these calculations, the Smiths will have 33 percent surface cover after subsoiling, winter decomposition, disking, and planting. This level is above the 30 percent surface cover required after planting to qualify as conservation tillage. However, it leaves little room for error and uncertainty in the weather. There is always the risk of excessive rain after seedbed preparation or replanting, forcing the Smiths to prepare the seedbed again, and burying more residue than they anticipated.

Don't forget in-field measurements

The percent surface cover method is an important planning tool, but it is no replacement for taking in-field measurements with the line-point method. Too many variables come into play to rely solely on the estimates done on paper with the percent surface cover method. When it comes down to it, compliance with your conservation plan depends on what's on the field, not on paper.

Residue remaining

Activities/events	Proportion of residue remaining *					
	FRAGILE residue [Soybeans]			NON-FRAGILE residue [Corn]		
	Low	Average	High	Low	Average	High
Moldboard plow	.0	.03	.05	.0	.05	.10
Equipment that fractures the soil						
Paratill/paraplow	.75	.80	.85	.80	.85	.90
"V" ripper/subsoiler (12" to 14" deep and 20" spacing)	.60	.70	.80	.70	.80	.90
Combination equipment that fractures the soil						
Subsoil-chisel (combination tool)	.40	.45	.50	.50	.60	.70
Disk-subsoiler (combination tool)	.10	.15	.20	.30	.40	.50
Chisel plows with						
Sweeps	.50	.55	.60	.70	.78	.85
Straight chisel spike points	.40	.50	.60	.60	.70	.80
Twisted points or shovels	.30	.35	.40	.50	.60	.70
Coulter chisel plows with						
Sweeps	.40	.45	.50	.60	.70	.80
Straight chisel spike points	.30	.35	.40	.50	.60	.70
Twisted points or shovels	.20	.25	.30	.40	.50	.60
Disk chisel plows with						
Sweeps	.30	.40	.50	.60	.65	.70
Straight chisel spike points	.30	.35	.40	.50	.55	.60
Twisted points or shovels	.20	.25	.30	.30	.40	.50
Offset disks for						
Heavy plowing, spacing greater than 10"	.10	.18	.25	.25	.38	.50
Primary cutting, spacing greater than 9"	.20	.30	.40	.30	.45	.60
Finishing, 7" to 9" spacing	.25	.33	.40	.40	.55	.70
Tandem disks for						
Heavy plowing, spacing greater than 10"	.10	.18	.25	.25	.38	.50
Primary cutting, spacing greater than 9"	.20	.30	.40	.30	.45	.60
Finishing, 7" to 9" spacing	.25	.33	.40	.40	.55	.70
Light disking after harvest, before other tillage	.40	.45	.50	.70	.75	.80
One-way disk with						
12" to 16" blades	.20	.30	.40	.40	.45	.50
18" to 30" blades	.10	.20	.30	.20	.30	.40
Single gang disk	.40	.50	.60	.50	.60	.70
Field cultivators (including leveling attachments) for primary tillage						
Sweeps or shovels, 6" to 12" spacing	.50	.60	.70	.35	.55	.75
Duckfoot points	.30	.43	.55	.35	.48	.60
Field cultivators (including leveling attachments) for secondary tillage following chisel or disk						
Sweeps or shovels, 6" to 12" spacing	.50	.55	.60	.70	.75	.80
Duckfoot points	.35	.43	.50	.60	.65	.70

Residue remaining, cont.

Activities/events	Proportion of residue remaining *					
	FRAGILE residue [Soybeans]			NON-FRAGILE residue [Corn]		
	Low	Average	High	Low	Average	High
Combination finishing tool with						
Disks, shanks, and leveling attachments						
(primary tillage)	.30	.40	.50	.50	.60	.70
Spring teeth and rolling baskets	.50	.60	.70	.70	.80	.90
Harrow finishing tool with						
Springtooth (coil tine)	.50	.60	.70	.60	.70	.80
Spike tooth	.60	.70	.80	.70	.80	.90
Flex-tine tooth	.70	.78	.85	.75	.83	.90
Roller harrow (cultipacker)	.50	.60	.70	.60	.70	.80
Packer roller	.90	.93	.95	.90	.93	.95
Rotary tiller finishing tool						
Primary or secondary operation 3" deep	.20	.30	.40	.40	.50	.60
Primary or secondary operation 6" deep	.05	.10	.15	.15	.25	.35
Rodweeders						
Plain rotary rod	.60	.65	.70	.80	.85	.90
Rotary rod with semi-chisels or shovels	.50	.55	.60	.70	.75	.80
Strip tillage equipment						
Rotary tiller, 12" spacing, tilled on 40" rows	.50	.55	.60	.60	.68	.75
Row cultivators (30" spacing and wider)						
Single sweep per row	.55	.63	.70	.75	.83	.90
Multiple sweeps per row	.55	.60	.65	.75	.80	.85
Finger wheel cultivator	.50	.55	.60	.65	.70	.75
Rolling disk cultivator	.40	.45	.50	.45	.50	.55
Ridge-till cultivator	.05	.15	.25	.20	.30	.40
Unclassified equipment						
Anhydrous applicator	.45	.58	.70	.75	.80	.85
Anhydrous applicator with closing disks	.30	.40	.50	.60	.68	.75
Subsurface manure applicator	.40	.50	.60	.60	.70	.80
Rotary hoe	.80	.85	.90	.85	.88	.90
Mulch treader	.60	.68	.75	.70	.78	.85
Drills						
Semi-deep furrow drill or press drill,						
7" to 12" spacing	.50	.65	.80	.70	.80	.90
Deep furrow drill, spacing greater than 12"	.50	.65	.80	.60	.70	.80
Single disk opener drills	.75	.80	.85	.85	.93	1.00
Double disk opener drills (conventional)	.60	.70	.80	.80	.90	1.00
No-till drills and drills with the following						
attachments *in standing stubble*						
Smooth no-till coulters	.70	.78	.85	.85	.90	.95
Ripple or bubble coulters	.65	.75	.85	.80	.83	.85
Fluted coulters	.60	.70	.80	.75	.78	.80

Activities/events	Proportion of residue remaining *					
	FRAGILE residue [Soybeans]			NON-FRAGILE residue [Corn]		
	Low	Average	High	Low	Average	High
No-till drills and drills with the following attachments *in flat residue*						
Smooth no-till coulters	.50	.60	.70	.65	.75	.85
Ripple or bubble coulters	.45	.55	.65	.60	.68	.75
Fluted coulters	.40	.50	.60	.55	.63	.70
Air seeders	Use the values of the seeder's soil-engaging device (field cultivator, chisel plow, etc.).					
Air drills	Use the values of the corresponding drill opener.					
Conventional row planter with						
Runner openers	.80	.85	.90	.85	.90	.95
Staggered double disk openers	.85	.90	.95	.90	.93	.95
Double disk openers	.75	.80	.85	.85	.90	.95
No-till planter with						
Smooth coulters	.75	.83	.90	.85	.90	.95
Ripple coulters	.70	.78	.85	.75	.83	.90
Fluted coulters	.55	.68	.80	.65	.75	.85
Strip-till planters with						
2 or 3 fluted coulters	.50	.63	.75	.60	.70	.80
Row cleaning devices (brushes, spikes, furrowing disks, or sweeps) to clear 8" to 14" wide bare strip	.50	.55	.60	.60	.70	.80
Ridge-till planter	.20	.30	.40	.40	.50	.60
Climatic effects — overwinter weathering following						
Summer harvest	.65	.75	.85	.70	.80	.90
Fall harvest	.70	.75	.80	.80	.88	.95

*The proportion of residue remaining is expressed as a range for every activity or event. Each range reflects the variable impacts of climate, soil type, type of residue, type of equipment, speed and depth of tillage, and timing of tillage on crop residue. The low range of values is more accurate for operators who run residue-destroying equipment at higher speeds and greater depths than average, while the high range of values is appropriate only for operators who run equipment at low speeds and shallow depths to preserve more residue. Most farmers should probably use the average values when planning their field operations. To gauge which range of values best fits your operation, take residue measurements in the field after every operation. Eventually, you may be able to replace the above estimates with actual field measurements.

SOURCE: Illinois Natural Resources Conservation Service, 1993.

Prepared with Rick Farnsworth, natural resources economics specialist, John Siemens, power and machinery specialist, and Robert Frazee, natural resources management educator, UI Extension.

CONSERVATION TILLAGE
REDUCES PESTICIDE RUNOFF—USUALLY

Runoff and residue

The quality of runoff has a lot to do with the quantity of residue cover. According to an extensive review of studies in Iowa, Wisconsin, Maryland, Kentucky, and Pennsylvania, no-till reduced the amount of herbicide in runoff water by an average of 70 percent when compared to conventional clean-till farming. Reduced tillage with the chisel plow cut the amount of herbicide in runoff water by 69 percent, and ridge till cut it by 42 percent.

Credit goes to the residue cover and increased water infiltration. The residue left with no-till, reduced tillage, and ridge till slows water runoff and helps reduce the sealing of the soil surface, both of which allow more water to filter into the soil. No-till also increases infiltration by increasing the development of "macropores"—large cracks, root channels, and worm holes. More infiltration means less runoff and, therefore, less pesticide moving with the runoff.

Another possible reason for the reduction in pesticide runoff is that conservation tillage increases organic matter content near the soil surface. This may increase pesticide adsorption and breakdown, which, in turn, reduces pesticide runoff.

However...

Some studies have shown that there are cases in which the amount of pesticide in runoff can *increase* with conservation tillage systems. For example, if the soil is compacted or has poor internal drainage, pesticide runoff may be greater with no-till than if the pesticide were incorporated with tillage.

Runoff can also be greater with conservation tillage when an intense rainfall occurs soon after herbicides are applied. The heavy crop residue that accompanies conservation tillage intercepts some of the herbicides applied. If an intense rainfall occurs soon after application, it washes herbicide from the residue and carries it away in runoff water. However, this problem doesn't show up if the rainfall is less intense. Small storms also can wash pesticide from the residue, but they do not generate enough runoff to carry the chemical away. Instead, the water and pesticide wash down into the soil.

What about leaching?

Because no-till increases the infiltration of water into the soil, some people wonder whether no-till simply trades one problem for another by threatening groundwater rather than surface water. Research is mixed on whether herbicide leaching is greater with no-till than with conventional tillage.

However, even if no-till does slightly increase pesticide leaching, it is important to keep the relative concentrations of pesticides in surface water and shallow groundwater in perspective. Concentrations of pesticides in surface runoff are often 100 times higher than concentrations in shallow groundwater.

Prepared with George Czapar, integrated pest management educator, UI Extension.

4 Estimate residue cover in the field

The line-point method

Beauty is in the eye of the beholder, and so is residue cover. In other words, visual estimates can vary greatly from one person to another, so eyeing your field is not an accurate way to estimate residue cover. In addition, making residue-cover estimates on paper may be a good way to plan your residue-management system, but it doesn't replace going out into your fields and measuring what's actually out there. As one Illinois farmer put it, "Until you measure, you don't know what you have."

Because residue cover is the key to any soil conservation plan, you want to be sure how much protection you're leaving on the land. Conservationists recommend you do this with the line-point method—an effective and simple procedure for measuring residue levels. The Natural Resources Conservation Service (NRCS) uses the line-point method to determine whether you have complied with the residue-level requirements in your conservation plan. By using this method to keep track of residue levels, you will have a good idea of how the NRCS personnel will evaluate your fields.

The only special equipment you need for the line-point method is a knotted rope or a tape measure. If you use a rope, make sure it has 100 evenly spaced knots ($1/8$-inch cord works very well). If you use a tape measure, it should have 100 clearly marked lines spaced either 6 inches or 1 foot apart. You can often get these ropes or tape measures from local conservation groups, pesticide or equipment dealers, or the local NRCS office.

The only other materials you need are a pencil, paper, and calculator. You may also want to bring a hand-held counter to make counting residue easier.

Measuring residue cover

The objective of the line-point method is to estimate the percentage of the soil surface covered with crop residue. To do this, take your equipment into one of your fields and follow this procedure:

1. Walk a predetermined distance into the field—such as 100 or 150 paces. This is your starting point. It should be away from end rows because residue levels in end rows are often not representative of residue levels in the majority of the field.

2. Secure one end of the knotted rope or tape measure halfway between two rows.

3. Stretch the knotted cord or tape measure diagonally at a 45-degree angle across the crop rows and stake the other end halfway between two crop rows (see illustration).

4. Walk back along the knotted cord or tape measure and, looking straight down, count the number of times you find pieces of residue directly underneath the knots or marks. If you use a rope, only count residue that is directly under the point where the straight part of the rope and the knot meet to

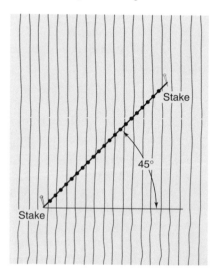

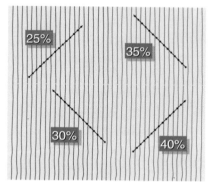

Conduct the line-point method at least four times in a field. To determine average percent cover for a field, add the percentages from each sample and divide by the number of samples. For the example above, average percent cover equals 32.5%.

(25% + 30% + 35% + 40%) ÷ 4 = 32.5%

Of the 7 knots shown, only 2 (⇨) should be counted as intersecting a piece of vegetation.

Count residue that is directly under one of the four corners of the knot. Look at the same corner of each knot.

form a "V" (see illustration on page 29). If you use a tape measure, select one side of the tape and only count residue that touches the marks on that side.

5. The percent of surface covered with residue equals the number of knots or marks that touched crop residue. For example, if you found crop residue underneath 40 out of a total of 100 knots or marks, then 40 percent of the soil surface is covered with residue.

6. Repeat steps 1 through 5 in at least three other areas of the field.

7. Once you have completed four or more measurements, add the results together and divide by the number of measurements made. This calculation gives you the average percent surface cover for the field. For example, consider the field shown in the illustration on page 29—a field where four residue measurements were taken randomly. The average percent surface cover equals 32.5 percent.

What counts?

If you are wondering how big a piece of residue should be before it can be counted, a simple rule is to ignore pieces of residue smaller than $1/8$ inch by $1/8$ inch. A typical pencil is roughly $1/4$ inch in diameter, so don't count residue smaller than half the thickness of a pencil.

If crop residue covers most of the field, it may be easier to count the number of times you do *not* find crop residue directly underneath a point on a knot or mark. Then, take that number and subtract it from 100 to get the percent surface cover. For example, if you found residue under every mark except for three, you would subtract three from 100. The result is 97 percent—the amount of soil surface covered with residue.

How often should you measure surface cover?

Check your residue cover throughout the season; that way, you can make whatever adjustments are necessary. For instance, if you find that your equipment is burying more residue than expected, you can slow your equipment speed or till at a shallower depth to leave more residue. It's a good idea to take line-point measurements and record them at these times:

- After harvest
- Following winter
- Before, during, and after primary and secondary tillage trips. (Taking measurements during tillage trips makes it easier to adjust your equipment.)
- After other residue-destroying activities
- Following planting

Prepared with Rick Farnsworth, natural resources economics specialist, and Robert Frazee, natural resources management educator, UI Extension.

Corn residue levels

20%

40%

60%

Photos courtesy of the Natural Resources Conservation Service—Iowa

Soybean residue levels

20%

30%

40%

Photos courtesy of the Natural Resources Conservation Service—Iowa

Wheat residue levels

20%

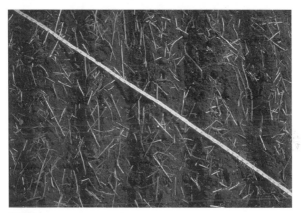

30%

50%

Photos courtesy of the Natural Resources Conservation Service—Kansas

ESTIMATING EROSION WITH RUSLE

Tracking soil

Scientists first developed a way to estimate the rate of soil erosion in 1936, using a strategy that looked at the soil type, the potential of rainfall and runoff to cause erosion, and the soil protection provided by plant cover. Since that time, there has been a long line of variations, culminating in the Universal Soil Loss Equation (USLE), which first appeared in 1965.

Today, we have the latest refinement. It's called RUSLE—the Revised Universal Soil Loss Equation.

First appearing in 1991, RUSLE includes new data and more involved calculations, resulting in a more accurate portrait of your erosion conditions. Because it is a more complex process, RUSLE has been designed to be a computer program adaptable to most personal computers with DOS operating systems.

RUSLE uses the same formula as the USLE:

R x K x LS x C x P = A (the average annual soil erosion rate in tons per acre)

Each letter still represents the same factor as before, but they have undergone some significant updating. Here's a brief summary of the changes.

R: Rainfall. R represents the erosion potential due to the rainfall patterns of a particular area. You can look up the R factor in the same way you did with the USLE—by simply checking the appropriate map. For RUSLE, however, the numbers and groupings have been somewhat changed. Also, a procedure was added that specifically targets the Pacific Northwest by considering the erosive forces of runoff from snowmelt and rain on frozen soil and from irrigation.

K: Soil erodibility. K takes into consideration that some soils are more easily eroded than others. With RUSLE, the soil erodibility factor now reflects changes in the soil due to freezing, thawing, and the extraction of moisture by the growing crop.

LS: Length and steepness of slope. LS reflects this basic principle: the longer and steeper the slope is, the more severe the erosion will be. For RUSLE, the LS formula is much more accurate and detailed.

C: Surface cover management. C, the impact of your cropping system on erosion, looks at prior land use, canopy cover, residue cover, surface roughness, and soil moisture. In RUSLE, the C factor has been refined to consider a wider range of conditions.

P: Support practices. P represents the reduction of erosion due to support practices, such as contouring, stripcropping, terracing, and subsurface drainage. In RUSLE, the P factor involves more detail than it did in the USLE. As an example, the P factor for contouring now includes the effect of storm severity, across-the-slope tillage, and ridge height. Also, formulas have been developed for both cropland and rangeland.

A: The average annual erosion rate. By multiplying all of the factors together, you come up with A, the average annual soil erosion loss in tons per acre.

What if your erosion rate is different under RUSLE?

Most conservation plans were developed using the USLE. But what if you use RUSLE and come up with a different rate of soil erosion? How will it affect your conservation plans?

As of October 1996, the Natural Resources Conservation Service offered these guidelines:

- If your conservation plan was developed using the USLE, you are not required to revise the plan, even if RUSLE shows greater soil loss than previously indicated with the USLE.

- If you are creating a new conservation plan or revising a plan, RUSLE will be used.

- If RUSLE shows that erosion is less than the tolerable, or sustainable, level (the T level), you can revise your plan up to the T level.

- New tenants or owners may accept the original conservation plan developed by the previous owner, as long as they continue to apply it.

Contact your conservationist with the Natural Resources Conservation Service for more information because approaches vary from state to state. In fact, some states have not yet begun to use RUSLE.

Prepared with Michael Hirschi, soil and water specialist, UI Extension, and Brett Roberts, conservation agronomist, Natural Resources Conservation Service.

5 Adjust equipment to preserve residue

Early adjustments

During the early years of conservation tillage, many producers thought that if they were using a chisel plow instead of a moldboard plow, they were using a conservation tillage system. They were now mulch-till farmers. But that notion was quickly shattered when producers discovered that in certain cases a chisel plow could bury too much residue for the system to be called mulch-till. Mulch tillage, as with all conservation tillage systems, requires that at least 30 percent of the surface be covered with residue from fall harvest through spring planting.

What these early experiences demonstrated was that your choice of equipment and your operation of the machinery both make a big difference in residue management. The following chart shows which deep and shallow tillage tools preserve the most surface cover and which preserve the least.

Tillage tools and residue		
Deep tillage equipment		**Shallow tillage equipment**
Ripper (subsoiler)	preserves	Field cultivator
Chisel plow	most residue	Combination tool
Coulter-chisel plow		Tandem disk harrow
Heavy offset disk	preserves	
Moldboard plow	least residue	

Exactly how much residue these tillage tools leave depends on several factors—some that you cannot control (the weather) and some that you can control (equipment). What follows is a discussion of the things you *can* control in preserving more surface residue.

Chisel plows

The three most common ground-engaging components attached to the standards of chisel plows are sweeps, spikes, or twisted shovels. Of the three components, sweeps leave the most residue on the soil surface, followed by chisel spikes, and then twisted shovels. Because sweeps lift and drop the soil, rather than invert it, they can leave up to 20 percent more residue on the surface than twisted shovels.

Percent of residue remaining after each pass Chisel plow with...		
Twisted shovels	Chisel spikes	Sweeps
Corn residue		
60%	70%	78%
Bean residue		
35%	50%	55%

Sweeps create a ridging effect, which can help to hold residue and snow cover in place, thereby reducing erosion. On sloping land, ridges can help channel surface runoff away safely after light to medium rains. This helps to control erosion, but only if you farm across the slope. If you farm up and down the slope (which is discouraged), the ridges can actually intensify erosion. In the furrows between the ridges, channels are created in which flowing water concentrates. As this water moves downslope, it builds up erosive power.

Coulter-chisel plows and disk-chisel plows

Chisel plows can clog with residue, especially if the residue is heavy or wet. That's why some chisels have a gang of coulters or disk blades mounted in front to cut the residue. These machines will bury more residue than a standard chisel plow, but they will bury less residue compared to chopping or disking the residue before chisel plowing.

When considering a coulter-chisel plow or disk-chisel plow, keep two things in mind:

- A gang of coulters in front of the chisel plow leaves more residue on the soil surface than a gang of disks.
- Consider a hydraulically adjustable disk or coulter gang. This will allow you to raise the coulter or disk gang when soil and residue conditions warrant. Raising the gang out of the soil can increase surface cover by 5 to 15 percent.

Disks

Offset disks generally are built heavier than tandem disks and tend to be a primary tillage tool, used for deeper tillage.

To preserve more surface residue with either type of disk, operate the gangs at a small angle and only as deep as necessary to perform the desired tillage and residue cutting. Operating depth can be varied either by adjusting the angle of the gangs or with adjustable depth gauge wheels. If you set an offset disk to till too deeply, you may end up burying as much residue as if you moldboard plowed.

Disks have two types of blades—spherical and conical. Spherical blades leave more residue on the soil surface than conical blades.

Field cultivators

A field cultivator is similar to a chisel plow, but it is lighter in construction and designed for less severe conditions. That's why it is typically used for secondary tillage. When there is a choice between a field cultivator and a disk for secondary tillage, the cultivator will tend to bury less residue. Also, sweeps with little lifting and throwing action do less soil mixing and leave more surface residue than sweeps with high lifting action. However, sweeps with high lifting action incorporate herbicides better.

Rippers (subsoilers)

Rippers are similar to chisel plows, although they generally leave more residue. Rippers typically have standards spaced 20 to 36 inches apart and are designed to operate 12 to 22 inches deep. They are primarily used to alleviate soil compaction, so use them when the soil is dry.

The farther apart you space the standards, the more surface residue you preserve. Also, narrower points will bury less residue than wide points. For rippers, available point attachments range from 2-inch-wide spikes to 8-inch-wide sweeps.

Combination tools

The set-up for different combination tools can vary considerably. However, many of them come with a disk gang in the front, followed by a series of cultivator shanks with sweeps or Danish tines, then followed by rolling baskets or drag harrows. To preserve the most residue, select the least aggressive attachments, set the disk blades to a shallow depth, and space the sweeps as wide as practical.

Tillage speed and depth

In most cases, the axiom holds true: If you till shallow at a slow speed, you leave more residue on the surface than if you till deep at a fast speed. One exception to this rule can be found with some of the newer rippers, designed since the late 1980s. These rippers have been designed to till deep without burying any more residue than if they were used to till shallow.

In most cases, however, shallow tillage results in less soil loosening and buries less residue. A chisel plow operated 6 inches deep in corn residue, for instance, can preserve up to 10 percent more surface cover than a chisel plow operated 10 inches deep. Field cultivating to a depth of 3 inches can preserve about 15 percent more soybean residue than field cultivating to a depth of 5 inches. Find a healthy compromise between deeper tillage to alleviate compaction or kill weeds and shallow tillage to preserve more surface cover.

Even if you do not want to slow your speed over an entire field, you may want to slow down on highly erodible areas. For example, if you reduced the speed of chisel plowing from 5 or 6 mph to 2 or 3 mph, you could preserve about 10 percent more corn residue in erosion-sensitive areas, depending on conditions. If you reduced your speed of field cultivation from 6 or 7 mph to 3 or 4 mph, you can increase soybean residue cover by up to 15 percent.

Angle of field operations

Many producers operate a tillage tool at an angle to the old rows to improve the flow of residue through the implement. With newer conservation tillage equipment, this is no longer necessary. You can till parallel to the rows—an approach that could preserve more residue, depending on how you operate the equipment.

If you operate the chisel plow so the points do not line up with the old rows—where residue is most concentrated—you should be able to preserve more residue than if you had tilled at an angle across the old rows. However, if you operate the chisel plow so the points *do* line up with old rows, you could end up destroying more residue than if you tilled at an angle.

Planting equipment

Several different soil-engaging components are now available for planters used in conservation tillage systems. These include single coulters, multiple coulters, fertilizer openers, row cleaners, and seed press wheels

Percent of residue remaining after each pass *No-till drill with...*				
	Fluted coulters	*Rippled coulters*	*Bubble coulters*	*Smooth coulters*
Corn residue	78%	83%	83%	90%
Bean residue	70%	75%	75%	78%

or seed firmers. Of these components, coulters, fertilizer openers, and row cleaners move the most residue and expose the most soil to erosion.

The wider the coulters on your planter, the greater the amount of soil exposed. Therefore, to preserve the greatest amount of surface cover, use narrow ripple, bubble, smooth, or ³/₄- to 1-inch-wide fluted coulters. The most commonly used coulter on no-till planters and drills is the ³/₄- to 1-inch-wide fluted coulter.

Row-cleaning attachments are typically most beneficial when planting a crop in heavy residue. Spiked wheels are the most common row-clean-

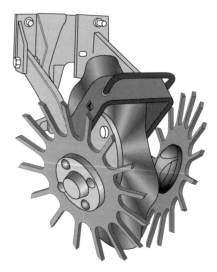

Row cleaner

ing attachments, but other available row-cleaning attachments include double-disk furrowers, brushes, sweeps, and horizontally mounted disks.

Row cleaners sweep residue to the side to improve planting and speed warming of the soil. If you use row cleaners, adjust them to move only residue (not soil). Take care not to create a furrow with your row cleaner or with other attachments. A furrow provides a place for water to accumulate, increasing the risk of soil crusting and runoff that will wash out seeds, soil, and plants.

Fertilizer attachments

Planters can be equipped with fertilizer attachments to apply starter fertilizer in no-till. These coulter or knife attachments can bury as much as 15 percent more residue than planters without starter fertilizer attachments, depending on such factors as the type of coulter and knife and the depth of operation. On the other hand, starter fertilizer can boost yields in no-till, and increased yields means increased surface cover.

CHECK IT OUT

To estimate how much residue different equipment leaves on the soil surface: page 23.

For details on how to estimate surface cover in the field: page 28.

Prepared with John Siemens, power and machinery specialist, and Robert Frazee, natural resources management educator, UI Extension.

NO-TILL BOOSTS SOIL TILTH

A complex system

Soil is anything but simple. On the contrary, it is a complicated physical, chemical, and biological system that can be altered by residue left on the surface with no-till and other conservation tillage systems. In general, no-till can create an environment that improves soil tilth, or soil health, and it can bring about changes that reduce the risk of surface-water contamination.

The following are some of the major changes that a heavy layer of crop residue can create in the soil environment. But be aware that there are often tradeoffs—benefits and drawbacks that depend on your own situation.

Residue and water availability

The layer of residue left with no-till reduces the rate at which water evaporates from the soil surface—sometimes by 40 to 50 percent. This means there will be more water in the upper portion of the soil profile, which can pose a problem in poorly drained soils.

However, the increased water availability in the soil can also be a benefit. Studies in central Iowa have shown that from mid-May to late June, when both corn and soybeans are undergoing the most rapid growth, plants grown in no-till or under other forms of conservation tillage have more water available and tend to grow without stress during periods of infrequent rainfall.

No-till also increases water availability by increasing the infiltration of water into the soil. Residue does this in several ways: by capturing surface runoff and giving it time to infiltrate through the soil; by reducing the sealing of the soil surface during a rainstorm; and by creating more "macropores"—tiny channels through the soil. Increased infiltration of water into the soil means there is less water on the soil surface to move as runoff.

✓ CHECK IT OUT

For information on how no-till affects pesticide runoff: page 26.

Residue and soil temperature

Because residue increases water storage in the upper soil profile and blocks the full effect of the sun on the soil, no-till reduces the daily range of soil temperatures. Residue also has a moderating effect, which means the soil undergoes less extreme variations in temperature. The effect is greater in the fall when residue is fresh than in the spring when the residue has decayed.

Compared to conventional tillage, no-till soils are slower to cool in the fall and only slightly slower to warm in the spring. This reduction in soil temperature can boost plant growth in southern latitudes but can delay seed emergence in the north.

As for water quality, the moderating effect on soil temperatures makes it possible for microorganisms to remain active in the soil for a longer time in the fall. This extended period of activity gives microorganisms more time to degrade pesticides, or break them down, into less toxic forms.

Residue and organic matter

Leaving crop residue undisturbed increases organic matter left by decaying root material. As the chart on page 45 shows, organic matter can benefit the soil in a number of ways, some of which will reduce the risk of water pollution. For example, microorganisms in the soil use carbon in the residue to produce polysaccharides, which help soil particles bind together. The result is a stable soil aggregate that is less likely to erode and move into nearby streams and lakes.

In addition, the increase in organic matter leads to an increase in beneficial microorganisms, which break pesticides down into less toxic chemicals. These microorganisms also create more sites for organic compounds to bind to soil particles. As chemicals become more likely to bind with soil particles, they are less likely to leach through the soil and into groundwater or drain tiles.

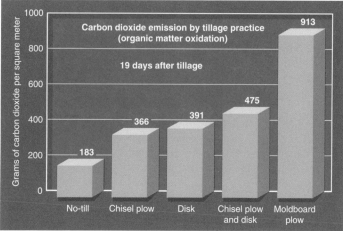

Short-term (annual) effect of tillage on organic matter

Carbon dioxide emission by tillage practice (organic matter oxidation)

19 days after tillage

Grams of carbon dioxide per square meter

- No-till: 183
- Chisel plow: 366
- Disk: 391
- Chisel plow and disk: 475
- Moldboard plow: 913

SOURCE: USDA/ARS, Morris, Minnesota, 1992.

Minnesota research shows how tillage during a single growing season can dramatically increase carbon dioxide emissions. Carbon dioxide emissions mean that organic matter is oxidizing, or being lost from the soil. In other words, more tillage means less organic matter in the soil.

Long-term effect of tillage on organic matter

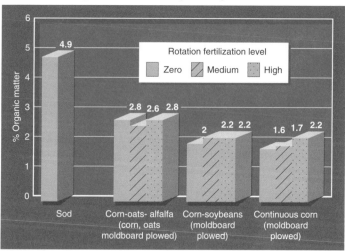

% Organic matter

Rotation fertilization level
- Zero
- Medium
- High

- Sod: 4.9
- Corn-oats-alfalfa (corn, oats moldboard plowed): 2.8, 2.6, 2.8
- Corn-soybeans (moldboard plowed): 2, 2.2, 2.2
- Continuous corn (moldboard plowed): 1.6, 1.7, 2.2

SOURCE: Morrow Plots, Urbana, Illinois, Fall 1992.

The long-term effect of tillage on organic matter can be seen in this research from the Morrow Plots, the oldest agricultural experiment field in the nation. This chart shows that after 100 years of moldboard plowing, about 2 to 3 percent of the soil's organic matter has been lost when compared to continuous sod. If no-till had been used during that time, organic matter levels might have remained close to the same level as the sod.

Potential effects of soil organic matter on soil properties

Nutritional properties

Soil property affected by organic matter	Beneficial effect of organic matter
Micronutrients	Provide copper, manganese, zinc, boron, chlorine, and molybdenum
Macronutrients	Provide oxygen, hydrogen, carbon, nitrogen, phosphorus, sulfur, iron, calcium, and magnesium

Chemical properties

Cation exchange capacity	Increases*
pH	Alleviates acidic and alkaline conditions

Physical properties

Soil aggregation	Increases
Aggregate stability	Increases
Water-holding capacity	Increases
Soil porosity	Increases
Water infiltration	Increases
Water percolation	Increases
Soil crusting	Decreases
Bulk density	Decreases

Biological properties

Beneficial microorganisms	Produce polysaccharides/antibiotics** Increase nutrient availability Suppress plant pathogens Decompose organic wastes
Earthworms	Populations increase

*An increase in the cation exchange capacity means an increase in the mobility and availability of nutrients.

**Polysaccharides help soil particles bind together.

Prepared with Jerry Hatfield, director of the National Soil Tilth Laboratory, Ames, Iowa.

6 Plant a cover crop

Why cover crops?

The effectiveness of a winter cover crop depends, in part, on the location of your farm and your reasons for planting the cover crop.

If your sole reason to plant a cover crop is to capture nitrogen and, therefore, save money on fertilizer, you may be in for a disappointment. University of Illinois research has shown that in the southern part of the Midwest, you may be able to break even financially with a cover crop, but the "fertilizer replacement" economics get shakier the farther north you move.

On the other hand, if you are planning to use the land for grazing or if you want to reduce your inputs and control soil erosion, then a cover crop may be a sign of good stewardship and wise management.

Cover crops, erosion, and runoff

Cover crops do an excellent job of controlling soil erosion during the winter and through the critical high-rainfall months of spring. This protection is provided by both the cover crop itself and by its residue when it is killed in the spring. On sandy soils, cover crops also significantly reduce wind erosion.

An Ohio study examined the impact of cover crops on 10 small watersheds by looking at a four-year corn-wheat-meadow-meadow rotation over the span of 28 years. For seven of those years, the winter cover was in wheat, and for 21 years the winter cover was in meadow (a grass-legume mixture). The study found that the average runoff from the 10 watersheds was 60 percent less when the cover was meadow than when it was wheat.

In Missouri, meanwhile, researchers found that soil losses on no-till soybean plots seeded to cover crops were 87 to 95 percent lower than plots that did not have a cover crop.

Grass cover crops

In the central and lower U.S. Corn Belt, rye is the preferred nonlegume for a winter cover crop. If the rye cover crop follows corn or soybeans, many producers have found that they can improve the germination of aerially seeded rye if they seed into standing corn or soybeans as the crop is maturing and before it drops its leaves. The leaves that drop provide a mulch that holds moisture in the soil.

The advantages of planting grasses such as rye as a cover crop include:

- Rapid establishment of ground cover in the fall
- Vigorous growth
- Effective recovery of nitrogen from the soil
- Good winter survival
- More extensive ground cover and, therefore, more erosion protection than with a legume cover crop. This is particularly true after soybeans or corn because they are harvested so late. If you follow with a legume cover crop, it will be very small throughout the winter. A rye cover crop will be larger and will provide better erosion protection.

  However, grasses do not have this same advantage over legumes if you plant a cover crop after a mid- to late-summer crop, such as wheat. In this case, the legume cover crop will have more time to grow and will be large enough to do a good job of erosion control.
- Possible weed control. Rye is allelopathic, which means it releases chemicals that may reduce the growth of some weeds. If you kill it a few weeks before planting corn or soybeans no-till, rye residue could help reduce weed pressure.

Despite these advantages, most research has shown that planting corn into a grass cover crop often yields less than when it is grown without a cover crop. There are several reasons for this:

- Residue from grass crops has a high carbon-to-nitrogen ratio. As a result, nitrogen from the soil becomes tied up by microbes and is unavailable to the crop.
- A vigorously growing grass crop such as rye can dry out the surface soil rapidly, causing problems with the next crop's stand establishment under dry planting conditions. If you use an irrigation system, however, you can eliminate this concern.
- When weather at planting is wet, the heavy amount of vegetation from a cover crop can cause soils to stay wet and cool, reducing emergence.
- Chemical substances released during the breakdown of some grass crops have been shown to inhibit the growth of a following grass crop such as corn. (These are the same chemicals that inhibit the growth of grass weeds.)

Legume cover crops

Legume cover crops are capable of nitrogen fixation; they can draw nitrogen from the air and provide it "free" to the following crop. Also, they have a lower carbon-to-nitrogen ratio than grasses, which means nitrogen will not be tied up as much when legumes break down.

However, the early growth of legumes can be somewhat slower than that of grass cover crops, and many of the legumes are not as winter-hardy as grasses such as rye. As a result, legumes seeded after the harvest of a corn or soybean crop often grow little before winter, resulting in low winter survivability, limited nitrogen fixation before spring, and (as mentioned earlier) inadequate ground cover to protect the soil from erosion. For improved ground cover, legume cover crops are normally seeded with spring oats.

Despite the limitations among legumes, hairy vetch has usually worked well as a winter cover crop in the southern Midwest. It offers the advantages of fairly good establishment, good fall growth, and vigorous spring growth, especially if it is planted early (during the late summer). When allowed to make considerable spring growth, hairy vetch has provided as much as 80 to 90 pounds of nitrogen per acre to the corn crop that follows.

Other legume species that may be used as winter cover crops include mammoth and medium red clovers, as well as ladino clover. However, these cover crops are not as effective as hairy vetch.

To get the maximum benefit from a legume cover crop, plant the crop early enough so that it grows considerably before the onset of cold weather in the late fall. The last half of August is probably the best time for planting these cover crops.

Retaining soil moisture is critical because dry weather after seeding may result in poor stands of the legume. Hairy vetch needs more rain than rye. In fact, you probably need a couple of $1/2$- to $3/4$-inch rains to get vetch started.

Some producers have attempted to seed legumes such as hairy vetch into corn at the time of the last cultivation. This may work occasionally, but a very good corn crop will shade the soil surface enough to prevent growth of a crop underneath its canopy, and cover crops seeded in this way will often be injured or killed by periods of dry weather during the summer.

All things considered, the chances for successfully establishing legume cover crops are best when they are seeded into small grains during the spring or after small-grain harvest or when they are planted on idle fields.

Cover crops and moisture

The primary risk that winter cover crops pose to the next season's crop is moisture depletion. That is why it is important to watch the weather and kill the cover crop if dry weather sets in.

Also, it's a good idea to kill a rye cover crop when it is between 1 and 2 feet high because it becomes difficult to work with if it is any taller. If your cover crop is vetch, let it continue to grow until the normal optimum planting date for the crop that follows; a larger plant means greater amounts of organic nitrogen. However, kill the vetch if the weather turns dry.

Incorporate residue?

Whether or not to incorporate cover-crop residue is a point of contention, with some research showing no advantages to incorporation; other results show some benefits.

If you plan to incorporate cover-crop residue, do *not* do it when the crop is tall (knee-high or taller). Incorporating heavy residue can hurt the seedbed. On the other hand, incorporating *light* amounts of residue can actually improve the seedbed. Also on the plus side, incorporation can improve the recovery of nutrients such as nitrogen under dry conditions, and it makes possible an additional weed-control option—cultivation.

Nevertheless, planting no-till into cover crops is the preferred option because incorporating cover-crop residue removes most or all of the erosion-control benefit of the cover crop between planting and crop canopy development—the period of highest risk for soil erosion. Tilling to incorporate residue can also stimulate the emergence of weed seedlings.

Prepared with Don Bullock, UI associate professor of crop production; Emerson Nafziger, crop production specialist, and Mike Plumer, natural resources management educator, UI Extension.

7 Rotate crops

The rotation effect

During the 1950s and 1960s, many people thought that synthetic fertilizers and pesticides could forever replace crop rotation without a loss of yield. But that opinion has changed. The current consensus is that crop rotation increases yield and profit and allows for sustained production no matter what amount of fertilizers or pesticides you use.

For example, a two-year rotation of corn and soybeans yields 5 to 20 percent more than continuous corn. And according to University of Minnesota research, a 5 percent increase in corn yields can translate into a 50 percent boost in profit for U.S. farmers.

Nobody knows precisely what accounts for the increase in yields with crop rotations—or "the rotation effect," as it is called. At times, an increase in nitrogen from legumes in the rotation is primarily responsible for the yield increase. At other times, the decrease in pest pressure under crop rotations has a major influence. But even these two factors do not entirely explain the yield boost.

In addition to yield benefits, crop rotation can significantly affect agriculture's impact on surface water. But exactly what kind of impact it has depends on whether you're looking at a short-term, corn-soybean rotation or an extended rotation that includes sod, pasture, or hay.

Short-term and extended rotations

Although the use of crop rotations dropped off with the advent of pesticides and fertilizers, about 80 percent of the corn crop continues to be rotated. What has gone down more dramatically has been the use of *extended*, or long-term, crop rotations, which include sod, pasture, or hay. The vast majority of corn land, for instance, is grown in a two-year rotation with soybeans or in a similar short-term (two- to three-year) rotation.

Many farmers shifted from extended rotations to short-term rotations because of the high labor requirements and generally low profitability associated with livestock production, which uses the sod, pasture, and hay ground. In addition, past government subsidy programs, which sometimes limited rotation options, may have forced some producers away from extended rotations.

But the shift to short-term rotations that consist of row crops has had some negative consequences, particularly in relation to soil erosion and water quality.

Rotation effects on erosion and water quality

Extended rotations that include sod, pasture, or hay crops can dramatically reduce soil erosion when compared to continuous monoculture—although the difference is not nearly as significant when you compare *no-till* continuous corn to a *no-till* extended crop rotation.

While extended rotations reduce soil losses, short-term rotations can actually *increase* soil erosion when compared to continuous monoculture. During an 18-year period, Ohio State researchers found that soil loss from a corn-soybean rotation was 45 percent greater than that from continuous corn.

The main reason for the increase in erosion with a corn-soybean rotation is the soybean crop. Soybean residue is a highly fragile residue that opens up the soil surface to the erosive impact of rain and runoff water.

However, even though short rotations that include soybeans lead to more erosion when compared to continuous monoculture systems, they still offer pest control benefits, reducing the amount of pesticides required.

Rotation and pest control

By shifting from one crop to another, rotations disrupt the best-laid plans of weeds, insects, and diseases.

Weeds. Ample evidence exists that crop rotation improves weed control, even when you use synthetic herbicides. For example, midwestern researchers found that after seven to eight years of standard chemical and mechanical weed control, continuous corn had between 137 and 275 weed seeds per square foot. Soil from a corn-soybean rotation, however, had only 18 to 64 weed seeds per square foot.

Insects. Crop rotation is particularly effective in controlling insects that target specific crops and are *not* highly mobile—such as the northern corn rootworm. When corn is grown continuously, corn rootworms reach the economic threshold about 30 percent of the time. But when corn is rotated with soybeans, rootworms reach the economic threshold less than 1 percent of the time.

However, note that in localized areas of the north-central United States, some corn rootworms are beginning to adapt to the two-year corn-soybean and corn-small grain rotations. As much as 9 percent of northern corn rootworm eggs are able to survive two or more winters before hatching.

Disease. Crop rotation effectively prevents the buildup of some diseases, particularly fungal diseases and nematodes and to a much lesser extent bacterial and viral diseases.

Other impacts of crop rotation

In addition to the effect on soil erosion and pest control, crop rotations have a variety of other impacts:

Nutrients. The contribution of nitrogen (N) from the legumes in crop rotations helps to increase yields. In addition, crop rotation increases soil microbial activity, and some researchers believe this increases the availability of other nutrients, such as phosphorus.

Soil organic matter and structure. Crop rotations that include long periods of sod, pasture, or hay crops usually increase soil organic matter. But short-term rotations, such as tillage-intensive corn-soybeans, lead to a destruction of organic matter.

In general, soil organic matter improves many soil qualities, such as the water infiltration rate and mineral availability.

CHECK IT OUT

For information on the nitrogen content of legume crops: page 139.

For information on the effect of no-till on soil organic matter: pages 43-45.

Allelopathy. Allelopathy is a process in which plants release compounds that affect other plants, either positively or negatively. Recent information suggests that with continuous corn, compounds develop in the soil that inhibit the yields of the next year's corn crop.

But once again, such theories do not fully explain why yields increase when crops are rotated.

Prepared with Don Bullock, UI associate professor of crop production.

8 Select vigorous perennial pasture species

Plant a mixture

An excellent stand of forage plants on highly erodible land (HEL) is unsurpassed in protecting surface water from eroding soil. But getting an excellent stand hinges on the selection of the right forage species.

Planting a pasture field to a single species is a risky venture because a single insect, disease, or environmental condition could easily destroy the entire pasture. Every forage has its own unique susceptibilities and resistances. Therefore, plant a mixture of forage perennial grasses and legumes in the same permanent pasture. This approach will provide stability in the midst of changing conditions.

It is best to select combinations that are adapted to a specific site instead of trying to manage a hodgepodge of species across different sites in the same field. Legumes are an especially important component of pastures because they fix atmospheric nitrogen.

In addition, you will get the most production and the most protection against erosion if you match perennial pasture plants to your animals, soil, and environmental conditions. To find the plants that fit best, you must:

- Match forages to the ruminant nutrient requirements
- Select perennial grasses based on their "booting date" and perennial legumes based on their "bud date"
- Match forages to soil drainage conditions
- Select forages according to other qualities, such as winter-hardiness, drought tolerance, flooding tolerance, and persistence

Matching ruminant nutrient requirements

Determine whether your livestock require very high levels of nutrients, high levels, medium levels, or low levels. Then select forages accordingly. For example, a high-producing dairy cow will need very high nutrient levels, while a beef cow will require low nutrient levels from the third trimester of pregnancy to just before (within two weeks) of the calf's birth.

The table on page 54 shows which forages will meet different nutrient requirements.

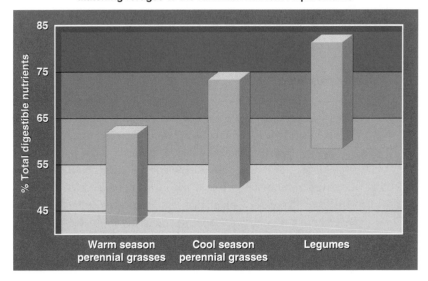

Matching forages to the ruminant nutrient requirements

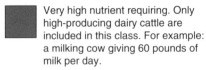 Very high nutrient requiring. Only high-producing dairy cattle are included in this class. For example: a milking cow giving 60 pounds of milk per day.

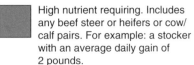 High nutrient requiring. Includes any beef steer or heifers or cow/calf pairs. For example: a stocker with an average daily gain of 2 pounds.

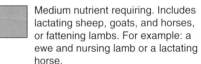 Medium nutrient requiring. Includes lactating sheep, goats, and horses, or fattening lambs. For example: a ewe and nursing lamb or a lactating horse.

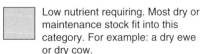 Low nutrient requiring. Most dry or maintenance stock fit into this category. For example: a dry ewe or dry cow.

Matching the "boot" or "bud" date

Select a forage that will yield during the season in which it will be principally used. This means matching the boot or bud date. The boot date is when the floral parts emerge through the whorl of the top leaf of grass, and the bud date is when a legume produces a flower bud.

The tables on page 55 list the boot and bud dates for different perennial pasture species. The dates listed are most appropriate for the southern Midwest, but they still provide an idea of how the different species compare. The dates listed are for Cairo, Illinois, which is at a latitude of 36 degrees and a mean sea level of 300 feet. As a general rule, add two days for every degree of latitude change north and one day for each 100-foot rise in mean sea level above 300 feet.

Even simpler, check with your Cooperative Extension Service office for the boot and bud dates for your region.

Perennial cool season grasses. Perennial cool season grasses produce most of their growth during the spring and fall. They mature early in the

"Boot dates" of perennial grasses

Perennial cool season grasses

Boot date*	Species
April 10	Creeping garrisongrass
April 26	Kentucky bluegrass
April 28	Orchardgrass
April 30	Tall fescue
May 8	Quackgrass
May 10	Perennial ryegrass
May 16	Reed canarygrass
May 18	Smooth bromegrass
May 26	Timothy
June 4	Redtop

Perennial warm season grasses

June 6	Eastern gamagrass
June 8	Switchgrass
June 10	Bermudagrass
June 12	Caucasian bluestem
June 20	Johnsongrass
July 4	Big bluestem
July 26	Little bluestem
August 12	Indiangrass

*Dates will vary, depending on the location.

"Bud dates" of perennial legumes

Bud date*	Species
May 1	Alfalfa (first harvest)
May 9	Red clover (first harvest)
May 17	White clover (ladino)
May 23	Alsike clover
May 27	Crown vetch
May 29	Birdsfoot trefoil
June 3	Sericea lespedeza
June 5	Alfalfa (second harvest)
June 17	Red clover (second harvest)
July 9	Alfalfa (third harvest)
July 27	Red clover (third harvest)
August 13	Alfalfa (fourth harvest)
September 5	Red clover (fourth harvest)
September 17	Alfalfa (fifth harvest)
October 23	Alfalfa (sixth harvest)

*Dates will vary, depending on the location.

growing season during April, May, and June. Only the tillers that initiate growth in the spring (first growth) produce a seed head. After the first tillers are grazed or cut, all growth comes from sterile or vegetative tillers, which do not produce a seed head.

Perennial warm season grasses. Perennial warm season grasses produce most of their growth during the summer months of June, July, and August. Only the tillers that initiate growth in the summer (first growth) produce a seed head. After the tillers are grazed or cut, all growth comes from sterile or vegetative tillers, which do not produce a seed head.

Perennial legumes. Perennial legumes are evaluated according to the bud date. Unlike perennial cool and warm season grasses, a bud is produced with each cycle of a legume's regrowth.

Matching soil drainage conditions

Some grass and legume species are better adapted to certain soil drainage characteristics than other species. The accompanying table indicates which forages adapt to poorly drained, moderately drained, and droughty soils.

Response of selected forages to drainage characteristics of soils

Perennial cool season grasses

Poorly drained soil	Moderately drained soil	Droughty soil
Reed canarygrass	Orchardgrass	Tall fescue
Redtop	Smooth bromegrass	
	Tall fescue	
	Timothy	

Perennial warm season grasses

Eastern gamagrass	Big bluestem	Little bluestem
	Indiangrass	
	Switchgrass	

Perennial legumes

Alsike clover	Alfalfa	Alfalfa
	Red clover	
	White clover	
	Birdsfoot trefoil	

General characteristics of perennial grasses and legumes

Perennial cool season grasses

Species	Winter-hardiness	Drought tolerance	Flooding tolerance	Persistence
Kentucky bluegrass	Good	Fair	Fair	Good
Orchardgrass	Good	Fair	Fair	Fair
Perennial ryegrass	Poor	Fair	Fair	Poor
Quackgrass	Excellent	Good	Fair	Good
Redtop	Fair	Fair	Good	Fair
Reed canarygrass	Good	Good	Excellent	Good
Smooth bromegrass	Good	Fair	Fair	Good
Tall fescue	Good	Good	Good	Good
Timothy	Excellent	Poor	Poor	Poor

Perennial warm season grasses

Species	Winter-hardiness	Drought tolerance	Flooding tolerance	Persistence
Bermudagrass	Fair	Good	Poor	Good
Big bluestem	Good	Good	Poor	Good
Caucasian bluestem	Fair	Good	Fair	Good
Eastern gamagrass	Good	Fair	Good	Good
Indiangrass	Good	Good	Poor	Good
Johnsongrass	Poor	Fair	Excellent	Fair
Little bluestem	Good	Good	Poor	Good
Switchgrass	Good	Good	Poor	Good

Perennial legumes

Species	Winter-hardiness	Drought tolerance	Flooding tolerance	Persistence
Alfalfa	Good	Good	Poor	Good
Alsike clover	Good	Poor	Good	Poor
Birdsfoot trefoil	Good	Poor	Fair	Good
Red clover	Fair	Poor	Fair	Fair
White clover	Good	Poor	Good	Poor

Other forage characteristics

The table above ranks perennial forage plants according to winter-hardiness, drought tolerance, flooding tolerance, and persistence. Match your forage to those qualities that are necessary to adapt to local environmental conditions. If you do, you increase the chances of seeing vigorous growth, high production, and increased erosion control.

Prepared with C.J. (Jim) Kaiser, UI associate professor emeritus, forage crop production and pasture management.

9 Protect the soil with special-use annual forage crops

Temporary production and protection

Annual forage crops are special, short-term forages that are often needed for temporary pasture, hay, or silage production. These special-use crops are often used as transitional crops in the following instances:

- When you are coming out of a corn or soybean crop in the fall and it is too late to plant a cool season perennial forage crop or too early for warm season perennials. A special-use annual forage crop can serve as a transitional crop until the following year, providing an effective cover to reduce soil erosion.

- When you switch from an old perennial forage stand to a new perennial forage crop with a higher production potential. You may need a transitional crop, depending on the planting date for the new perennial crop.

- When you face delayed planting in the spring due to abnormally wet soil conditions and the growing season is too short for planting certain row crops.

- When you are facing a feed emergency

To provide the best protection against erosion, special-use annual crops should be no-tilled. Instead of disking the seedbed, as is often done with annual crops, plant directly into an untilled seedbed.

Meeting production needs

Special-use annual forage crops complete their entire life cycle in one year or less. They are grouped into summer annual crops and winter annual crops.

Summer annuals are planted in the spring through early summer and mature before frost. Winter annual forage crops are planted in the early fall. Winter annuals often produce forage in the late fall or early winter, with the major forage yield coming the following spring or early summer.

You get the most erosion control if you select the appropriate species for your production goal and seed by no-till methods. The accompanying tables will help you select the right species.

The boot, bud, and availability dates listed in the tables are most appropriate for the southern Midwest; they are based on standard planting dates in Cairo, Illinois. However, they still provide an idea of how the different species compare. Check with your Cooperative Extension Service office for the dates for your region.

Summer annuals

Summer annual grasses are seeded in April through June and are ready for use by mid-summer. Later plantings will be available later in the growing season but with smaller yields.

Summer annual volunteer grasses are good forages for animal production if used in the vegetative stage. They are not useful for animal production if left unused until maturity.

Summer annual legumes are excellent forage plants for animal production. They are seeded in late winter to late spring. White sweet clover and lespedeza are often broadcast seeded, and soybeans and cowpeas are frequently no-tilled.

"Boot and bud dates" of summer annuals

Summer annual grasses

Boot date*	Species
June 30	Sudangrass (first harvest)
July 2	Spring oat
July 6	Sorghum/sudangrass (first harvest)
July 16	Pearl millet (first harvest)
July 18	Silage sorghum
August 14	Silage corn
August 22	Silage grain sorghum

Summer annual volunteer grasses

June 14	Giant foxtail
July 8	Crabgrass
August 16	Fall panicum

Summer annual legumes

Bud date*	Species
June 1	Forage field pea
June 15	White sweet clover
July 13	Berseem clover
August 11	Lespedeza
August 19	Soybean (hay or silage)
August 27	Cowpea (hay or silage)

*Dates will vary, depending on the location and planting dates.

First harvest date of non-grass, non-legume summer annual forages	
First harvest date*	Species
June 30	Rape/canola (spring seeded)
July 8	Chicory
*Dates will vary, depending on the location and planting date.	

Non-grass, non-legume forages are seeded in the spring. Like summer annual volunteer grasses, they must be used for animal production in the vegetative stage.

Winter annuals

Winter annual grasses contain both volunteer grasses and seeded species. They begin their life cycle in the fall but seldom produce any forage in the fall. They mature quickly in the spring and are good for forage production for only a short time.

Winter annual legumes contain both volunteer legumes and seeded species. They are seeded in late summer for establishment before winter. Forage production is mostly during the spring.

"Boot and bud dates" of winter annuals	
Winter annual grasses	
Boot date*	Species
April 24	Cheat
May 3	Field brome
May 9	Wild barley
May 20	Ryegrass
Winter annual legumes	
Bud date*	Species
April 17	Hop clover
May 3	Crimson clover
May 7	Hairy vetch
May 11	Bigflower vetch
June 1	Yellow sweet clover (also biennial)
*Dates will vary, depending on the location and planting date.	

Winter annual cereal grasses are seeded in the late summer or fall, often by no-till methods. Many of the cultivars used for forage production are the same cultivars used for grain production.

Availability dates of winter annual cereal grasses

Availability date	Species
October 28	Rye (first grazing)
November 8	Barley (first grazing)
November 16	Triticale (first grazing)
November 22	Oat (first grazing)
November 28	Wheat (first grazing)
April 20	Rye (hay or silage)
May 2	Barley (hay or silage)
May 6	Triticale (hay or silage)
May 22	Oat (hay or silage)
May 24	Wheat (hay or silage)

*Dates will vary, depending on the location and planting date.

Winter annual brassicas are seeded in the late summer. No-till seeding is the preferred method of establishment. Their forage production comes quickly in the fall, and little or no forage is available in the spring.

First grazing of winter annual brassicas

First grazing*	Species
November 15	Rape/canola
November 20	Chinese cabbage hybrid
November 30	Turnip
December 10	Kale

*Dates will vary, depending on the location and planting date.

Prepared with C.J. (Jim) Kaiser, UI associate professor emeritus, forage crop production and pasture management.

10 Protect the soil with rotational grazing

Maximum benefits

Rotational grazing is a process of planned grazing that encourages pasture growth, provides maximum benefits to the animals, and prevents overgrazing. By preventing overgrazing, a rotationally grazed pasture provides better cover to reduce soil erosion.

Rotational grazing makes use of a large number of paddocks—subdivisions of the larger pasture. The paddocks give the animals access to grazeable forage at all times during the season. Animals rotate from paddock to paddock, so each area of land undergoes a short grazing period, followed by a longer rest period. The pasture is grazed while it is leafy and nutritious, still in the vegetative stage, and before the forage matures.

Although rotational grazing requires more labor, its benefits are numerous:

- By limiting grazing in each paddock to short time intervals (one to three days), pasture plants are given a chance to fully regrow before they are regrazed. In fact, rotational grazing allows a pasture to rest for 90 percent of the time.

- Grazing for short periods results in a more even grazing of all plants. This is partly because animals have less time to foul the plants with dung and urine. In a continuous grazing system, on the other hand, animals will tend to graze heavily in one area, fouling the area with dung and urine. They will then avoid that area, and the result is uneven grazing.

- Rotational grazing maximizes the quantity of forage harvested by reducing the trampling losses.

- Rotational grazing decreases the amount of land required because it can handle more animals per acre.

- A short grazing period followed by a long rest period maintains a large root mass, which allows for a quicker recovery of top growth. Continuous grazing, in contrast, keeps the grass very short over a long period of time. The result is reduced root mass, which prevents a quick recovery of top growth.

- Rotational grazing better distributes recycled soil nutrients because dung and urine are more evenly distributed. This, along with a large root mass and dense top growth, will help protect the soil from erosion.

Forage growth curve: Quality and yield

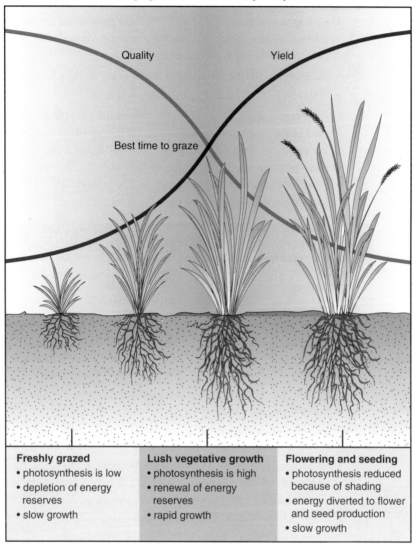

Freshly grazed	Lush vegetative growth	Flowering and seeding
• photosynthesis is low	• photosynthesis is high	• photosynthesis reduced because of shading
• depletion of energy reserves	• renewal of energy reserves	• energy diverted to flower and seed production
• slow growth	• rapid growth	• slow growth

With rotational grazing, cattle graze the pasture at the ideal time—while it is leafy and nutritious, still in the vegetative stage, and before the forage matures. Rotational grazing also reduces overgrazing.

- By reducing overgrazing, rotational grazing maintains more residual leaves on the pasture plants. The greater the leaf area that remains, the faster plants recover from grazing. Increased leaf area allows plants to use photosynthesis for energy instead of drawing solely on root reserves for regrowth. This can improve the health and productivity of the pasture.

Determining the number of paddocks

Deciding on the number of paddocks to be grazed and the size of the paddocks are key factors in creating a grazing plan. The number of paddocks needed depends on two things:

- The length of time the animals are to graze an individual paddock
- The rest period needed by the pasture plants

A "grazing cycle" is equal to the rest period plus the grazing period. Most legume-grass combinations used in the Midwest work well with rest-to-graze periods similar to alfalfa-orchardgrass. An alfalfa-orchardgrass pasture needs about 30 days of rest, although the rest period may be longer during July and August. The accompanying table shows four possible grazing cycles for an alfalfa-orchardgrass pasture.

Four possible grazing plans for an alfalfa-orchardgrass pasture

Rotational plan	Rest (days)	Graze (days)	Grazing cycle (days)	Rest per cycle (percent)	Paddocks needed (number)
Plan 1	33	3	36	92	12
Plan 2	30	3	33	91	11
Plan 3	27	3	30	90	10
Plan 4	28	4	32	88	8

Determining the paddock size and stocking rate

Paddock size primarily has to do with the yield of the pasture and the stocking rate of animals. Paddock layout will vary from farm to farm because of topography, available water, animal traffic, and individual management concerns. The illustration on page 65 shows two possible ways to subdivide a 160-acre tract into 12 paddocks.

Plan the paddock layout to reduce lane use and cowpath erosion. Determine paddock size and livestock numbers per paddock by trial and error for each set of pastures. Start with the minimum stocking rate per acre that would be used for the same pasture under continuous grazing management.

In the Midwest, experience has suggested that on productive soils with good legume-grass mixtures, rotationally grazed pastures can support about 2,000 pounds of live animal weight per acre. This means they can support ten ewe-lamb units per acre, two cow-calf pairs per acre, or six stockers per acre.

Subdividing a paddock

Two possible subdivisions of a 160-acre tract into 12 paddocks of 13.3 acres each

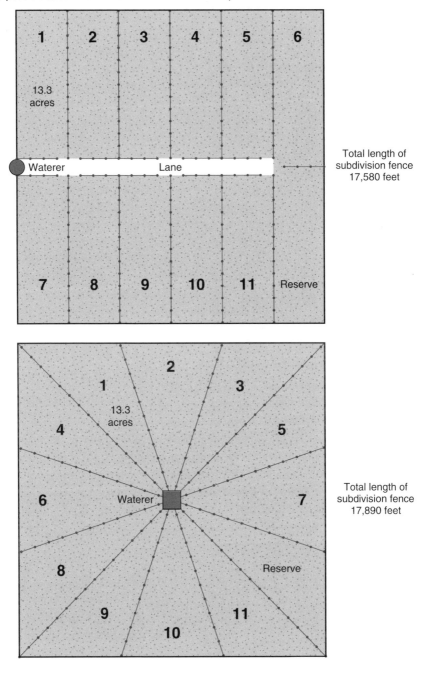

Total length of subdivision fence 17,580 feet

Total length of subdivision fence 17,890 feet

Prepared with C.J. (Jim) Kaiser, UI associate professor emeritus, forage crop production and pasture management.

11 Use no-till when renovating pasture

Keep slopes covered

Erosion can have a field day when you're renovating a pasture—unless you renovate it the no-till way.

"Pasture renovation" usually means changing the plant species in a pasture to increase pasture quality and productivity. However, before seeding new grasses and legumes, you need to reduce the competition from existing pasture plants, and many producers do that by tilling the slopes. The result: Slopes are exposed to erosion. This is a significant concern because pastureland is often steep land that is not suitable for row crops; therefore, extensive tillage during renovation can expose bare soil to extremely high levels of erosion.

With developments in herbicides and no-till seeders, the no-till option is an effective alternative to tilling the slopes. Using a herbicide to subdue existing pasture plants and then seeding with a no-till seeder has proven very successful in many research trials and farm seedings. It also keeps the slope better protected from the erosive forces of rain and runoff.

No-till pasture renovation

There are eight basic steps to no-till pasture renovation.

1. Graze the pasture intensively for 20 to 30 days before the seeding date to reduce the vigor of existing pasture plants.

2. Lime and fertilize, using a soil test as your guide. Soil pH should be between 6.5 and 7.0. Although desirable levels of phosphorus and potassium will vary according to the soil type, phosphorus should be in the range of 40 to 50 pounds per acre and potassium in the range of 260 to 300 pounds per acre.

3. One or two days before seeding, apply a herbicide to further subdue the vegetation—if necessary.

4. Seed the desired species, using high-yielding varieties. The legumes alfalfa and red clover have high-yield potential; they are often the species seeded into a pasture that has a desirable grass species.

5. Seed with a no-till drill that places the seed in contact with the soil. In general, seedings may be made in early spring through the northern Midwest and late August in the southern Midwest. Check with the local Cooperative Extension Service office for your area's seeding date guidelines.

6. Apply insecticides as needed. Insects that eat germinating seedlings are more prevalent in the southern part of the Midwest than in the northern part, and an insecticide may be needed.

   Leafhoppers will usually appear in early summer and be present during most of the growing season. They must be controlled where alfalfa is seeded, especially in spring-seeded pastures, because leafhopper feeding is devastating to new alfalfa seedlings. Well-estasblished alfalfa plants are injured but rarely killed by leafhoppers. Red clover and grass plants are not attacked by leafhoppers.

   For information on insecticide selection, contact your local Cooperative Extension Service office.

7. Initiate grazing 60 to 70 days after spring seedings, but not until the next spring for late-August seedings. Spring-seeded alfalfa and red clover should be at about 50 percent bloom at the first grazing, while late-August seedings should be in the late-bud to first-flower stage of growth when grazing begins.

   Use rotational grazing, in which animals rotate from paddock to paddock. With this system, each area of land undergoes a short grazing period, followed by a longer rest period.

   Rotational grazing offers greater animal product yield than continuous grazing, results in a more even grazing of all plants, and decreases the amount of land required because it can handle more animals per acre. Use one or two strands of electric fencing for interior fencing to separate paddocks. Movable fencing is very practical for interior fencing of rotational grazing paddocks.

8. Fertilize pastures annually according to the amount of nutrients that the crop removed. Each ton of dry matter from a pasture contains about 12 pounds of phosphate and 50 to 60 pounds of potash. Do not use nitrogen on established pastures in which at least 30 percent of the vegetation is alfalfa, red clover, or both.

   About 20 to 80 percent of the nutrients removed by a pasture crop may be returned to the pasture in the form of urine and manure, so fertilization rates will be less than for hay production. Rotational and intensive grazing improve the uniformity of distribution of manure and urine on pasture, thus increasing the efficiency of nutrient recycling and further reducing the need for supplemental fertilization.

   Test the soil of pastures thoroughly every four years and adjust your fertilization program according to results.

Prepared with Don Graffis, forage crops specialist, UI Extension.

12 Manage timberland to protect soil

A stabilizing force

Trees represent strength and stability, which is only fitting because trees bring stability to an ecosystem in a way unmatched by any other type of vegetation. Therefore, you do well to manage your timber wisely, no matter if your timber is part of a narrow "riparian zone" running alongside a stream or lake or is part of a denser woodland from which you harvest trees.

Trees serve any number of purposes on your land, acting as filters, transformers, sources of energy, and sources of shade.

Filters. Streamside forests act as filters by capturing sediment, nitrogen, phosphorus, and other pollutants before they reach the water. When streams clog with sediment, the risk of flooding increases and the sediment can interfere with the feeding and reproduction of bottom-dwelling fish and aquatic insects.

Transformers. Streamside forests act as transformers when the bacteria and fungi of the forest transform nitrogen from runoff and decaying organic debris into minerals—valuable food for plants. Denitrifying bacteria can also convert dissolved nitrogen into gases, which are then released into the atmosphere. Meanwhile, a variety of biodegrading forces, active on the forest floor, break down pesticides, transforming them into generally less toxic compounds.

Sources of energy. Streamside forests act as sources of energy for aquatic life. In small, well-shaded upland streams, as much as 75 percent of the organic food base for aquatic life comes from dissolved organic materials, such as fruit, limbs, leaves, and insects that fall from the forest canopy. This benefit passes up the food chain.

Sources of shade. Streamside forests act as sources of shade, which optimize the light and temperature conditions for aquatic plants and animals. The loss of shade increases the demand for dissolved oxygen by certain fish, but reduces the amount of dissolved oxygen available in the water.

To keep your trees in business, doing what they do best, a good place to start is to keep cattle out of timber areas.

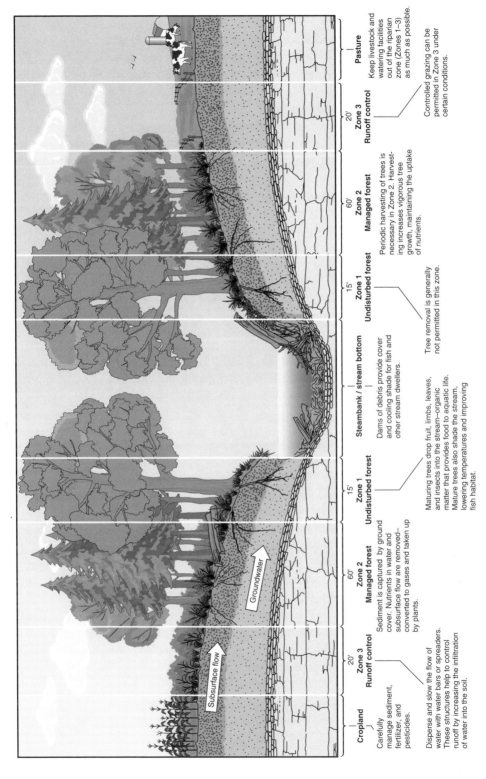

Cropland

Carefully manage sediment, fertilizer, and pesticides.

Disperse and slow the flow of water with water bars or spreaders. These structures help to control runoff by increasing the infiltration of water into the soil.

Subsurface flow

20'
Zone 3
Runoff control

Sediment is captured by ground cover. Nutrients in water and subsurface flow are removed–converted to gases and taken up by plants.

Groundwater

60'
Zone 2
Managed forest

15'
Zone 1
Undisturbed forest

Maturing trees drop fruit, limbs, leaves, and insects into the stream–organic matter that provides food to aquatic life. Mature trees also shade the stream, lowering temperatures and improving fish habitat.

Steambank / stream bottom

Dams of debris provide cover and cooling shade for fish and other stream dwellers.

15'
Zone 1
Undisturbed forest

Tree removal is generally not permitted in this zone.

60'
Zone 2
Managed forest

Periodic harvesting of trees is necessary in Zone 2. Harvesting increases vigorous tree growth, maintaining the uptake of nutrients.

20'
Zone 3
Runoff control

Controlled grazing can be permitted in Zone 3 under certain conditions.

Pasture

Keep livestock and watering facilities out of the riparian zone (Zones 1–3) as much as possible.

Avoid grazing timberland

It's been said, tongue-in-cheek, that cattle would need 20-foot-wide mouths and would have to graze at speeds up to 6 miles per hour to obtain an adequate supply of nutrients when being pastured in a timberland area. The vegetation in a forested area simply does not provide the nutrition needed for cattle.

What the vegetation does provide is a protective cover on the soil surface. But you lose some of this protection if you let your cattle graze it away. The result will be an increased movement of sediment and other pollutants. In addition, the trees will be harmed by the compaction caused by the cattle's hooves, and the animals will hinder the regrowth of new tree seedlings.

The bottom line: When you pasture cattle in timberland, your animals and trees suffer, and so does the quality of any water running through and alongside the forested area.

If livestock pasture adjoins forested lands, block access with fencing or other physical barriers. If shade and wind protection for livestock are important considerations, scatter shade trees and shelter plantings across the pasture and at least 100 feet from the forest edge or from any streambank.

CHECK IT OUT

For ideas on fencing animals away from streams and ponds: page 157.

Managing riparian zones

In addition to keeping cattle out of timberland, you can protect a streamside woodland by carefully managing the various zones within it (see illustration on page 69). The principles summarized in the illustration also apply to more extensive forested areas near lakes and streams. However, the denser woodland areas call for additional management when harvesting, constructing haul roads, felling trees, skidding, and locating landings near wetland areas.

The sidebar on pages 71-72 summarizes some of the key management practices when harvesting trees. By observing best management practices, you minimize the impact of harvesting on the environment and maintain forest productivity.

Prepared with Mike Bolin, forest management specialist, UI Extension.
SOURCE: *Riparian Forest Buffers*, USDA Forest Service, Northeastern Area, 1991.

HARVESTING TREES: KEY BEST MANAGEMENT PRACTICES IN WETLAND AREAS

Haul roads
- Avoid road construction and road use during wet periods.
- Avoid placing wetland and stream crossings through known rare, threatened, and endangered species habitat, as well as through the headwaters of public water supplies.
- To minimize the disturbance of temporary roads and to make their removal easier, use fabric mats or pads under fill.
- Minimize road width to the size necessary, typically 12 feet wide.
- Maintain roads and minimize the creation of ruts. Design the road so water drains off to either side, rather than allowing it to drain to the middle of the road.
- Divert any drainage from the road away from the wetland or stream.

Felling trees
- Avoid felling trees into standing water. This can damage habitat and disturb the breeding and spawning areas of amphibious and aquatic species.
- Keep slash (branches, limbs, and pieces of the trunk) out of streams and wetlands with standing water. Slash left in these areas uses up oxygen during decomposition, limiting the oxygen available to fish and other aquatic animals.

Skidding (dragging of timber)
- Confine skidding to a few main trails to reduce the amount of area affected.
- Keep equipment out of small wetlands.
- If you must enter large wetlands with skidding equipment, schedule the harvest during the drier seasons or when the ground is frozen. Dry or frozen ground is less likely to be eroded by equipment. If excessive rutting (deeper than 6 inches) of the land occurs, halt the skidding.
- Use cable skidding whenever possible to keep equipment out of the wetland area.
- Use low ground pressure equipment when possible; in the wettest areas, consider using tracked vehicles. Use conventional tires on skidders (tractors used to drag timber) only when the ground is dry or frozen.

- When skidding in wet areas, minimize soil compaction and rutting by putting brush down on the skid trail as a cushion. Another option is to build a "corduroy road" by laying logs across the road.
- Do not skid through vernal (temporary) ponds, spring seeps, or stream channels.
- Reduce the volume of material when skidding through wetland areas.
- Where stream crossings are unavoidable, cross only in areas that have a solid (rock) streambed bottom. Always cross at right angles to the stream. Where a solid bottom is not available, construct a temporary bridge that will accommodate the skidding equipment and the logs. Use bumper trees to keep the logs on the skid trail or bridge and off the streambanks.
- If the movement of sediment from the skid trail into the stream could present a problem at stream crossings, put down brush or create a corduroy road right before and after the crossing to help "filter" and trap sediment coming from the tires and logs.

Landings (areas where logs are piled)

Avoid locating landings in wetlands. But if no other locations are practical, follow these guidelines:

- Place landings on the highest ground possible within the wetland and use them only when dry or frozen conditions exist.
- Keep landings to a minimum size and number.
- Use proper erosion-control methods and avoid spills of oil and other hazardous materials. To minimize erosion and compaction, consider using fabric mats and pads at landing sites.
- After completing an operation, remove temporary fill or pads used for landings in wetlands.

Prepared with Mike Bolin, forest management specialist, UI Extension.

SOURCES: *Forested Wetlands,* USDA Forest Service, USDA Natural Resources Conservation Service, U.S. Army Corps of Engineers, U.S. Environmental Protection Agency, and U.S. Department of the Interior Fish and Wildlife Service, 1995; and *Best Management Practices for Silvicultural Activities in Pennsylvania's Forest Wetlands,* School of Forest Resources, College of Agricultural Sciences, Pennsylvania State University and the Pennsylvania Hardwoods Development Council, May 1993.

Controlling the flow of water

*Tag your soil with radioactive material. Then, when you quit
farming, take a Geiger counter, go down to Louisiana, identify
your soil, and retire on it."*

—Anonymous farmer

Eroding soil's primary mode of transportation is moving water.
The rills and gullies in the fields are the highway system for soil
particles, which travel with runoff water to other parts of the
countryside.

The bottom line: After managing surface cover to reduce the
impact of raindrops, the second major way to reduce erosion is to
control the flow of runoff water. Surface cover provides some
control of runoff because residue can capture and slow water on
the soil surface. But sloping land often calls for additional strategies, such as terraces and contouring.

This section examines the primary options for controlling
runoff water. It also offers ideas on how to deal with the erosive
flow of water in rivers and streams.

13 Reduce soil compaction and increase infiltration

The cost of compaction

Soils can tolerate a tremendous amount of abuse and still grow a good crop. For example, some soil compaction is beneficial at planting time for good seed-soil contact, rapid germination, and slower moisture evaporation. But when soil compaction becomes excessive, you inevitably end up paying in a number of ways—potentially lower crop yield and greater soil erosion and water runoff.

The surface of compacted soils is more likely to seal, which means water has a harder time moving down through the soil. Water accumulates on the surface and moves downslope, carrying with it eroded soil, nutrients, and pesticides.

Excessive compaction also poses these problems:

- Compacted soil reduces the space for roots to grow and the amount of oxygen getting to the roots, resulting in poor root and plant development and lower crop yields.

- If compaction restricts root development, reduced nutrient intake can limit plant growth.

- Compaction can lower yields during years of high moisture. With too much moisture, a compacted soil becomes too wet or saturated because of poor drainage. Roots of most crops do not grow well in soil that is too wet. In a saturated soil, roots die in only a few days.

Preventing compaction

Recent studies have shown that deep soil compaction, below the operating depth of commonly available primary tillage tools, persists for many years and is often impractical to remove. Therefore, compaction *prevention* is the best course of action. Here are some suggestions.

- Avoid, if at all possible, heavy wheel traffic and tillage of soils that are too wet. Remember that in the spring, the soil just below the surface is often too wet to till, even when the soil surface looks dry and suitable for tillage. If it is necessary to till such a soil for timely planting, till as shallowly as possible with no extra ballast on the tractor.

- Use wide tires or dual tires. Although wide tires and dual tires compact a greater percentage of the field surface, they will reduce the severity and depth of compaction, as long as they are not used to carry more weight or are not used to work wetter soils.

- Minimize tractor weight to provide the optimum wheel slippage for the load pulled and operating speed. In general, the higher the operating speed, the lower the tractor weight needed for optimum performance.

- Maintain the minimum tire inflation pressure needed for an acceptable tire life. Tire and tractor research engineers recently found that radial tires could operate at much lower levels of inflation pressure than previously thought. For improved tractor performance, the new tables recommend an inflation pressure as low as 6 pounds per square inch (psi) for certain tire loads.

- Avoid using oversized equipment. If your 100-horsepower tractor can do the job, don't use a 200-horsepower tractor.

- Try to combine or eliminate field operations so you make fewer passes over the field. About 90 percent of the soil compaction occurs during the first pass of traffic. So, if multiple passes are needed, try to operate in the same traffic path for all passes.

- Minimize spring tillage operations, especially on fields that were tilled in the fall.

- Keep the soil-engaging components of your equipment sharp. Dull points on a chisel plow cause more compaction below the operating depth and loosen less soil than sharp, new points.

- Add and maintain soil organic matter. Organic matter helps to bind soil aggregates together so they are not as easily broken down and compacted.

- Vary the depth of primary tillage operations from year to year to reduce the formation of a "plow pan"—a compacted layer that can develop just *below* the tillage zone.

- Use tractors with four-wheel drive or mechanical front-wheel drive (when available), instead of two-wheel drive tractors. When both the front and rear wheels are powered and line up to follow the same path, overall compaction is less. With more of the total tractor weight on the powered front wheels of these types of tractors, soil compaction is reduced when compared to the same size and properly weighted two-wheel drive tractor. Tractors with mechanical front-wheel drive or four-wheel drive also have a higher power efficiency and weigh less per pound of pull than two-wheel drive tractors.

- Consider track-type tractors. Track-type tractors leave a long, narrow "footprint" and exert a low pressure on the soil. Therefore, they provide an excellent way to reduce soil compaction problems.

Compaction and tillage

Under a no-till system, the level of soil compaction will tend to move to a natural equilibrium state for the plants grown on it. In other words, even with no wheel traffic, a loose soil will slowly become *more* compacted, while a compacted soil will slowly become *less* compacted until it reaches this natural state. (However, if heavy transport traffic and harvest vehicles continue to cross the field when soil is moist, compaction could increase.)

Although a compacted soil will tend to become less compacted with no-till, it can take several years for this to happen. Therefore, no-till is generally not regarded as a way to alleviate soil compaction. The process is slow because under a no-till system any decreases in soil density depend on natural causes: wetting and drying, freezing and thawing, and the channels created in the soil by roots and earthworms. Many specialists recommend that you take care of soil compaction problems before starting no-till.

In an excessively compacted field, you can use the subsoiler or paraplow to sufficiently loosen the soil. However, studies have shown that except for possibly improving drainage, it is not necessary to loosen the soil to the depth that some of these implements—especially the subsoiler—are designed to operate. For best results, the soil should be dry at the time you use the implement.

Also, keep in mind that the effect of subsoiling may only be temporary. For the first few rainfalls after subsoiling, the infiltration of water into the soil will be high. But eventually the rain will cause the surface to seal, and runoff may be the same as if you hadn't subsoiled. What's more, the soil can be easily recompacted by secondary tillage and subsequent wheel traffic.

If subsoiling is necessary, it is best to do it and other field operations on the contour. Contouring can reduce erosion by 50 percent as compared to subsoiling up and down the slope.

Measuring compaction

Some techniques for measuring compaction depend on highly subjective estimates. However, a soil cone penetrometer can give a more objective indication of the degree of soil compaction.

A cone penetrometer, available for about $150, measures the amount of resistance encountered when probing the soil, but its readings are affected by soil moisture and require careful interpretation before they have any practical meaning. Also, with a penetrometer it is difficult to tell if a dry soil is compacted; dry soils are often very hard, but they are not necessarily compacted. A penetrometer is often used successfully to identify compacted areas by comparing results with readings from a known noncompacted area in the same field.

Another way to assess the severity of compaction is to study plant rooting patterns. Deformed or flattened roots are a good indication of compaction. The roots grow down until they encounter a compacted zone, then grow horizontally and become deformed or flattened as they try to penetrate it.

To accurately assess the effect of compaction on a crop, examine plants at a number of locations in the field. Here are some key symptoms of compaction:

- Plants grow slowly, especially if compaction causes poor drainage.
- You find only shallow roots.
- The soil breaks out in abnormally hard, horizontal layers (or "plates").
- Roots grow primarily on the top of these plates.
- You see signs of denitrification (yellow corn plants in the compacted areas).

Prepared with John Siemens, power and machinery specialist, UI Extension.

Install grassed waterways

Natural watercourses

You probably know your fields better than the backs of your hands—every slope and soil. And you probably know the natural paths that water follows as it meanders across your fields in search of a place to drain. These natural watercourses do not always pose problems. But if you notice that a watercourse is creating excessive erosion, year after year, it may be time to convert it into a grassed waterway.

In addition to controlling erosion, grassed waterways drain storm water safely off the land into designated outlets. They can also be used as outlets for the concentrated water coming from terraces, diversions, or adjacent properties.

If you decide that a grassed waterway is needed, you have four main tasks ahead: designing and constructing the waterway, establishing vegetation, and maintaining the waterway.

Designing the waterway

Grassed waterways are generally shaped in one of three ways (see illustrations):

- Parabolic (dish-shaped bottom)
- Trapezoidal (flat bottom)
- Triangular (V-shaped)

Parabolic is usually the shape of choice for several reasons: (1) It is the shape found in natural watercourses; (2) small flows of water are not as likely to meander in a parabolic-shaped waterway; (3) the parabolic shape is the easiest waterway to cross with farm equipment; and (4) contractors find the shape easy to visualize and build.

However, some situations warrant drainageways of other shapes.

During the design stage, work closely with your soil conservationist at the Natural Resources Conservation Service (NRCS). The NRCS technician will help to calculate the grade of the watercourse, measure the drainage area, select and size the waterway, and calculate the number of acres in the grassed waterway. The minimum grassed waterway for small drainage areas is 30 feet wide and 1.2 feet deep (see illustration).

Also, depending on your outlet, soils, grade, and the length of the proposed waterway, the NRCS technician may include other structures as part of the design—grade control structures, tile lines, diversions, and checks, for example.

Shapes of grassed waterways

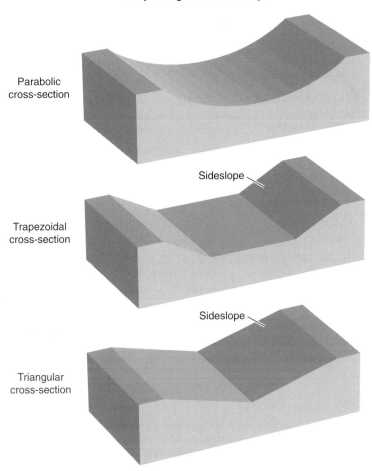

Parabolic cross-section

Sideslope

Trapezoidal cross-section

Sideslope

Triangular cross-section

The most common shapes for grassed waterways are parabolic, trapezoidal, and triangular.

A standard waterway design

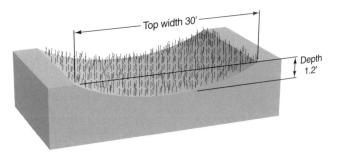

Top width 30'

Depth 1.2'

A standard waterway design is a 30-foot-wide, 1.2-foot-deep parabolic waterway.

Grade control structures. If the outlet of the proposed waterway has overfalls (small waterfalls) or if it drops more than 2 feet, your waterway needs a grade control structure at its outlet.

✓ CHECK IT OUT

For more information on grade control structures: page 105.

Tile drainage. Naturally wet soils make it hard to establish a stand of vegetation and perform maintenance activities on grassed waterways. The NRCS technician will likely recommend tile lines to reduce the problem.

Diversions and checks. To protect the waterway from erosive water flow during grass establishment, the NRCS technician may recommend side diversions to keep the flow out of the channel (see illustrations below). However, side diversions can cause erosion along the edge of the waterway, are costly, and will have to be removed at a later date, so the NRCS technician may suggest rock or fabric checks instead (see illustration on page 81).

Side diversion channels

Diversions are a temporary measure to protect the waterway from excess flow during grass establishment. After grass is established, they are removed so that runoff water flows into the waterway.

The NRCS technician may also recommend the use of "kickers." Kickers are excavated depressions or "speed bump" mounds constructed perpendicular to the waterway. They direct water flow into the grassed channel instead of allowing it to run along the side of the grass (as it has a tendency to do over time).

Rock checks

To install a rock check:
1. Dig at least 15 inches deep and the width of a backhoe bucket.
2. Fill with rock.
Rock checks protect the waterway during grass establishment; but unlike side diversions, they do not have to be removed. Rock checks are normally placed in the center of the watercourse to a depth of 15 inches. Their width is usually one-half the top width measurement. They are spaced as follows:

Grade of waterway	*Maximum spacing between checks*
• *0 to 1.5 percent*	• *100 feet*
• *1.5 to 3 percent*	• *75 feet*
• *greater than 3 percent*	• *50 feet*

Constructing the grassed waterway

To ensure quality work, obtain several cost estimates for the job and make sure your contractor is a member of the professional association of land improvement contractors. Confirm that the contractor regularly attends workshops to learn about new construction techniques.

Check with your neighbors to find out whom they have used and how satisfied they have been with the contractor's work and rates. Also, check with adjacent landowners if construction of the waterway involves blending earthwork across property lines.

Establishing vegetation

When to seed. Time the construction to coincide with a suggested seeding period—spring, late summer, or winter. Seed a waterway immediately after earth moving is complete as long as it is during the recommended seeding period.

Which seeding period is best depends on your climate and schedule of farm activities. Taking into account climate only, a late summer seeding is not likely to be washed out because dry soil will absorb most of the rainfall. Also, weed competition is lower in late summer.

A spring seeding has the advantage of ample moisture and time for plants to establish deep root systems and thick cover. Weed pressure, however, is very high and may require chemical control or extensive mowing.

Winter seeding is the least preferred, but it may be useful because it does not interfere with other farm activities. Mulch these seedings to provide erosion protection until grass is established. The seeds lie dormant until spring when soil temperature and moisture trigger their emergence. Seed mixes that sprout early obtain a foothold over weeds. However, herbicides or frequent mowing will likely be required to reduce weed pressure.

Seed mixes. Make sure your seed mix is approved by the NRCS and matches your soil type. The accompanying chart shows some approved seed mixes in Illinois and the types of soil with which they work best. It is usually not a good idea to use a standard pasture mix.

Grassed waterway seeding mixtures (Illinois)

Seeding mixture

	Rate pounds per acre	Site suitability Wet [1]	Well-drained [2]	Desirable for wildlife habitat
1. Smooth bromegrass	20		x	x
Timothy	4			
2. Smooth bromegrass	8	x	x	
Tall fescue	16			
3. Reed canarygrass	16	x	x	x
Timothy or redtop	4			
4. Smooth bromegrass	16	x	x	x
Reed canarygrass	8			
5. Reed canarygrass	12	x	x	
Tall fescue	8			
Redtop	1.5			
6. Tall fescue	16	x		
Redtop	3			
7. Kentucky bluegrass[3]	35		x	
8. Kentucky bluegrass[3]	4	x	x	
Red fescue	20			
9. Redtop	8	x		x

[1] This includes sites that are excessively wet for only a portion of the growing season.
[2] This includes sites that are well-drained with tile, as well as naturally well-drained and droughty sites.
[3] These mixtures are suitable for areas where close mowing is desired—residential areas, for example. For shady areas, use mixture number 8.

This chart presents the seed mixes approved for grassed waterways in Illinois. Check with the Natural Resources Conservation Service for approved mixes in your state.

SOURCE: Illinois Natural Resources Conservation Service, 1992.

Nutrients and weed control. Your new seeding will need added nutrients to ensure a vigorous stand of grass. Fertilize according to soil test requirements or use the standard rate recommended by the Cooperative Extension Service. The local Extension office can also provide weed-control recommendations.

Preparing the seedbed. When preparing the seedbed for planting, you must till across the waterway. Otherwise, large tillage tools such as a field cultivator or disk harrow will destroy the constructed shape of the waterway. Furthermore, tillage marks along the length of the waterway will encourage the development of rills or gullies before vegetation is fully established.

To incorporate the nutrients and lime, work the seedbed thoroughly to a minimum depth of 3 inches. As a finishing touch, use a cultipacker or other suitable tillage tool to firm the seedbed.

Seeding. Press seeds into the soil to a depth of $^1/_4$ to $^1/_2$ inch. If you broadcast the seed, use a cultipacker or another similar tool to cover the seed with soil.

Just as you did with seedbed preparation, perform seeding operations across the waterway. If you cannot seed across the waterway, use the "figure 8" seeding pattern (see illustration on page 84).

Mulching. Mulching the seeded waterway with straw reduces erosion and evaporation losses. Straw also shades young seedlings, protecting them from drying out. The recommended rate is 2,000 pounds or about 50 bales of straw per acre. Distribute straw uniformly and anchor it to the soil with a disk harrow. To anchor straw, set the blades straight and drive very slowly.

Maintaining the waterway

To avoid damaging a waterway, follow these guidelines:

- If you allow grazing, do not reduce grass height below 2 inches.
- Do not use the waterway as a roadway. Wheel tracks quickly become gullies.
- Practice conservation tillage on adjacent cropland to limit the amount of sediment reaching the waterway.
- Disengage tillage equipment when you cross a waterway.
- Do not use farming activities that hinder the flow of water into a waterway. For example, do not plant end rows along waterways.
- Shut off pesticide spray rigs before entering a waterway.
- Do not use water-soluble chemicals in waterways. These chemicals can contaminate surface water supplies.
- Do not burn waterways.

- As a general rule, examine your waterway two or three times yearly as well as after storms.
- Mow when needed because it stimulates certain grasses, improves the stand, and controls weeds. Some types of grasses, if not mowed, regularly form clumps and make the waterway vulnerable to erosion.

  With proper maintenance, a grassed waterway can last for decades.

Figure 8 seeding pattern

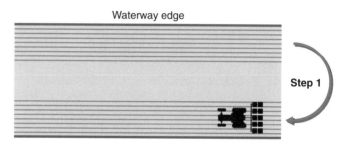

Step 1. Seed along the outer edges, leaving the center one-third unseeded.

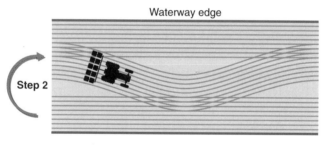

Step 2. Seed the center by gently steering from side to side to make one-half of the figure 8.

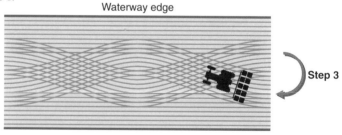

Step 3. On the return trip, seed the remaining areas and make the other half of the figure 8 by steering from side to side.

Prepared with Harry Means, Illinois state conservation engineer, and Leon Wendte, district conservationist, Natural Resources Conservation Service; Rick Farnsworth, natural resources economics specialist, UI Extension; and Kent Mitchell, UI professor of agricultural engineering.

15 Plant vegetative filter strips or make critical area plantings

Vegetative filter strips

Vegetative filter strips serve as the last line of defense against the movement of nutrients and pesticides into streams and lakes. These strips of grass, trees, and/or shrubs, planted between water and cropland, provide four basic forms of protection:

- They capture sediment eroding from adjoining cropland before it reaches the stream or lake.
- They capture the nutrients and pesticides moving from adjoining cropland. Instead of entering a waterway, the nutrients and pesticides are taken up by the buffer strip's grass, trees, or shrubs.
- They increase denitrification, a process in which soil organisms convert nitrate-nitrogen into a form that is lost to the atmosphere. Denitrification reduces the amount of nitrate available to move into groundwater and surface water supplies.
- They increase the infiltration of runoff into the soil.

As a bonus, vegetative filters can serve as a natural "classroom" for children, a corridor for wildlife movement, and an important breeding ground for birds and other wildlife.

Filter strip placement

Runoff water should reach a vegetative filter strip as a shallow, uniform flow. Filter strips are not recommended in areas where water moves in a concentrated flow. (Terraces or grassed waterways are more suited to carrying concentrated flow.)

In addition, a filter strip is most effective on slopes of 5 percent or less, where controlling the surface movement of sediment, fertilizers, and pesticides is the goal. Where controlling the *subsurface* movement of fertilizers and pesticides is the goal, filter strips are most effective on land that does not have subsurface drainage. Subsurface drain tiles simply bypass a filter, delivering water and pollutants directly into waterways.

The accompanying table, which draws data from numerous studies throughout the United States, shows the reductions that researchers have observed using strips of varying widths on land without subsurface drainage.

Reductions in nitrogen and phosphorus in surface runoff				
Nutrient	Filter strip type	Filter strip width (in feet)	% reduction	Year of study
Nitrogen	Forest	98	98	1977
Nitrogen	Forest	164	79	1984
Nitrogen	Grass	16	54	1989
Nitrogen	Grass	30	73	1989
Nitrogen	Grass	89	84	1980
Phosphorus	Forest	52	50	1987
Phosphorus	Forest	62	74	1984
Phosphorus	Forest	164	85	1984
Phosphorus	Grass	16	61	1989
Phosphorus	Grass	30	79	1989
Phosphorus	Grass	89	83	1980

Filter strip width

Filter strip width is affected by slope steepness, soil type, and the shape and size of the land draining into the filter. For example, the Natural Resources Conservation Service in Ohio recommends the following minimum strip widths for different slopes:

Minimum filter strip widths (Ohio)	
Slope	Minimum filter strip width (in feet)
Less than 1%	10
1 to 10%	15
10 to 20%	20
20 to 30%	25

If the sediment entering the filter contains considerable amounts of clay, strip widths must be wider because it takes a greater distance to filter out clay particles than it does silt and sand. Research supports filter strip widths in the range of 10 to 40 feet. Also, make sure the ratio of field drainage area to filter area is no greater than 50:1. Ideally, the ratio should be between 3:1 and 8:1.

Planning and managing a filter strip

The plants in a vegetative filter should have dense top-growth to provide good, uniform soil cover, and a fibrous root system for stability. Grasses are more effective than broadleaves in filtering sediment because they form a dense sod, have a fibrous root system, and provide more ground cover. Also, sod-forming grasses are preferred over bunch-grasses because they provide more uniform ground cover.

The type of vegetation you select for a filter strip will depend on its main purpose. For example, are you establishing the strip around a sink-hole, to control runoff from a feedlot, or to filter runoff from cropland?

Be sure you install adequate soil conservation measures above the filter strip or it can become clogged with sediment. Once the filter strip is planted, observe these guidelines:

- Do not use the strip as a roadway.
- Consider keeping livestock off the filter. When strips are dry and firm, controlled grazing may not cause excessive erosion, but it may increase the risk of microbrial contamination (see page 161).
- Inspect the filter strip frequently, especially after intense rains.
- Mow or remove hay as required.
- Repair rills and small channels that can develop in the filter strip.
- Test the soil periodically.
- Control trees, brush, and noxious weeds.

CHECK IT OUT

For information on using vegetative filters to handle runoff from livestock areas: page 175.

Critical area planting

While vegetative filter strips provide protection along waterways, a critical area planting is used to protect small, isolated areas in a field that are being damaged by excessive erosion. These plantings of grass, legumes, trees, shrubs, or vines also can capture nutrients and chemicals running off farmland, and they can provide small areas of nesting cover for birds and small animals.

Before considering a critical area planting, ask the following questions:

- If left untreated, will these areas cause severe erosion or sediment damage?
- Can the area be stabilized with other conservation methods?
- Will protection provided by the critical area planting be adequate?
- Are proper soil conservation practices installed above the planting area?
- Will you want to provide wildlife cover?

Planning and managing a critical area planting

As you establish a critical area planting, consider these points:

- Protect the area from erosion with annual grasses until establishing permanent cover.

- On areas disturbed during construction or on barren slopes 4:1 or steeper, mulch to provide temporary protection before seeding. Mulches include grass, hay, grain straw, and shredded cornstalks.

- Apply lime and fertilizer, if needed, in the top 3 inches of soil before planting.

- Prepare a firm seedbed that is free of large clods, stones, and debris larger than 6 inches in diameter.

- Use proper rates and recommended seeding dates.

- Severely eroded areas may need a nurse crop like oats. Seed oats at a rate of 1 to 1^1/$_2$ bushels per acre. Mow oats before they head out, if possible. Mow high to avoid clipping the permanent seeding.

- To improve the establishment of vegetative grass cover on critical areas, topdress a late-summer seeding during the following spring with 100 to 150 pounds per acre of actual nitrogen; topdress spring seedings in late August or early September.

- Allow no grazing for at least 18 months. After the 18-month period, you can allow moderate grazing on sites where doing so will not damage the vegetative cover, cause excessive runoff, or lead to severe erosion. Fence if needed.

- Permanently exclude livestock from extremely steep slopes.

- Native or warm season grasses can benefit from periodic burning, which stimulates growth by reducing and removing competing plant growth.

Prepared with David Kovacic, UI associate professor of landscape architecture and natural resources and environmental sciences; Kent Mitchell, UI professor of agricultural engineering; and Harry Means, Illinois state conservation engineer, Natural Resources Conservation Service.

ADDITIONAL SOURCE: *Vegetative Filter Strips: Application, Installation and Maintenance,* Rob Leeds, Larry C. Brown, Marc R. Sule, and Larry VanLieshout, The Ohio State University Extension, 1993.

CONSTRUCTED WETLANDS
SHOW PROMISE AS FILTER

An optional tool

If current studies provide positive results, constructed wetlands may prove to be an effective tool that farmers can use to prevent nitrogen from reaching streams—although the question of their effectiveness has generated some controversy.

University of Illinois researchers are evaluating the use of constructed wetlands as filters to absorb and to prevent nitrogen from moving into adjacent streams. To study the effectiveness of wetlands of different sizes, researchers constructed $1^1/_2$- to 5-acre wetlands 50 feet from the river bank. A berm, built up along the edge of the river, contains the runoff water, causing it to pool in the wetland. By retaining runoff, there is more chance for nitrogen to be removed either by the plants or by denitrification, and there is less chance of nitrogen reaching the stream.

Currently, UI researchers believe 1 acre of wetland can handle the nitrogen moving from 20 to 40 acres of field, but they will not know the actual efficiency of wetlands for several years. As of November 1996, data indicate that wetlands can remove more than two-thirds of the nitrogen entering them.

The wetland advantage

But why wetlands? Why not use a grass or forest filter strip? One disadvantage of grass buffer strips is their ineffectiveness on land drained with tiles. The tiles carry subsurface water directly to streams and other outlets, bypassing the filter strips. But with constructed wetlands, tile flow is directed into the wetland where plants and denitrifying bacteria can directly use the nitrogen. A constructed wetland would present a formidable barrier to nitrogen-laden drainage water moving toward streams.

The most likely areas for constructed wetlands are marginal lands— spots that flood easily or have high rates of erosion. Nonetheless, devoting the land to constructed wetlands may be a difficult proposition for some farmers economically. Financial incentives for this management strategy could be provided through such programs as the Conservation Reserve Program and the Wetlands Reserve Program.

Also, keep in mind that a constructed wetland, if proven practical, would be just one tool among many. Many situations call for a combination of options, such as grass filter strips, constructed wetlands, changes in tillage practices, and fertilizer management. As a bonus to controlling nitrogen flow into rivers, constructed wetlands would provide fish and wildlife habitat, scenic and recreational benefits, and some degree of flood control.

Prepared with David Kovacic, UI associate professor of landscape architecture and natural resources and environmental sciences.

16 Farm on the contour

The shape of things

From the air, contour farming presents dramatic patterns on the land. But in terms of erosion control, the real drama takes place closer to earth.

With contouring, you perform farming operations across the slope, following the shape or contour of the land. The small furrows and ridges that you create act like dams, trapping runoff water, sediment, nutrients, and pesticides, and directing them along graded crop rows to outlets such as grassed waterways or field borders. The result, some say, are reductions in soil erosion up to 50 percent on gentle slopes when compared with farming up and downhill. On very steep slopes, the erosion reduction will be less—possibly as low as 10 percent.

Contouring also offers possible savings in fuel and reduced wear and tear on machinery and equipment; some farmers report that it takes less power to farm across the slope than up and down hills.

However, tilling, planting, and harvesting fields along the contour become increasingly difficult as the number of dips, draws, ridges, and elevation changes increase. The number of point rows, short rows, and rows requiring turning and doubling back also increases.

To put it another way: Contouring is both a science and an art.

Maximum slope lengths

As a slope lengthens, the ability of runoff water to build momentum and erode the soil increases. Therefore, longer slopes mean that contouring will be less effective. So check with your local Natural Resources Conservation

Maximum allowable slope lengths for contouring (Illinois)		
Slope of the land	Percent of surface covered with residue	
	50% or less	Greater than 50%
percent	maximum slope length in feet	
1 to 2	400	500
3 to 5	300	375
6 to 8	200	250
9 to 12	120	150
13 to 16	80	100
17 to 20	60	75
21 to 25	50	63

Service office for maximum slope lengths. The table on page 91 shows the maximum lengths in Illinois.

If slopes exceed these maximum lengths, contouring must be paired with other practices such as terraces and diversions. These practices divide the slope length into shorter segments.

Key lines

The key to contouring can be found in the "key line"—the guideline that you establish along the contour of the slope, using a hand level or a contour gauge, and flags to mark the line. As you perform your farm operations, the goal is to try to stay parallel with this line.

The key line runs across the slope, dropping slightly in elevation toward a waterway, watercourse, field border, or other protected outlet for runoff water. The grade of a key line must not be more than 2 percent, which means that over the span of 100 feet, the drop in elevation cannot exceed 2 feet. (One exception: The first and last 100 feet of a key line can slope downward at a 3 percent grade. This makes it easier to enter and exit waterways and field borders.)

If your land is very steep or irregular, you may need to establish more than one key line, which means your field will have more than one contour pattern. Place the first contour guideline about one-third from the top of the slope, but no more than 150 feet from the top. Additional key lines are generally needed about every 200 feet, as measured down the drainageways.

If you cannot always follow the key line exactly when operating along rows, be sure the row grades do not exceed the smaller of the following:

- one-half the slope's percent, or
- 4 percent grade

Location of key lines for contouring

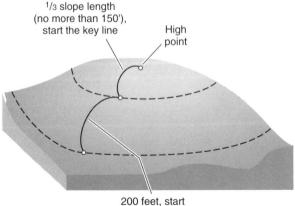

¹/₃ slope length
(no more than 150'),
start the key line

High
point

200 feet, start
the next key line (if needed)

Also, to avoid laying out new key lines every year, it's a good idea to establish a narrow permanent strip of grass along each key contour line.

Field borders

You defeat the purpose of contouring if you plant end rows up and down hill. Therefore, use field borders—a band or strip of grass that can be used as a turn row at the ends of your field.

Field borders also make good cover for wildlife. They benefit wildlife most if you delay mowing until July 15, thus allowing young ground-nesting birds to leave their nests.

To be most effective, field borders should be at least 16 feet wide, but they may be more useful as turn areas for large machinery if they are wider.

Farming on the contour

The accompanying illustration shows the standard technique for farming a contoured slope. Hopefully, you will be able to farm most of each contoured field in a straightforward way; but it is inevitable that some odd areas will develop—areas that cannot be farmed without extensive maneuvering of farm equipment. These odd areas form:

- Between two key lines where two different contour patterns meet
- On slopes where curves become too sharp to negotiate with equipment
- On hilltops where the land flattens out
- Near the bottom of sloping land where contoured rows and straight rows meet

Pattern to contour farm a field

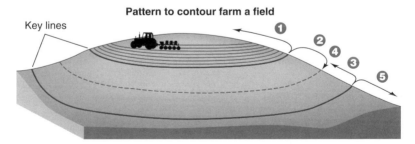

This pattern for contour farming keeps you as close to a key line as possible. The arrows on the diagram show the direction for tilling and planting.

1. Farm above the first key line.

2. Farm below the first key line about one-half the way down to the second key line.

3. Farm above the second key line to meet the area already farmed.

4. Handle any odd areas using turnstrips or butt rows.

5. Farm below the second key line.

For harvesting, the best approach is to start at the bottom and harvest up to the top. Harvest odd areas after both ends of the rows in the odd area are exposed.

The two most common techniques for dealing with odd areas are turnstrips or butt systems (see illustrations). For details, consult with your local soil conservationist and compare the income potential, production costs, and time associated with the different methods.

Techniques for farming odd areas between key lines

Turnstrip

1. Farm below the upper key line and above the lower key line until the narrowest point is 20 to 30 feet wide.

2. Add the point rows using the turnstrip to turn the equipment.

3. Farm the turnstrip or plant in protective cover.

Upper key line

Turnstrip

Lower key line

Butt system

1. Farm from the key line until you hit the area that will be butted.

2. Farm the remaining area, butting the rows as necessary.

Key line

Turnstrip and butt systems are the primary techniques for farming odd areas between contour lines. Turnstrips are preferred where odd areas have unusual boundaries caused by widely divergent key lines. Turnstrips may be planted to grass or farmed. A butt system is preferred when rows from different key lines meet at an angle. Judgment and experience will help you tailor these techniques to fields.

Prepared with Harry Means, Illinois state conservation engineer, and Jerry Misek, district conservationist, Natural Resources Conservation Service; and Kent Mitchell, UI professor of agricultural engineering.

17

Use contour stripcropping and contour buffer strips

Contour stripcropping

Contour stripcropping combines the erosion control benefits of two time-tested conservation strategies—contouring and crop rotations that include small grains.

Contour stripcropping is a system of alternating strips of meadow or small grains with strips of row crops on the contour. This combination of contouring and crop rotation can reduce soil erosion by up to 75 percent when compared to planting row crops up and down the slope.

The details of contouring, including the acceptable slope gradients, are described in Chapter 16 and also apply to a contour stripcropping system. However, the maximum allowable slope lengths are different, so check with your local Natural Resources Conservation Service (NRCS). The following chart gives the maximum slope lengths and the maximum strip widths in Illinois.

Maximum allowable slope lengths and strip widths for contour stripcropping (Illinois)		
Slope of the land	Maximum strip width	Maximum slope length
percent	feet	
1 to 2	130	800
3 to 5	100	600
6 to 8	100	400
9 to 16	80	240
17 to 20	60	160

If you must exceed the maximum strip width to accommodate your equipment, do not exceed the figure by more than 10 percent. If slope length exceeds the maximum, you must pair contour stripcropping with other practices, such as terraces or diversions. These other practices divide the slope's length into shorter segments.

Contouring and contour stripcropping also differ in the way you set up the key lines and farm the systems. So check the illustrations on page 96 for ideas on how to locate key lines and farm a contour stripcrop system.

Location of key lines for contour stripcropping

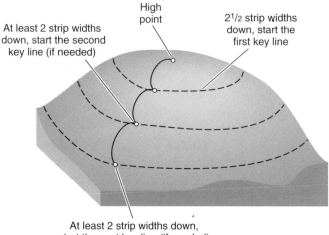

High point

At least 2 strip widths down, start the second key line (if needed)

2¹/₂ strip widths down, start the first key line

At least 2 strip widths down, start the next key line (if needed)

More than one key line is necessary when row grade exceeds the maximum specification. To determine when a new key line is necessary, strip widths must be laid out and flagged. When row grade is excessive, measure downhill at least 2 stripwidths from the last strip with acceptable row grades; then add another key line.

Pattern to contour stripcrop a field

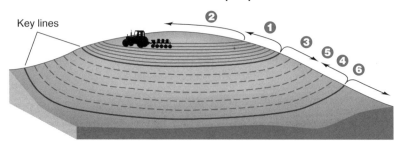

Key lines

This pattern for contour stripcrop farming keeps you as close to a key line as possible. The arrows on the diagram show the direction for tilling and planting.

1. Farm one strip width above the key line.

2. Farm the hilltop.

3. Farm strip widths below the first key line until you are two or three strip widths above the second key line.

4. Switch to the second key line and farm up the remaining strip widths.

5. Handle any odd areas using turnstrips or butt rows.

6. Farm strip widths below the second key line following the procedure in steps 3 and 4 above.

To harvest, start at the bottom of the slope and work your way up to the top. Harvest odd areas after both ends of the rows in the odd area are exposed.

Contour stripcropping is as much an art as it is a science.

The following are some other considerations when stripcropping:

- Strips of row crops should be the same width, or nearly the same, as the strips of close-grown crops and hayland. Strip width can vary by up to 10 percent.
- To be most effective, no more than half the field should be in row crop in any one year. That's why it is important to determine in the planning stage how many acres of row crops you need.
- Keep strip widths consistent from year to year. The chart on page 98 helps you match equipment widths with strip widths.
- Once the strips are established, pick up the flags that you used to mark them; this prevents the wires from getting into the machinery and crops.
- If a meadow crop fails or is killed during the winter, the NRCS can help you adjust your rotation schedule.
- Alternating strips of corn and hay will keep the strip edges visible.
- When applying herbicide, consider using additional spray nozzles on the ends of the boom with separate control valves. This helps to ensure adequate herbicide application at the strip edges.
- Use field border strips to avoid planting end rows up and down hill. The field borders also provide access to all strips throughout the growing season.

Matching strip widths with equipment widths

4-row equipment 36" rows	4-row equipment 38" rows	4-row equipment 40" rows	6-row equipment 30" rows	Implement trips
strip widths in feet				
72	76	80	90	6
84	89	93	105	7*
96	102	107	120	8
108	114	120	—	9*
120	—	—	—	10

8-row equipment 30" rows	8-row equipment 36" rows	8-row equipment 38" rows	12-row equipment 30" rows	Implement trips
strip widths in feet				
60	72	76	90	3*
80	96	101	120	4
100	120	127	—	5*
120	—	—	—	6

12-row equipment 36" rows	12-row equipment 38" rows	16-row equipment 30" rows	24-row equipment 30" rows	Implement trips
strip widths in feet				
72	76	80	120	2
108	114	120	—	3*

*Strip widths that require an odd number of equipment passes may require you to make a return trip up the next strip of row crops or an "empty" return trip.

- Because contour strips provide excellent erosion control, you might be able to reduce residue levels. Check with the NRCS to plan appropriate residue levels.

- Contour stripcropping benefits wildlife by increasing "the edge effect." Wildlife is generally attracted to the edges where different types of plant covers meet. By alternating among different crops, contour stripcropping provides numerous "edges" where different crops meet. Contour stripcropping also is aesthetically attractive and provides visual proof of your conservation efforts.

Contour buffer strips

Contour buffer strips are strips of sod, alternated with strips of row crops. This may sound basically the same as contour stripcropping, but there is an important difference. Unlike contour stripcropping, in which all strips are roughly the same width, buffer strips are narrow while the strips of row crop are wide. (Buffer strips typically make up about 20 to 30 percent of a slope.)

Although contour buffer strips offer less erosion control than contour stripcropping, the principle is the same: The strips of sod slow runoff, increase the infiltration of water into the soil, and trap sediment moving from the crop strips above.

Each buffer strip must be at least 10 feet wide to be effective. Keep vegetation tall in the spring and early summer to help slow runoff flow; and if it is not used for hay, delay mowing until July 15 to help ground-nesting birds and mammals.

As with contouring and contour stripcropping, you can end up with odd areas in the field when setting up contour buffer strips. One way to deal with these odd areas is to put them in sod and keep all of the row crop strips an even width. Eliminating point rows will make the system easier to farm, although less of the slope will be in row crops.

Finally, check with your local NRCS office for recommendations on the maximum distance between sod strips. In Illinois, the NRCS recommends the following distances:

Maximum distance between sod strips (Illinois)	
Slope	**Maximum distance between sod strips**
percent	*feet*
1 to 2	130
3 to 8	100
9 to 16	80
17 and over	60

Prepared with Harry Means, Illinois state conservation engineer, and Jerry Misek, district conservationist, Natural Resources Conservation Service; and Kent Mitchell, UI professor of agricultural engineering.

18 Install terraces

The long and short of it

Long slopes give runoff water a chance to build up momentum and energy, increasing its power to slice into the land. For example, the soil eroded from 1 acre of land with a 4 percent slope *550 feet in length* will be about twice the amount eroded from an acre with a 4 percent slope *100 feet in length*.

One of the best ways to shorten long slopes is with terraces—embankments, channels, or combinations of embankments and channels constructed across a field slope. Terraces not only shorten slopes; they channel runoff water into a stable outlet where it is carried safely away.

Types of terrace outlets

Terraces are sometimes described according to the type of outlet they use:

Gradient terraces with a grassed waterway outlet. Water is channeled downslope to a grassed outlet.

Terraces shorten slopes, channeling runoff into a stable outlet, such as a grassed waterway.

Gradient terraces with underground outlets, or parallel-tile-outlet (PTO) terraces. With this system, runoff water is channeled to a storage section of the terrace where it is released slowly through a surface inlet and underground pipe or tile. Underground outlets increase the farmability of a terrace and reduce the amount of land needed for a grassed waterway outlet.

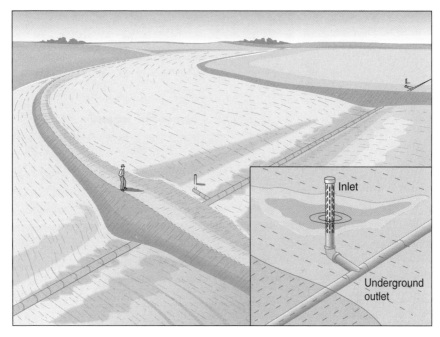

Inlet

Underground outlet

Underground outlets increase the farmability of a terrace and reduce the amount of land needed for a grassed waterway outlet. Locate the tile inlet on a short branch connected to the main tile line (see inset).

Types of terrace cross-sections

In addition to defining terraces by their type of outlet, terraces are sometimes categorized according to their cross-section types (see illustrations on page 102).

Broad-base terraces. All slopes on this type of terrace are designed to be farmed. For best farmability, make sure the terrace spacing and length of the front slope are multiples of the planter width.

Broad-base terraces are best used on long, uniform, gentle slopes up to 5 or 6 percent. Because the entire terrace can be farmed, make sure the terrace slopes are not too steep for your equipment. Know the slope limitations of your equipment and be sure to inform your technical adviser and contractor so they can help you plan a safe, farmable system. It is possible to flatten a terrace by moving more earth during construction, but this will add to the cost.

Grassed-back-slope terraces. The back slope is graded to a steep pitch and grassed. The front slope, which is farmed, is flattened and is usually the width of your planter. Consider grassed-back-slope terraces on slopes of 6 to 15 percent.

Narrow-base terraces. The entire ridge is grassed instead of just the back slope. Because the ridge is narrow, only a small area of the field is removed from production.

Narrow-base terraces disturb less soil than the other two types of terraces; therefore, they are often the best choice when topsoil is shallow and subsoils less productive. They are usually less expensive to construct.

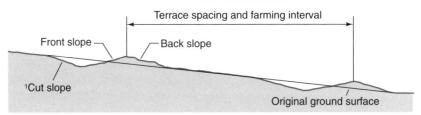

Broad-base terraces

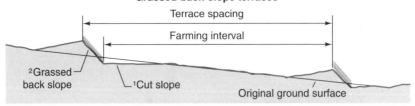

Grassed-back-slope terraces

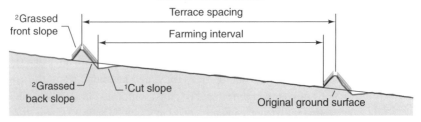

Narrow-base terraces

[1]Slopes 4:1 or flatter
[2]Slopes 2:1 or flatter

Make it easy to farm

Terraces constructed many years ago were often hard to farm because they had many sharp turns and odd areas. Modern terraces, however, are designed to be parallel and to match farm equipment dimensions and are therefore much more farmable. The following are some tips in making a terrace system farmable:

- Make sure terraces are parallel wherever possible with few (if any) point rows.

- Make terraces parallel or perpendicular to the field boundaries, wherever possible.

- Make sure terraces have gentle, circular turns with minimum curvature.

- Design the spacing and cross sections to fit the farm's equipment. Terrace spacing should be multiples of the width of your present planting and harvesting equipment and, if possible, should be suitable for future equipment.

- Space terraces as far apart as possible. This could mean changing the tillage practices or crop rotations between terraces. For example, you might be able to increase terrace spacing and still control erosion if you use some form of conservation tillage between terraces.

- Design terraces so that roads or field border strips provide access to all parts of a field. Field boundaries and ridges are ideal locations for access points.

- Irregular areas between terraces can be farmed using the same principles outlined for contour farming.

Will inlet pipes obstruct equipment?

There are some relatively simple ways to reduce the obstruction caused by terrace inlets:

- For farmable terraces, make sure the distance from the terrace ridge to the intake pipe allows your equipment to make a specific number of passes (usually one or two).

- With narrow-base terraces, place the inlet close to the grassed ridge where it is less likely to interfere with equipment.

CHECK IT OUT

For information on setback zones around tile inlets: page 279.

For information on farming irregular areas with contouring: page 94.

- Install a removable connection between the inlet and underground outlet near the ground surface. This makes it easy to remove the inlet before planting. It also makes it easier to repair if equipment damages it.
- Locate the tile inlet on a short branch connected to the main tile line (see illustration on page 101). This reduces the potential for damaging the main lines.

Designing and constructing a terrace system

If you decide to install terraces, you will need technical help, a qualified land improvement contractor, and perhaps financial assistance. For technical assistance in designing your system, contact the soil conservationist with the Natural Resources Conservation Service.

Because the installation costs may be more than you want to invest in a single year (and federal assistance has annual limits), you may want to install the terrace in segments.

Maintaining a terrace system

- Remove sediment from the terrace channel. This reduces the risk of "overtopping"—water overflowing and spilling over the top of terrace ridges.
- Redistribute sediment that is deposited near the intake of an underground outlet system and soil that has banked up around the intake during tillage operations. Make sure the intake is always located at the lowest point of the terrace storage section.
- Remove debris around intakes. Debris around intakes increases the time that water will stand in the terrace storage section before being channeled away. This can result in terrace failure and crop damage.
- Clean and repair intakes after each storm and promptly repair any damage done by machinery.
- Limit primary tillage on farmable terrace ridges and periodically regrade farmed ridges to maintain their original height.
- Repair damage to the terrace ridge promptly.
- Mow grassed terrace slopes periodically and control the growth of brush to avoid attracting rodents.

Prepared with Harry Means, Illinois state conservation engineer, and Leon Wendte, district conservationist, Natural Resources Conservation Service; and Kent Mitchell, UI professor of agricultural engineering.

19 Install grade control structures

Making the grade

Grade control structures drop water safely from one level to another, preventing it from gouging out gullies. They can also help to control flooding and trap the sediment moving with runoff water. If they are designed to store water, they can provide a water source and habitat for wildlife.

Grade control structures are typically built across an existing gully, a grassed waterway, or the outlet of a waterway. They come in three basic types: weirs, chutes, and pipes.

Weirs

A weir is a structure that allows water to run over the edge like a miniature waterfall, dropping down onto a concrete apron. The apron safely absorbs the impact of the falling water, and then the water streams to an outlet. Although weirs come in many forms, one of the most popular and cheapest of weirs is made of corrugated metal with a concrete apron (see photo).

A weir structure is very stable and is not as likely to become clogged with debris as other structures; it is also easy to construct. If the drop is greater than 10 feet, however, it is not as efficient as other structures.

One of the most popular and cheapest weirs is made from corrugated metal. Water flows over the weir, and its impact is cushioned by the concrete apron below.

The concrete-block–lined chute is one of the easiest types of chutes to construct. It is also the most economical.

Chutes

When the drop in grade is more dramatic, you can use a chute to prevent severe erosion. As the name implies, water moves down a chute made of concrete or lined with rocks or concrete blocks. The concrete block-lined chute (see photo) is one of the most popular and economical of chutes. The simplicity of construction and the availability of material make it easy for farmers to do the installation themselves.

Pipes

Like chutes, pipes are effective in handling water when the drop in grade is dramatic. They are designed to carry water through or under an earth embankment to a lower elevation; there may or may not be a permanent pool of water above the embankment.

The inlet for pipes comes in two basic forms: a drop inlet and a hood inlet (see illustrations). With a drop inlet, water does just that; it drops down into the inlet and then flows through the pipe. With a hood inlet, water flows directly into the pipe; the end of the inlet either has a hood on the top or is cut at an angle so the top of the pipe acts as a hood.

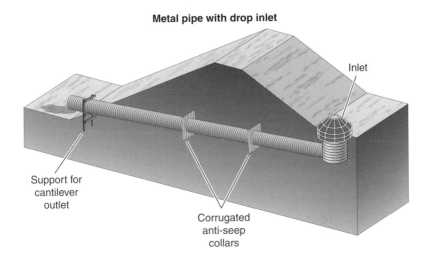

Metal pipe with drop inlet

Inlet

Support for
cantilever
outlet

Corrugated
anti-seep
collars

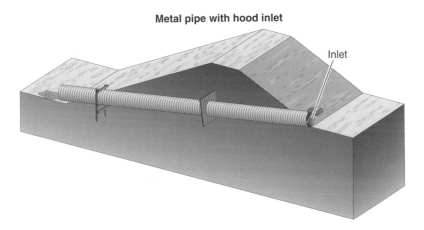

Metal pipe with hood inlet

Inlet

Planning a grade control structure

Some key points:

- Control runoff and erosion on the land above the grade control structure. Excessive runoff or erosion can seriously reduce the effectiveness of the structure.

- If you are building a grade control structure across a gully that produces large amounts of sediment, consider an earth dam to capture debris. Design the basin to store the eroded soil rather than allow sediment to damage valuable land or structures below.

- Design the grade control structure to carry a specific peak rate of runoff water. This rate will depend on the characteristics of your particular watershed.

- Use a grassed waterway or diversion as an approach to the grade control structure.
- Consult with the Natural Resources Conservation Service when locating, designing, and constructing a grade control structure.
- Obtain any necessary easements or permits.

Constructing and maintaining a grade control structure

Some key points:

- Seed earthen supporting structures. Prepare a good seedbed for sod, sprigs, seed, small plants, cuttings, or vines.
- Fertilize the vegetation on earthen structures as needed.
- Eliminate competition from undesirable weeds and grasses in vegetative plantings.
- If the gully banks are not too steep or do not receive large amounts of runoff, use mulches of straw, hay, light brush, or other organic materials to protect newly planted vegetation from being eroded away by rain. In some areas, you may need to prevent mulches from being blown away by wind.
- Remove all trees and shrubs within 30 feet of the structure.
- Route any tile outlets around the structure and not through it.
- Protect all plantings from grazing until they are established.
- When the vegetation is established, mow, spray, or allow limited grazing to prevent tall grass, weeds, briars, and brushy growth from taking over. Maintaining the vegetative cover is as important as the original establishment.
- Use sod or seed to deal with any spot failures in the vegetative plantings.
- Protect the structure from fire and trampling.
- Keep outlets, drop inlets, and weirs free of debris.
- Remove sediment that builds up in front of or downstream of the structure.
- Keep burrowing animals out of earthen structures.
- Inspect the sides, corners, and wingwalls of all structures and repair any cracks in concrete.

Prepared with Harry Means, Illinois state conservation engineer, and Leon Wendte, district conservationist, Natural Resources Conservation Service; and Kent Mitchell, UI professor of agricultural engineering.

20 Install water and sediment control basins

If a terrace isn't possible . . .

If installing a terrace is impractical on your land, you might want to go with a water and sediment control basin—a short, earthen dam built across a drainageway.

A water and sediment control basin is similar to a terrace in that it traps sediment and runoff from farmland above the structure and prevents them from reaching farmland below. A basin also reduces flooding and gully erosion and improves the farmability of a field.

However, water and sediment control basins should not be used as a substitute for terraces in areas where you can use terraces.

Designing a basin

Work with the Natural Resources Conservation Service (NRCS) to obtain a design. The following are some of the key design considerations:

The cross section. The cross section of the basin's ridge, or embankment, can vary according to the farmability of its slopes. For example:

- Both slopes and the top of the embankment can be suitable for farming.
- One slope can be steep and vegetated, while the other is suitable for farming.
- Both slopes can be steep and vegetated.

The grade of vegetated slopes should not be steeper than $2^{1}/_{2}$:1. To allow for the soil to settle, the height of the embankment should be 5 percent higher than the height you are aiming for. To determine the effective width for the top of a basin embankment, check the following chart.

Alignment. The embankment of each basin should be almost perpendicular to the principal slope, permitting rows to be farmed as closely on the

Basin effective top width	
Embankment height	Effective top width
feet	feet
0 to 5	3
5 to 10	6
10 to 15	8

contour as possible. If you construct a system of water and sediment control basins, try to keep them parallel.

Spacing. The spacing between basins depends on the predominant slope, the cross section, and the tillage and management systems used.

Capacity. Build the basin large enough to control the runoff, without overtopping, during a 10-year, 24-hour storm (the heaviest 24-hour rainfall that can be expected, on average, every 10 years).

Unless you periodically clean the basin to maintain the proper capacity, you should design the basin so it also can collect 10 years of accumulated sediment. If a basin is designed to provide flood protection, make sure it can meet the potential hazard.

The uncontrolled area draining into the basin should not exceed 30 acres.

Outlets. All water and sediment control basins should have a principal spillway. The spillway controls the rate of water flowing from the basin. It also dewaters the temporary detention storage area before the next storm.

Vegetation. Disturbed areas that are not to be farmed should be planted in grass as soon as practicable after construction. If soil or climatic conditions prevent the use of vegetation and if some form of protection is needed, consider mulches or gravel.

Check with the NRCS for design assistance, as well as seeding, fertilizing, and mulching rates.

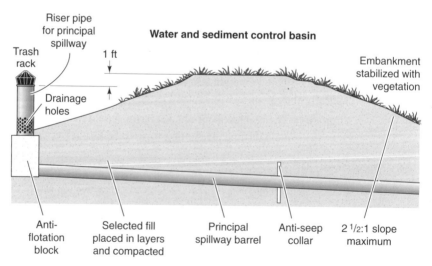

Like terraces, water and sediment control basins trap sediment and runoff. But they are not substitutes for terraces. Do not use them in areas where you can use terraces.

Constructing and maintaining the basin

Some key points:

- Use cultural and management practices, such as conservation tillage, to adequately reduce soil erosion above and between the basins.
- Seed the earthen structure. Prepare a good seedbed for sod, sprigs, seed, small plants, cuttings, or vines.
- Fertilize the vegetation on earthen structures as needed.
- Eliminate competition from undesirable weeds and grasses in vegetative plantings.
- If the gully banks are not too steep or do not receive large amounts of runoff, use mulches of straw, hay, light brush, or other organic materials to protect newly planted vegetation from being eroded away by rain. In some areas, you may need to prevent mulches from being blown away by wind.
- Route any tile outlets around the structure and not through it.
- Protect all plantings from grazing until they are established.
- Once the vegetation is established, mow, spray, or allow limited grazing to prevent tall grass, weeds, briars, and brushy growth from taking over. Maintaining the vegetative cover is as important as the original establishment.
- Use sod or seed to deal with any spot failures in the vegetative plantings.
- Check the basin after each large storm and make any needed repairs.
- If the storage for sediment has reached capacity, clean out the basin or raise the ridge to restore capacity.
- Protect the structure from fire, trampling, and heavy grazing.
- Remove debris from inlets.
- Keep burrowing animals out of earthen structures.

Prepared with Harry Means, Illinois state conservation engineer, and Leon Wendte, district conservationist, Natural Resources Conservation Service; and Kent Mitchell, UI professor of agricultural engineering.

21 Use diversions

The purpose of diversions

A diversion is a graded channel constructed across the slope with a ridge running along its lower side. It conveys water away from its present source to another location.

From this description, diversions sound a lot like terraces, and they often function like terraces. But whereas a terrace is part of a larger system of terraces, a diversion often stands alone, serving one specific purpose. Also, a diversion typically handles a greater flow of water coming from a larger area than an individual terrace does.

If land requires terraces for erosion control, diversions should not be used as a substitute. Diversions have many uses of their own, such as:

- To divert water away from gullies, preventing erosion
- To divert water away from farm buildings or feedlots
- To divert runoff away from bottomlands
- To collect or direct water to a pond
- To break up concentrations of water on long, gentle slopes, and on slopes too irregular or flat for terracing
- To protect a terrace system by diverting water away from the uppermost terrace. This use comes into play when topography or ownership rights prevents you from terracing the land above your terrace system.
- To protect lowlands from flooding or sediment damage by diverting floodwater from small tributaries

Planning a diversion

The following are some key points in planning a diversion:

- Diversions should be designed by the Natural Resources Conservation Service.
- Make sure you take the proper erosion-control precautions to prevent your diversion channel from filling with sediment.
- Diversions must be built to carry at least the peak amount of runoff generated by a 10-year, 24-hour storm (the heaviest 24-hour rainfall that can be expected, on average, every 10 years). The capacity of a diversion will depend on several factors, such as the size of the channel as well as the type and growth habits of vegetation lining the channel.
- The minimum width for the top of a diversion ridge is 4 feet.

- Each diversion must have an outlet, such as a grassed waterway, grade stabilization structure, or underground outlet.
- The diversion should discharge at a legal outlet, as defined by state drainage law.
- If you are using a vegetative outlet, establish it before you construct the diversion.
- If you use a diversion to protect cropland from the runoff of adjoining grassland on the same farm, build it close to the boundary between grassland and cropland.
- When diverting runoff water across irregular slopes, reinforce the diversion where it crosses draws.
- The best time to build diversions is when the watershed area is mainly in grass or other good cover so runoff will be at a minimum.

Construction and planting

Constructing and establishing vegetation for a diversion is much the same as for a grassed waterway. For details, see page 81.

Maintenance

Fertilize the vegetation on the diversion as needed and keep the outlet free of debris. Mowing, spraying, or limited grazing of the diversion channel is essential to prevent tall grass, weeds, briars, and brushy growth from obstructing water flow. This growth generally occurs where diversions empty into wooded areas.

When woody growth becomes too extensive, mowing becomes impossible and the diversion channel gradually becomes clogged with tall grass and brush. If this happens, water may seep through the ridge, causing it to fail.

You may also need to remove sediment that builds up in spots of the diversion channel. If the sediment fills long stretches of the diversion, you may need to rework it with the appropriate construction equipment.

Diversions left in permanent vegetation sometimes attract rodents and other burrowing animals. Examine the ridge frequently for breaks or holes and then repair them.

For further details on maintenance, refer to the chapter on grassed waterways (page 83). Maintenance for grassed waterways and diversions is basically the same.

Prepared with Harry Means, Illinois state conservation engineer, and Leon Wendte, district conservationist, Natural Resources Conservation Service; and Kent Mitchell, UI professor of agricultural engineering.

Install a farm pond

Controlling runoff

A farm pond can provide function as well as recreation. It can be both scenic and highly practical. For instance, a farm pond can capture runoff water, preventing it from doing erosive damage or it can provide water for livestock, household use, irrigation, fire fighting, and orchard spraying. As for recreation, it can offer fishing, swimming, picnicking, ice skating, and wildlife habitat.

You can create a farm pond by building a dam across an existing gully or low-lying area. Using heavy machinery, dig out a bowl-shaped

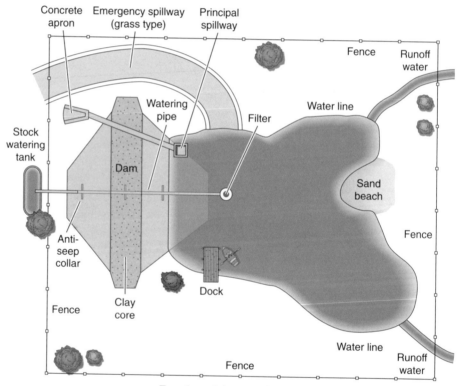

Top view of dam and farm pond

When building a pond, the soil must contain enough clay to provide a watertight dam and a basin through which a minimum of water will seep. If there is not enough watertight soil for the entire dam, you may need to put a clay core in the center of the dam or install a prefabricated pond liner.

basin above the dam and then use the soil to build the dam. Within a year, the ponded area should fill with water.

The first step in designing a farm pond, however, is to select a suitable site. This means finding a site that has suitable topography and an acceptable soil type and one that will provide sufficient water.

Topography

The ideal topography is a wide, gently sloping basin with rather steep banks that come closely together at the dam site. The idea is to impound the largest amount of water with the smallest dam.

For successful fish management, the general rule is that ponds should have a surface area of at least 1 acre and 10 to 12 feet of water in 25 percent of the pond basin. Ponds less than 1 acre can handle relatively little pressure by fish populations. Also, if water is not deep enough, fish can be killed by oxygen depletion during hot days in the summer and when the lake is covered with ice and snow during winter.

Extensive shallow areas encourage aquatic weeds and those unappreciated visitors, mosquitoes.

Soil type

The soil must contain enough clay to provide a watertight dam and a basin through which a minimum of water will seep. Test the subsoil by squeezing a moist piece into a hard ball. If it does not crumble after some handling and squeezing, it should be satisfactory.

Check the depth of the clay to see if there is enough beneath the dam site and in the pond basin. Usually, 3 feet of clay soil is needed below the excavation level to prevent seepage. It may be necessary to haul clay for the dam from a nearby area.

If there is not enough watertight soil for the entire dam, you may need to put a clay core in the center of the dam or install a prefabricated pond liner.

Water supply

A watershed is the area surrounding the pond that drains into it. The ideal watershed will provide enough siltfree water to keep the lake full at all times with water seldom running over the spillway.

In some areas, the goal is to aim for about 20 acres of watershed area for every acre of pond surface. However, local conditions can alter this figure. If you have too much watershed area draining into the pond, you can move water *away* from the pond with terraces or diversions; and if you do not have enough watershed area, you can divert water *toward* the pond.

Managing the pond

- Install adequate soil conservation measures near the pond to prevent it from filling with sediment.
- Provide a natural or constructed spillway to allow water to spill through the dam without causing erosion. Clear all trees and shrubs within at least 30 feet of the dam's spillway and embankment.
- Divert runoff from feedlots, barnyards, and septic tanks away from the pond.
- Fence the pond from livestock. Grazing can tear down the shoreline and bank vegetation, resulting in erosion and muddy water. The amount of sediment entering the pond will increase, eventually filling the basin. Also, continuous muddy water will destroy the habitat for fish because certain game species will not be able to see their food.
- If the water is used for livestock, pipe it to a tank located outside the fence and below the dam.

CHECK IT OUT

For more information on fencing to keep livestock out of water: page 157.

For information on water sources for livestock: page 158.

- Use extreme care when applying pesticides near the pond because the chemical could move with runoff, posing a toxic hazard to fish and those using the pond's water for drinking and swimming. For information on setback zones, see page 279.
- Keep the outlet free of debris.
- Keep trees, shrubs, and burrowing animals out of the dam.
- Maintain grass cover on the dam. You might also consider a grass cover on the shoreline where it can add beauty, control soil erosion, and act as a final filter for water running into the pond.

Prepared with Robert Frazee, natural resources management educator, UI Extension; and Harry Means, Illinois state conservation engineer, Natural Resources Conservation Service.

Managing land means managing water

Ralph Neill remembers that when he was a child, he and his father would ride horses across their land in Adams County, Iowa, and his father would point to areas that needed to be in pasture. His father, a cattle feeder, kept all of his hill ground in grass because that was the best use from both a production and environmental perspective.

Neill still lives on the farm where he was born, and he has learned his father's lessons well. Ralph and his wife Joyce keep their 300 acres or more of rolling ground primarily in hay or pasture, while they produce row crops on about 1,000 acres of flat, river-bottom land. The flatter land is split by the Middle Nodaway River.

"Not all of the hilly ground that surrounds our valley is classified as highly erodible," Neill points out. "But by our classification, it is erodible. If it has slope, it's erodible."

Neill says their goal is to hold all of the water they can on their land, thereby bringing erosion as close to zero as possible and protecting the stretch of river and two intermittent streams on their land. These are ambitious goals, but the Neills are ambitious planners. Since the late 1960s, they have installed eight farm ponds, which they prefer to call "water-retention structures." The ponds are located at the lower end of waterways in their sloping pastures to capture water moving downhill.

Above the ponds are grassed waterways and short terraces with tile intakes that outlet into the ponds. In turn, the ponds have intakes that convey water to the closest stream.

Neill says they are always doing some soil conservation work in and around their pastures, as they steadily make improvements year by year—one pasture at a time.

The Neills are also busy fencing out their ponds, a job that Ralph says they should have done from the very beginning. They fenced cattle away from the first pond that they created and the most recent one, but not the other six.

"It's crystal clear to me that the water quality is much higher in the ponds that I fenced out," he notes. "In Texas, studies have shown that calves will grow faster when they're drinking water that they don't stand in. So we need to fence out ponds. There are other ways to get water to the cattle."

To provide water to his 80 cow/calf pairs, Neill is planning to use a solar-powered unit to generate the 12 to 24 volts necessary to pump water to a tank. His goal is for every pasture or paddock to have its own water system.

In addition to these projects, the Neills created a windbreak last year and plan to create an additional one each year for the next three years. In 1996, they planted 400 new trees below one of their ponds as a wildlife area. Three years down the road, they aim to begin planting hybrid willows along the streambanks to control streambank erosion.

As the trees and bushes go in, the Neills have seen the wildlife respond. They have seen bald eagles off and on for the past five years, and great blue herons have been nesting up and down the river for the past 15 years. The land is also a refuge for pheasants and quails, and the Neill family is accustomed to looking out their window and seeing up to 10 deer at a time.

With all of this work going on, it's no surprise that the Neills were awarded the 1993 Environmental Stewardship Award for their region by the National Cattlemen's Association. At the time, Ralph confesses that he felt a bit smug— until he met the winners from other regions.

"I thought we were doing everything we could," he says. "But when I met those other people, I saw how much could really be done. I felt a little sheepish. Some of the things people are doing are incredible. So we always have to look at ourselves with a hard eye to see where we are and where we are going."

As he puts it, "Farmers are natural environmentalists. We don't just talk about the environment. We work with nature all of the time, and we depend on the environment for a living. If we let it deteriorate, we will be out of business."

23 | Maintain your drainage system to protect surface water

Production, profit, protection . . . and problems

There can be two sides to drainage systems.

On the positive side, a properly designed drainage system lowers the water table and takes care of excess water on the soil surface, improving production and profits on millions of acres of fertile cropland.

Another plus is that drainage systems have the potential to protect surface water. They can prevent excess water on the soil surface from getting out of control—eroding soil and carrying sediment, pesticides, and fertilizers into streams and lakes.

On the negative side, however, University of Illinois research has shown that there are cases in which a subsurface drainage system can contribute to contamination problems. It can channel nitrate through its drain tiles and directly into streams, rivers, and lakes.

UI studies along the Little Vermilion River in east-central Illinois reported excessive levels of nitrate-N in water flowing out of the tile drains—levels reaching up to 35 parts per million (ppm), with the mean ranging from 7 to 16 ppm, depending on the nitrogen, tillage, and cropping management. The maximum contaminant level for nitrate-N in drinking water is 10 ppm.

There are no easy answers to this problem, but the method and timing of nitrogen applications play a key role in any solution.

✓ CHECK IT OUT

For details on how to manage nitrogen to minimize contamination: Chapters 26-31.

For information on using setback zones to keep nitrogen and pesticides from entering drainage systems: page 279.

Meanwhile, if you hope to reap both the economic and environmental benefits of your drainage system, proper maintenance is essential. What you need to do to maintain your system depends on whether you use subsurface or surface drainage.

Maintaining a subsurface drainage system

Subsurface drainage is used where the soil is permeable enough to economically space drains and productive enough to justify the investment. Water moves through a system of laterals to the main drains, which then take the water to either a surface or subsurface outlet.

Although subsurface drainage systems require very little maintenance, the maintenance that is required is very important. Regular inspection of the drainage system is essential, so check for these problems:

Outlet ditches. The outlet ditch may become blocked by sediment. If the outlet ditch becomes filled with sediment, determine how much clean-out work will be required and find out whether you need to use some type of conservation practice to keep soil from moving into and filling the ditch.

Surface inlets. Poorly constructed surface inlets are subject to severe damage and require frequent repair. Also, surface inlet covers may become sealed with debris and should be checked frequently. Clean the covers after a heavy rain and replace them carefully. If a cover is removed but not replaced, debris can enter and block the line.

Extra connections. Do not connect the gutters from buildings to the drainage system inlet. A drainage system is not designed to handle the extra water coming from the gutters. In addition, do not allow manure runoff to drain through the tile. Not only can the manure pose serious contamination problems as it leaves the drainage outlet, but it will eventually clog the tile lines.

Blow-outs. Holes known as "blow-outs" can develop over subsurface drains, resulting in large amounts of soil washing into the line and blocking the entire system. Blow-outs often form above spots where a drain tile is broken or where the joints or slots are too wide.

If the tile is broken, replace it. If the joint is too wide, place tile bats (pieces of broken tile) over the joint to prevent soil from washing into the line.

To replace crushed or punctured corrugated plastic tubing, cut the damaged segment from the line and replace it with new tubing, using the manufacturer's couplers.

Sediment. If you encounter sandy or silty soils while laying drain tile, you can use sediment traps to keep soil from filling the lines. Clean the traps every few days just after the lines are laid because sizable quantities of fine soil will at first wash in through the joints between tiles or through perforations in plastic tubing.

After one freezing and thawing cycle, soil will wash in more slowly and you will need to check the traps only once or twice a year. You can gain access to drainage lines and flush them through inspection wells.

Tree roots. Willow, elm, soft maple, cottonwood, and other water-loving trees may damage a drainage system and should be removed within 100 feet of the drain. Maintain a clearance of 50 feet between the drain and other species of trees.

Ochre accumulations. Ochre, an iron oxide, may block the drain. Ochre usually enters drains through organic soils, but has been known to occur in other soils as well.

There is no foolproof solution to the ochre problem (except for the construction of open ditches). Jetting the drain with an acid solution has proven successful in some areas, but it is costly.

Maintaining a surface drainage system

A surface drainage system may be suitable for slowly permeable soils and for soils with fragipans or clay subsoils. Water is carried to an outlet channel by lateral ditches, which receive water from drainage ditches in the field or sometimes directly from the surface of the field.

Clean the outlet channel, lateral ditches, and field ditches as needed to keep them functioning properly. Small deposits of silt can greatly reduce the capacity of a surface drainage system and cause partial or complete failure of the system.

Inspect the outlet channel and ditches after each heavy rain and re-move silt deposits or other obstructions. Brushy types of vegetation, such as cattails, willows, and cottonwoods, are a menace to surface ditches. Remove them once or twice each year as needed. (If you intend to use herbicides to remove them, check the label for any restrictions.)

For the first year or two after constructing a surface drainage system, maintain the areas of land that have been graded or reshaped. Some-times, areas that you have filled with soil will settle, creating depressions and impeding drainage. To remedy this problem, you may need to make several land smoothing operations, using special equipment such as a land plane or land leveler.

Prepared with Michael Hirschi, soil and water specialist, and George Czapar, integrated pest management educator, UI Extension; and Kent Mitchell, UI professor of agricultural engineering.

24 Control streambank erosion with the willow-post method

Blow-outs

Some of the streams that children could have jumped across just a generation ago have exploded in size to the width of a football field or more. This is not uncommon as streambank erosion takes sizable bites from the banks of creeks, streams, and rivers.

Streambank erosion occurs whenever the erosive power of a stream or river is so great that it cuts large chunks of soil from the bank. As the stream cuts deeper into the foot of the bank, the bank is weakened and eventually collapses into the stream. These incidents have been called "blow-outs."

Streambank erosion can take sizable bites out of productive farmland.

When streambanks erode, productive topsoil sloughs off into the stream. This topsoil is ultimately deposited in rivers, lakes, or backwater areas, choking them with sediment, inhibiting the growth of aquatic plants, and disturbing the habitat of fish, ducks, and other wildlife.

Streambank erosion is an age-old problem that is growing in severity because changes on the landscape have increased the velocity of water in the streams and increased the runoff of water from adjacent fields. These landscape changes include:

- Straightening, or channelizing, of creeks and streams. When a stream is straightened, its natural, winding form is eliminated, increasing the velocity of moving water.

✓ CHECK IT OUT
For more information on channelization: page 127.

- Clearing vegetation from streambanks. Stands of perennial grasses, shrubs, and trees stabilize streambanks.
- Less land in the soil-conserving crops of hay, pasture, and cereal grains
- More land in the erosive row crops of corn and soybeans
- Removal of fencerows, hedgerows, and windbreaks
- Lack of proper management on steep, sloping pasture and timber areas
- Increased surface drainage to eliminate "wet holes" in fields

The willow-post method

The traditional way to control streambank erosion has been to place rock, concrete, or steel along the eroding bank. These methods typically cost $50 to $200 per foot and require maintenance and repair through the years.

A more economical and equally effective method for small streams is the willow-post method. It can be installed for only $7 to $15 per foot.

The willow-post method controls streambank erosion through the installation of native willow cuttings to stabilize the bank. To install the willows, follow these simple steps:

1. Slope the streambank to a 1:1 grade.
2. After willows have gone dormant for the winter, cut down the ones that measure about 3 to 4 inches in diameter.
3. Shear off their branches, leaving a 10- to 12-foot section of trunk.
4. Place willow posts into holes made by an excavator equipped with a hydraulic auger. Dig the holes in rows about 4 feet apart beginning in the water and extending up the sides of the streambank. Most likely, the first row of willow posts will eventually die, but by that time they will have served their function.

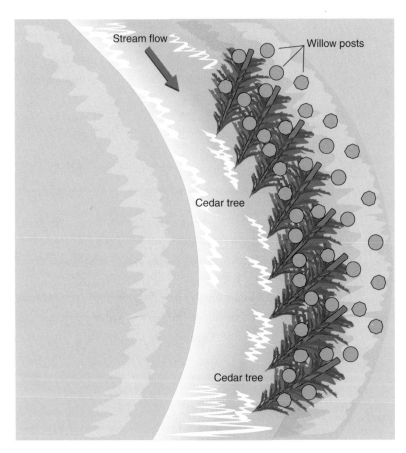

Stream flow

Willow posts

Cedar tree

Cedar tree

*Cedar trees are placed in the first two rows of willows to act as a "revetment" —
a vegetative structure that adds stability to the lower bank until the willow posts
have had a chance to regrow roots and branches. The base of each cedar tree
faces upstream.*

The willow posts must be planted in the holes when the willows are
dormant—usually mid-November to mid-March in the Midwest. Also,
for long-term protection, the posts in the first two rows should be 2 to 3
feet below the deepest section of the streambed.

5. Within each row, space willow posts 3 to 4 feet apart, depending upon
the severity of erosion at the site.

6. Use cedar trees as a "revetment"—a vegetative structure that adds
stability to the lower bank. Cut cedar trees (about 10 to 14 feet tall) and
use $3/8$-inch polypropylene rope to tie them to the lowest two rows of
willow posts (see illustration). Also, make sure the base of each cedar

tree faces upstream and the branches overlap the downstream cedar. The cedar trees act like a shock absorber; they reduce the ability of flowing water to erode the streambank until the willow posts have had a chance to regrow roots and branches.

7. Seed the soil on the streambanks with native prairie grasses, perennial grasses, and legumes.

It's important to correctly design and install the system so the stream does not cut away the bank behind the willow posts.

The advantages

In addition to the reduced cost when compared to traditional bank stabilization methods, the willow-post method offers these rewards:

- Dormant posts sprout roots, and this root network binds the soil together, reducing erosion.
- The foliage that grows on the posts slows floodwater near the bank.
- The use of all native materials encourages natural habitats in and around streams and enhances scenic beauty.
- Maintenance costs are low because the willow-post method creates a natural environment that is self-sustaining.
- The system has been tested and proven effective in Illinois under flood conditions, even when heavy spring floods carry ice floes.
- After the willows slow streambank erosion, more valuable trees can grow along the bank.

Will the willows spread into adjacent fields?

When the system is used at severe erosion sites, the willows have remained at the water's edge, which is their preferred environment. They have not spread upward into adjacent fields, nor have they clogged the channel.

How do you know if you need a system?

To decide if you need to take action to control streambank erosion, follow these steps:

1. Make site visits to the creeks that flow through your land. Starting upstream from your property, walk the entire length of the creeks and identify the locations and severity of streambank erosion sites.
2. Examine each streambank erosion site carefully and assess the potential for additional damage and future property loss.

3. Find out where to obtain more information and assistance. You can contact the local soil and water conservation district or local offices of the Cooperative Extension Service and Natural Resources Conservation Service. Some states offer cost-share assistance for streambank erosion control. Also, local land improvement contractors can provide the equipment and expertise for installing the right system for your property.

Where should you use the system?

In the Midwest, the willow-post method has been used most successfully along streams in agricultural floodplains without tree cover. However, it is not recommended for drainage ditches.

The willow-post method is also most effective when used with a "systems approach" to land and water management. A systems approach means that you control erosion on the land upstream from the stabilized streambank. In cropland areas, you can achieve this goal with no-till and mulch-till farming systems.

Prepared with Robert Frazee, natural resources management educator, UI Extension; and Don Roseboom, director of the nonpoint pollution program, Illinois State Water Survey.

25 Avoid channelization of streams and creeks

An idea whose time has gone

Channelization sounded like a good idea at the time.

From the 1920s through the 1960s, it wasn't unusual for farmers to channelize, or straighten, the streams meandering through their land. By straightening out the kinks in the course of a stream, they increased the speed of water moving downstream, thereby increasing the rate at which water drained away from their land. Straightening the channel also made their fields more farmable because now they could farm along a straight waterway rather than along a curving stream.

As many of them discovered, however, channelization often makes things worse in the long run. By increasing the velocity of water moving in the stream, the flowing water scours the streambed and deepens the channel. This means the banks are higher and, in many cases, more unstable. The result: Huge chunks of the bank may suddenly crumble into the stream. It is streambank erosion at its worst.

So what starts out as an idea to increase farmability often turns into an idea that results in the loss of farmland. The problem is especially severe on banks where there are deep glacial deposits of sand and gravel.

As channelization increases streambank erosion, more sediment enters and clogs the stream. What's more, an accelerated velocity of water increases flooding downstream and decreases a stream's ability to recharge groundwater. (Streams recharge groundwater when water seeps from the channel into underground water supplies.)

In addition to the loss of farmland, fish and wildlife pay a price for channelization. Channelization reduces the amount of vegetation along the streambank, which means less food and cover for wildlife. It can also drain wetlands and destroy bottomland hardwoods. Meanwhile, increased sedimentation makes it difficult for some fish to feed and spawn, and the increased velocity of the stream drives out fish that cannot tolerate fast-moving water. Studies have found some channelized stretches of streams devoid of fish for five years after the waterway was altered.

The consequences of channelization are often long-term, and they can affect areas both upstream and downstream from the channelized segment of stream. For instance, 60 years after the Blackwater River in Johnson County, Missouri, was channelized, the resulting erosion continues to be a problem, farmland continues to be lost, and downstream flooding continues to increase.

What to do

Landowners, in general, no longer channelize streams and creeks, and some landowners are even working with agencies to convert streams back to their normal flow. However, there are still cases in which channelization may be necessary. And in those cases, a special permit process is required. Unfortunately, some landowners alter streams on their own.

The best course of action is to let the stream follow its normal path. Streambank erosion is an inevitable process, but by letting the stream meander naturally, at least the process will be a slow one. With channelization, it can take only 10 years for streambank erosion to do the amount of damage it might have taken 100 years to do naturally.

By letting the stream flow naturally, however, you may have to stabilize certain parts of the bank to protect it from erosion. To stabilize a bank, use the willow-post method, described in Chapter 24. If the stream running through your land is deep or its watershed is larger than 20,000 acres, you may also need to stabilize the underwater portion of the bank with rock "riprap."

Another way to help stabilize the bank of a meandering stream is to reduce the energy of water running off your land and into the stream. You can do this by switching to no-till because crop residue increases water infiltration and slows the movement of surface runoff into the waterway. You can also do this by planting buffer strips alongside the stream. In addition to filtering out contaminants, buffer strips slow the runoff moving into the stream and give you the straight edge along which to farm—the straight edge that many farmers are looking for when they channelize a stream.

CHECK IT OUT

For more information on buffer/vegetative filter strips: page 85.

Prepared with Don Roseboom, director of the nonpoint pollution program, Illinois State Water Survey; and Michael Hirschi, soil and water specialist, and Robert Frazee, natural resources management educator, UI Extension.

Managing nutrients effectively

The low cost of nitrogen was one of the driving forces behind the boom in nitrogen use and soaring production during the 1960s and 1970s. As an example of how economical nitrogen fertilizer became by that time, one bushel of corn could purchase only 5 pounds of nitrogen fertilizer in 1940. By 1970, one bushel of corn could purchase 20 pounds of nitrogen.

In the 1980s and 1990s, tighter budgets called for a closer look at fertilizer expenditures. In addition, an increasing number of producers began to see that although nitrogen was still relatively cheap, it could be costly in other ways. Excessive nitrogen rates had an environmental cost. Nitrogen washing into water can boost nitrate levels, posing health risks and sometimes forcing water suppliers to take expensive measures to treat water. Nitrogen and phosphorus can also overfertilize lakes, and they can act together to produce excessive algae growth. Excessive algae, in turn, can steal the oxygen available to aquatic life.

The practices described in this section offer ideas on how to cut both the economic and environmental costs of phosphorus and nitrogen use.

26   Set realistic yield goals

The price of overoptimism

In farming, it can be expensive to be overoptimistic, especially when it comes to nitrogen (N) application.

Because soil tests for nitrogen are not entirely reliable, N application recommendations are based on yield goals. If your yield goals are unrealistically high, the recommended application rates for nitrogen will be high. The result: increased expense, increased levels of nitrogen in the soil, and increased risk to surface water and groundwater.

Some studies show that farmers do tend to be overoptimistic about yield goals. According to a four-year survey of 158 farmers in Nebraska, only 10 percent reached their yield goals. About half the farmers reached 80 percent of their yield goals, whereas another 40 percent of them fell more than 20 percent below their goals.

Guidelines for setting realistic yield goals

- Recognize that exceptionally good years are the exception.
- Establish realistic yield estimates for each field based on soil type, your own three- to five-year yield records, county average yields, and yields on neighboring farms. When figuring the average yield on a field, do not count years of abnormally low yields that resulted from drought or other weather-related conditions.
- Set your yield goal 5 to 10 percent above your average yield of the past five years. That way, if it's a good year, the crop will have enough nutrients to become a bumper crop. If it's an off year, the amount of excess nitrogen in the soil will be kept to a minimum.

Yield monitors

High-tech systems offer the promise of greater precision in setting yield goals. For example, yield monitors are becoming increasingly common features on combines. In fact, as technology continues to develop, yield monitors may follow the example of harvest loss systems, which started out as options and eventually became standard.

Yield monitors estimate grain flow into the combine every 1 to 3 seconds; this data can then be merged with information from a global positioning system (GPS) unit, which pinpoints the combine's precise location on the field. The result is an accurate yield map for each field.

When the yield map is created, it can be combined with a soil map, also generated by GPS technology. By putting yield and soil information together, you can set application rates with much greater accuracy. However, you will want to map yields for several years before using the information to vary the rate of fertilizer applications.

CHECK IT OUT

For more information on global positioning systems: page 148.

Prepared with Robert Hoeft, soil fertility specialist, UI Extension.

Monitor the level of nutrients

Soil testing

Soil testing is the single most important guide to the profitable application of lime and fertilizer. It helps you to find the balance—applying enough fertilizer to maintain productivity without applying so much that it becomes uneconomical or environmentally hazardous.

To ensure that your soil test is accurate, follow these guidelines:

Collect samples to the proper depth. The proper depth of sampling for pH, phosphorus (P), and potassium (K) is 7 inches. For fields where you use reduced tillage systems, proper sampling depth is especially important because there will be a less thorough mixing of lime and fertilizer than with a tillage system that includes a moldboard plow.

Collect an adequate number of samples. You want to collect enough samples to get an accurate assessment of nutrient levels, but not so many that costs become prohibitive. As a compromise, take a sample from each $2^1/_2$-acre area.

Collect samples from precisely the same areas of the field that were sampled in the past. To make sure you sample from the same locations, use a global positioning system (GPS) or accurately measure the sample points with devices such as a measuring wheel. Once the sample points have been identified, collect and mix five soil core samples, 1 inch in diameter, to a 7-inch depth, from an area with a 10-foot radius at each location.

CHECK IT OUT

For information on global positioning systems: page 148.

Collect samples at the proper time. Sampling every four years is strongly suggested. Late summer and fall are the best seasons to collect soil samples because potassium test results are most reliable at these times.

Testing for nitrogen

Because of nitrogen's high mobility in the soil, testing for nitrogen has not been consistently reliable. However, the drier parts of the Corn Belt (west of the Missouri River) have had some success with both the early spring nitrate-nitrogen test and the pre-sidedress nitrogen test.

Early spring nitrate-N test. For this test, collect soil samples in 1-foot increments down to a 2- to 3-foot depth in early spring.

Although guidelines vary from state to state, Wisconsin specialists recommend that you reduce standard nitrogen recommendations by the amount found in the soil profile sampled. But first, you should correct the test values for "background" soil nitrate content by subtracting 50 pounds of N per acre from the initial soil test. For example:

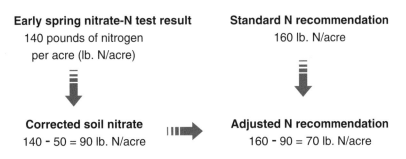

Early spring nitrate-N test result
140 pounds of nitrogen
per acre (lb. N/acre)

Standard N recommendation
160 lb. N/acre

Corrected soil nitrate
140 - 50 = 90 lb. N/acre

Adjusted N recommendation
160 - 90 = 70 lb. N/acre

For all initial soil tests of 200 pounds per acre or less, Wisconsin specialists recommend a minimum application rate of 50 pounds of N per acre. If the soil tests *over* 200 pounds of N per acre, they recommend no additional nitrogen.

Research in Michigan and Wisconsin in the late 1980s found success with the early spring nitrate-N test, but Iowa researchers concluded that the procedure did not accurately predict nitrogen needs.

The test should be most useful in continuous corn because it will be able to measure the potential for nitrogen carryover from the previous corn crop. If rain is heavy in late spring or early summer, the test will be less helpful because a lot of the N will be lost before it can reach the plant.

Pre-sidedress nitrogen test. Some studies have found that the pre-sidedress nitrogen test is most helpful on soils where manure has been applied—areas where there is a greater risk of excessive nutrient levels.

With the pre-sidedress test, take a sample from the top 1 foot of soil when the corn is 6 to 12 inches tall from the ground to the whorl. Take at least 16 to 24 core samples from each 10-acre area. Then follow these guidelines.

- If test results show nitrate-N levels of 25 parts per million (ppm) or more, several universities advise that you don't need to apply any more nitrogen. (In Wisconsin, agronomists use 21 ppm as the break-off point.)

- If nitrate levels are below 10 ppm, apply the full rate.
- If nitrate levels fall between 10 and 25 ppm, follow state recommendations.

In Iowa, specialists recommend that if your soil test reports a level between 10 and 25 ppm, you can determine the application rate by subtracting the soil test value from 25 and then multiplying by 8. For instance, if you have a soil test of 15 ppm nitrate-N, subtract 15 from 25 to get 10. Then multiply 10 x 8 to get 80. The recommended N application rate would be 80 pounds per acre.

In Wisconsin, on the other hand, specialists recommend the following rates for soil test levels less than 21 ppm:

Corn nitrogen recommendations based on the pre-sidedress soil nitrate test (Wisconsin)

| Nitrate-nitrogen | Soil yield potential* | |
	Very high/High	Medium/Low
(ppm)	(N application rate, pounds per acre)	
18 to 20	60	40
15 to 17	100	40
13 to 14	125	80
11 to 12	150	80
10 or less	160**	120**

*For assistance in determining a soil's yield potential, contact your local Cooperative Extension Service office.

**Unadjusted nitrogen application rate.

NOTE: For first-year corn following alfalfa, the maximum N recommendation rate is 40 pounds per acre for all pre-sidedress soil nitrate test results less than 21 ppm.

SOURCE: *Soil Nitrate Tests for Wisconsin Cropping Systems*, University of Wisconsin Extension, 1994.

What about cornstalk tests?

Tissue testing of *young* cornstalks is not reliable for indicating N availability in the field, but tissue testing of *mature* cornstalks shows promise, reported Iowa State researchers in the September-October 1992 issue of *Agronomy Journal.* Iowa State researchers stated that the end-of-season cornstalk test "deserves attention" as a tool to compare and refine N fertilizer recommendations.

End-of-season cornstalk tests can indicate whether corn has received too little or too much N. If a plant has received too little N, it will draw on nitrogen from the lower part of the plant to support grain fill at the top of the plant. If a plant has received too much N, the nitrogen will build up in the lower part of the plant.

Iowa State guidelines say that the optimum range of nitrate concentrations in the stalk is 700 to 2,000 ppm. Plants with less than 700 ppm have received too little N, while plants with levels over 2,000 ppm have received too much N.

What about chlorophyll meters?

Research indicates a close link between leaf chlorophyll content and N content in the leaves. Therefore, some specialists in the drier parts of the Corn Belt recommend that you monitor N levels with a chlorophyll meter beginning a little before tasseling.

The meter must be calibrated for each field, previous crop, hybrid, fertilizer and/or manure application, and differing soil types. To do this, create a reference strip in each field and make sure the strip receives an adequate level of nitrogen fertilizer. On the rest of the field, University of Nebraska specialists recommend that you fertilize with one-half to two-thirds of the total N recommended by standard soil test procedures.

Take weekly chlorophyll meter readings from both the reference strip and at least three locations in the rest of the field. At each location, take an average reading of 30 plants. By comparing results from the reference strip and the rest of the field, you can determine whether additional N is required. As one person put it, "Use the chlorophyll meter to schedule your *last* 50 pounds of nitrogen per acre, not your *first*."

Because the nitrogen readings are not taken until tasseling time, the chlorophyll meter has been most effective for farmers who irrigate fields. Adding fertilizer through an irrigation system can be practical at tasseling, but it is often too costly to apply nitrogen in any other way at such a late stage of crop growth.

Testing for P and K

In contrast to testing for N, soil tests for P and K are well established and quite effective for determining phosphorus and potassium needs.

The most useful test for phosphorus is the P-1 test, which estimates the amount of P in the soil that is available to the plant. The most frequently used and best calibrated test for K is ammonium acetate exchangeable K.

Testing for pH

Fluctuations in soil acidity can affect the availability of nutrients to plants, not to mention the levels of toxic metals in the soil and the amount of microorganism activity.

Phosphate, in particular, reacts to soil pH and is more available to the plant in slightly acidic to neutral soils. If the soil is too acidic (pH below 5.5) or too alkaline (pH above 7.3), much of the phosphate is converted to a form that is unavailable to the plant.

Researchers have found that the most effective use of nutrients occurs in corn and soybeans when the pH level is 6.0 to 7.0.

Prepared with Robert Hoeft, soil fertility specialist, UI Extension.

FERTILIZER PHILOSOPHIES: WHAT'S THE DIFFERENCE?

Should you feed the crop or feed the soil?

Behind this question lie two basic approaches to fertilizer application—approaches that can affect both crop production and water quality. In brief, here are the two schools of thought:

Feed the crop. With this approach, producers aim to maximize the yields of a particular crop for that year, assuming average growing conditions.

Feed the soil. With this approach, producers build up the soil to a level at which you attain maximum yields under the most ideal conditions and for the most demanding crop.

The first approach decreases the risk of applying excessive amounts of fertilizer because your goal is to maximize yields under average growing conditions. In contrast, if you assume the most ideal conditions, but the growing conditions are not ideal, you can end up applying more fertilizer than needed.

It is generally recognized that nitrogen always should be applied using the first approach: Feed the crop. The bigger question is whether to apply phosphorus and potassium under the "feed the crop" or "feed the soil" philosophy.

If you have a short-term land tenure or a very limited financial base, the first approach is the best way to minimize the investment in P and K and still optimize the yield potential. In these cases, you may want to consider a band application for most of the phosphorus and potassium to maximize the benefits from a "limited" application rate for the year.

The drawback is that by assuming average growing conditions, you may not provide enough nutrients to maximize yields if the year turns out to be one of the best ones. Also, a "feed-the-crop" approach will not improve or build up the supply of nutrients in the soil, and it may not meet the nutrient needs adequately if you use new and improved practices and varieties.

Therefore, many states recommend that you add enough P and K to build up the soil to a level at which you can optimize yields with the most demanding crop, plus enough to replace what the crop will remove. Some agronomists even set the desired soil test level slightly *above* the point at which yields are maximized as an added insurance. The argument is that this one-time investment to initially build up the soil can be prorated over a number of years. This cost will be much less than a yield decrease that might occur if your soil's nutrient level cannot meet the needs of a demanding crop in an ideal year.

However, the "feed-the-soil" approach means higher levels of P and K in the soil—at least initially. And this could mean more phosphorus moving with eroding soil. P readily attaches to soil particles, so when soil erodes, the phosphorus goes with it.

Prepared with Robert Hoeft, soil fertility specialist, UI Extension.

28 Credit other nitrogen sources

Where credit is due

When most soil-test laboratories recommend nitrogen (N) application rates, they usually base recommendations on the crop yield goal. So it's up to you to adjust these recommendations to account for N supplied by previous legume crops, manure, other organic wastes, or residual soil nitrate. If you do not credit other sources of nitrogen, you may end up applying more N than is agronomically necessary or environmentally wise.

Adjusting for legumes

To take into consideration the amount of nitrogen supplied by legume crops during the previous year, use the following table. The table shows how many pounds of nitrogen per acre can be reduced from your application rate.

Adjusting nitrogen: after legumes

Crop to be grown	After soybeans	First year after alfalfa or clover			Second year after alfalfa or clover	
		plants per square foot				
		Fewer than 2	2 to 4	5	Fewer than 5	5
		nitrogen reduction, pounds per acre				
Corn	40	0	50	100	0	30
Wheat	10	0	10	30	0	0

Adjusting for manure

The best way to gauge the nutrient content of manure is to have samples chemically analyzed. A laboratory analysis will tailor information to your specific farm. If you don't have manure samples analyzed, use the tables on pages 180-181 to credit nitrogen and other nutrients in manure.

✓ **CHECK IT OUT**
For more information on having manure samples analyzed: page 178.

Keep in mind that when you incorporate dry or liquid manure immediately following application, approximately 50 percent of the nitrogen will be available to the crop. Therefore, your manure credit should be about 50 percent of the figures listed in the tables.

If manure is allowed to lie on the soil surface for several days after application, a portion of the nitrogen will be lost. Although it is difficult to predict how much will be lost, it's recommended that your nitrogen credit be less than 50 percent of the figures in the tables.

Adjusting for other organic wastes and residual nitrate

If you apply other organic wastes to the soil, such as sludge, material from municipal wastewater treatment plants, or waste materials from food processing plants, you should have those wastes analyzed to account for nutrient content. Also, you can take into consideration residual nitrate in the soil with a preplant soil test.

CHECK IT OUT

For more information on nitrogen testing: page 132.

Adjusting for time of planting

Research at the Northern Illinois Research Center for several years showed that as planting was delayed, less nitrogen fertilizer was required to get the most profitable yield.

Based upon this research, Illinois agronomists suggest that for each week of delay in planting after the optimum date for the area, you can reduce the nitrogen rate 20 pounds per acre. The minimum rate would be 80 to 90 pounds per acre for very late planting in a corn-soybean cropping system.

The planting date adjustment is possible, of course, only if the nitrogen is sidedressed. Also, because of the importance of the planting date, you are encouraged not to delay planting just to apply less nitrogen fertilizer.

Prepared with Robert Hoeft, soil fertility specialist, UI Extension.

29 Select nitrogen fertilizers wisely

Nitrate on the move

Nitrogen (N) doesn't do much traveling in the ammonium form. Ammonium compounds grab hold of soil particles and generally stay put. But in the nitrate form, nitrogen begins to move and it's usually downward—leaching into the soil where nitrate can slip past the root zone and enter groundwater or drain tiles. Drain tiles can provide a direct route for the nitrate to reach lakes and streams.

Eventually, ammonium forms of nitrogen will transform into nitrate through the nitrification process (see illustration). But nitrogen sources that contain a greater percentage of ammonia will be *less* likely to leach

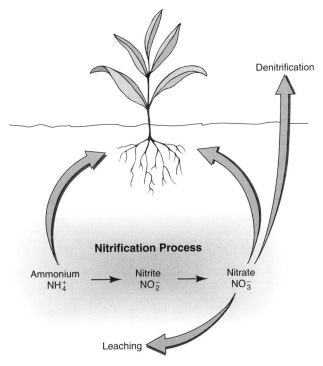

A high percentage of the nitrogen applied in the Midwest is in the ammonium form, or it converts to ammonium soon after application. During the nitrification process, ammonium nitrogen changes to nitrite, which then converts to nitrate. In the nitrate form, nitrogen can be lost by denitrification or by leaching. Nitrification inhibitors slow the conversion of ammonium to nitrite.

initially after application. Here is how the different sources of nitrogen compare in that regard:

Anhydrous ammonia. Anhydrous ammonia is manufactured by combining N from the air with hydrogen under pressure. It is applied beneath the soil surface and immediately reacts with soil water to form ammonium. Of all nitrogen fertilizers, anhydrous ammonia is the least likely to leach initially after application.

Urea. Urea is formed when ammonia and carbon dioxide are combined, and it is usually incorporated to prevent it from dissipating into the atmosphere. Of nitrogen fertilizers, urea is the second least likely to leach initially after application.

Urea ammonium nitrate (UAN) solutions. One-fourth of UAN solutions is in the nitrate form, a form that could leach immediately after application.

Ammonium nitrate. Half of ammonium nitrate is in the nitrate form. This makes ammonium nitrate the fertilizer in which the greatest amount of nitrogen is ready to leach immediately after application.

On sandy soils, the differences between these forms of nitrogen will be especially significant because water and nitrate can leach quickly through such coarse-textured soils. Therefore, you will want to use nitrogen in which a greater percentage is in the ammonium form.

On heavy soils, however, it's a different picture. It generally takes about four weeks for ammonia to transform into nitrate. During this time, water will not leach very far into heavy soils. Therefore, the differences between nitrogen forms may not be as significant—unless you use a nitrification inhibitor. The inhibitor delays the transformation from ammonium to nitrate well beyond the four-week period, greatly reducing the risk of nitrate contamination.

Nitrification inhibitors

Nitrification inhibitors can be used with any of the nitrogen materials. But they are primarily used with anhydrous ammonia and, to a limited extent, with UAN solutions.

One reason for this is that anhydrous is injected, while the other forms of nitrogen are usually broadcast-applied. With a broadcast application, you need to increase the rate of the inhibitor, so cost can become a stumbling block. Also, anhydrous ammonia is more likely to be applied earlier, which makes a nitrification inhibitor more important.

The following are some guidelines in deciding whether a nitrification inhibitor pays off.

Effective uses for inhibitors. Consider a nitrification inhibitor in these cases:

- Inhibitors should slow the processes in which N is lost if the soil is moderately or well-drained and is in an area of heavy rainfall or frequent flooding.
- Using a nitrification inhibitor offers the greatest potential benefits when you fall-apply nitrogen. When you apply nitrogen in the fall, ammonium forms of N have more time to convert into nitrate forms. As a result, there is more risk of leaching or denitrification. With the use of inhibitors, you can reduce these problems because most of the nitrogen may remain in its ammonium form throughout the winter.
- If you plan to apply nitrogen with inhibitors in the fall, it works best to make applications after the soil temperature has dropped below 60° F and the soil is likely to be frozen for most of the winter.
- Inhibitors work best when nitrogen is applied at or below optimum levels.
- Inhibitors should not be viewed as a way to reduce the amount of nitrogen applied to a field, but rather as a tool for reducing N loss.

Questionable uses. The following are cases in which an inhibitor may *not* make sense:

- Inhibitors are not necessary if the nitrogen is applied right before the crop needs it. Nitrogen without inhibitors would work just as well in this case.
- Inhibitors do not work as well in extremely coarse soils. In these soils, the ammonium nitrogen has a tendency to move away from the inhibitors. However, inhibitors can be effective in coarse soils when nitrogen applications are managed carefully.
- Fall-applied inhibitors are not effective if the soil remains unfrozen for most of the winter. In such cases, bacterial processes will eventually denitrify the N. By the time spring comes, the nitrogen will be in nitrate form and will leach through the soil during spring rains or be lost through denitrification.

Urease inhibitors

The first urease inhibitor to be available commercially reached the market in 1996. Urease inhibitors slow the conversion of urea to ammonia, thus reducing volatilization, the process in which ammonia on the soil surface is lost into the atmosphere as a gas.

By using a urease inhibitor, producers can now broadcast urea and UAN without incorporation—thus preserving more crop residue. They also no longer need to apply excess amounts to compensate for volatilization.

University research has shown urease inhibitors to be very effective when they're needed. The main instance in which an inhibitor would *not* have been needed is if a rain had followed urea application—but rainfall, of course, is fairly unpredictable.

The following charts, based on Purdue University and University of Illinois studies, show promising yield results with urease inhibitors.

Urease inhibitors and yields, University of Illinois
No-till corn after soybeans, Shelbyville, Illinois

Nitrogen source	80 lb. per acre N	160 lb. per acre N
	corn yield (bushels per acre)	
Unfertilized	—	134
Urea	164	175
Urea with inhibitor	170	191

Urease inhibitors and yields, Purdue University
Five locations in Indiana

N management system	One-year average for all locations
	corn yield (bushels per acre)
Control plot	85
Urea surface applied	117
Urea with inhibitor	132
UAN	124
UAN with inhibitor	128
UAN knifed-in	136

Prepared with Robert Hoeft, soil fertility specialist, UI Extension.

30 Apply nitrogen in the spring

Fall versus spring

Your best bet is to apply nitrogen (N) as close as possible to when your crop needs it most.

When you apply nitrogen in the fall, a portion of the N may be lost through denitrification before the next year's crop can use it, possibly reducing yields. Denitrification is a process in which soil organisms convert nitrate-nitrogen into a form that is unavailable to the plants.

Fall application also could give nitrogen time to leach through the root zone and into groundwater or subsurface drainage tile. (Nitrogen is more likely to reach rivers, lakes, or streams by moving through drainage tile than by moving with runoff water on the soil surface.)

Researchers estimate that with fall application, nitrogen losses from denitrification and leaching can range from 10 to 20 percent on fine- and medium-textured soils and 20 to 50 percent on coarse-textured soils. University of Illinois research has also shown that it can take 120 pounds of fall-applied nitrogen to produce the same yield increase as 100 pounds applied in the spring.

On sandy soils: Sidedress

As a general rule, an inch of rain can leach about $1/2$ foot through a heavy soil and about *1 foot* through a sandy soil. This means that 6 inches of rain can leach 6 feet down through a sandy soil, putting it out of the root zone.

The increased risk of leaching on sandy soils means you need to take special care to prevent nitrogen from leaching into groundwater or drain tiles. A sandy soil may call for sidedressing—applying nitrogen right before the peak demand of the plant. With sidedressing, the plant absorbs N before it has much time to leach or denitrify.

Sidedressing also gives you the option of adjusting your application rates to crop conditions. For instance, you can lower rates if you have a reduced stand, delayed planting, severe weed problems, or any other situation that will reduce yields.

But timing is critical with sidedressing. The period in which corn takes up nitrogen most rapidly is from about three to twelve weeks after planting. Therefore, if the weather is too wet and you have trouble getting application equipment on the field in time, the benefits of sidedressing are greatly reduced. You could also run into problems if you sidedress N on dry soil that remains dry. According to research, the best strategy is to sidedress the nitrogen as soon as corn rows are visible.

If you irrigate your sandy soil, one option is to apply a small amount of nitrogen at planting time (30 to 40 pounds per acre), one-third of it through the irrigation system no later than two weeks after tasseling, and the remainder as a sidedress application before corn is 8 inches tall. If you do *not* irrigate, you can split your N applications by applying one-third preplant and the other two-thirds sidedress.

Prepared with Robert Hoeft, soil fertility specialist, UI Extension.

BROADCAST, INCORPORATE, OR INJECT?

Phosphorus

Phosphorus binds easily to soil particles, which means that if you broadcast P, it can move to streams by hitching a ride with eroding soil. Therefore, anything you can do to control erosion will reduce the movement of phosphorus to streams, lakes, and rivers. This also means that incorporating broadcast-applied phosphorus is *not* recommended. Incorporation buries crop residue, which increases soil erosion and the movement of phosphorus with the soil.

By *injecting* at least a portion of the phosphorus in starter fertilizer with the planter, however, you can keep P off the surface without destroying much surface residue. Ample evidence indicates that including phosphorus in starter fertilizer at planting will be beneficial, especially on no-tilled fields. But research has not shown that the *deep* injection of phosphorus (5 to 6 inches deep) pays for itself with increased yield.

Also, injecting phosphorus in a concentrated band can affect soil sampling. So don't sample next to the row where the concentrated band could give misleading results; sample between rows.

Nitrogen

Unlike phosphorus, nitrogen is much more soluble; it moves into the soil much more easily and doesn't bind to soil particles on the surface as easily as phosphorus. As a result, nitrogen isn't as likely to move with runoff water; it reaches lakes and streams primarily through drain tiles and other subsurface flow. The major cases in which you would see a lot of nitrogen movement with surface runoff are on frozen soils or on steep slopes when you have a sudden, intense rainfall.

What all of this means is that from an environmental perspective, broadcasting nitrogen on the surface is *not* as great a risk as broad-casting phosphorus. But, of course, there are still good economic reasons for choosing injection or incorporation over broadcasting N. For example, to prevent nitrogen losses due to volatilization, any product containing urea should be injected or incorporated, unless a urease inhibitor is used. (Volatilization is a process in which nitrogen is converted to a gas and lost to the atmosphere.)

The incorporation of ammonium nitrate is *not* necessary, however, because it is not a volatile compound. By incorporating ammonium nitrate, you could bury a substantial percentage of the residue that protects the soil surface from erosion.

Prepared with Robert Hoeft, soil fertility specialist, UI Extension.

31 Apply fertilizer with a global positioning system

GPS: How realistic?

When the idea of using satellite signals to improve the precision of chemical applications began receiving attention in the late 1980s, many people thought it sounded more like science fiction than scientific fact. It also sounded expensive.

But when John Deere and Rockwell International announced their entry into the field of precision farming in 1994, interest in global positioning systems (GPS) took off. For many producers, GPS suddenly seemed a little more down to earth. John Deere began testing GPS receivers in the spring of 1994 on the tractors of about one hundred select customers. In the spring of 1996, they made them available to the general public.

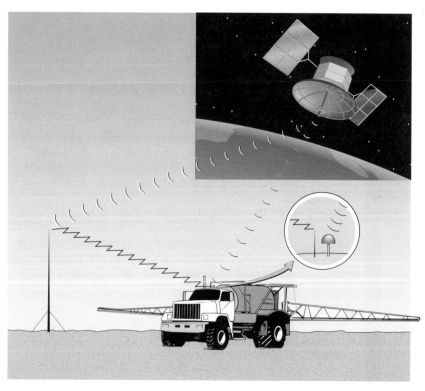

With some global positioning systems, satellites send signals to both a ground-based station and to the tractor. In turn, the ground-based station transmits a signal to the tractor. A computer on board the tractor pieces together all of the transmitted information to determine the location of the equipment.

How it works

Think of GPS as a triangle of transmitter signals. The three points to the triangle are:

- A set of satellites
- A receiver on the tractor
- A ground-based station

The satellites send signals to the ground-based station, as well as to the receiver on the tractor. In turn, the ground-based station sends a "correction signal" to the tractor. Then the tractor's on-board GPS receiver puts all of this information together to pinpoint the area of the field that the equipment is passing over. When the computer knows the precise part of the field it is covering, it can adjust fertilizer rates to meet the soil's needs. Because of this ability to vary the application rate on the go, it is called "variable rate technology" or other such names—site-specific application, prescription farming, or precision farming, to list a few.

Most farmers using GPS connect their equipment to standard systems that can locate their position on the field within a diameter of about 6 to 20 feet. But a newer system, known as "kinematic GPS," can locate your position with even greater accuracy—within a circle 1 foot in diameter.

Kinematic GPS boosts accuracy by measuring the number and length of the radio waves being sent to the tractor by the satellite. It is more expensive than standard GPS, but the price is coming down.

Obtaining a correction signal

One of the keys to the system is finding a ground-based station to send the correction signal to the tractor's receiver. Currently, farmers have four basic ways to obtain a correction signal:

Obtain a signal transmitted by Coast Guard stations. This signal is free, but the farmer's receiver must be located within 250 miles of a Coast Guard station. Stations are strung along the coasts and up the Mississippi River.

Receive a signal that is broadcast on the side band of a commercial radio station signal. A farmer must pay a subscription fee for this signal. The signal has about a 50-mile range and can be more susceptible to interference.

Subscribe to a service that provides a correction signal. One subscription system transmits its correction signal through its own system of satellites. This arrangement makes it possible to receive the correction signal no matter where you are located in the United States.

Operate your own ground-based station. Developing your own station to transmit the correction signal can be costly. In addition, the range of such a signal tends to be limited to about 12 to 15 miles.

What can GPS be used to do?

So far, two of the primary uses for systems based on GPS have been soil testing and fertilizer application. The custom applicator takes soil samples using an all-terrain vehicle equipped with a GPS receiver. Then the computer creates a soil map that shows the phosphorus (P) and potassium (K) levels for each zone on a grid. The zones have generally ranged from 2.5 to 3.3 acres in size, depending on the company doing the soil sampling. With these soil maps, the computer can adjust the application rates to meet the P and K needs for each specific area, based on the crop to be planted, expected yield, and the base fertility level of the soil.

Using this kind of technology to map nutrient needs works well with P and K, which are not highly mobile. But it has limited use with N, which readily moves through the soil and is easily lost through denitrification and volatilization. If you map N levels in a field, those levels will most likely be different by the time you actually apply the nitrogen.

Other uses for GPS include:

Yield monitoring. In addition to soil testing and fertilizer application, the other major use for GPS technology so far has been yield monitoring. A yield monitor on the combine estimates grain flow into the combine every 1 to 3 seconds. By combining this data with GPS information that pinpoints the equipment's position in the field, producers can develop an extremely accurate yield map for each part of the field.

The yield map can be used for troubleshooting and for adjusting the seeding rate on the go. In addition, yield information can be combined with the soil map for even more precise fertilizer application rates.

Herbicide application. Using variable rate technology to adjust herbicide rates is more limited than with fertilizer application. But it is being used to adjust the rates of some herbicides according to particular soil characteristics.

Does variable rate technology reduce surface-water contamination?

It's generally assumed that more precise fertilizer applications translate into less nutrients moving into groundwater and surface-water supplies. However, there has been little research on the environmental impact of variable rate technologies that use GPS.

If variable rate technology becomes more practical for nitrogen and pesticides, the environmental benefits could potentially be great. But the environmental benefits for applying P and K are not as clear-cut.

Because phosphorus and potassium are not highly mobile nutrients, the primary way they move into surface water supplies is by hitching a ride on eroding soil. Therefore, variable rate technology is most likely to reduce the amount of P and K reaching surface water if it lowers the P and K application rates on erosive areas of a field.

Unfortunately, this is not always the case. Variable rate technology can sometimes *increase* application rates in certain parts of the field. If those areas happen to be highly erosive, the amount of P and K reaching surface water could actually increase.

If GPS technology is eventually used to map the erodibility of various parts of a field, the environmental benefits will become more dramatic. In fact, GPS may someday be used to map a wide array of environmental factors throughout a field—proximity to streams, susceptibility of the soil to surface-water runoff, depth to groundwater, etc. An on-board computer could combine this information with other data, such as nutrient and yield goals, to come up with an optimum application rate.

Does it pay?

In most cases, variable rate technology will apply P and K in a field more efficiently than if you applied them uniformly across a field. But does the increased efficiency and the potential for higher yields provide enough payback to make up for the added costs of variable rate technology? It depends primarily on two things:

- How variable the fertility levels are within a field
- The average level of fertility in a field

In 1994, University of Illinois research compared variable rate application methods with *uniform* applications of P and K. Generally, variable rate technology became more economical as the average fertility level and the fertility variability in the field increased.

When fertilizer application rates were based on standard, agronomic rates, the variable rate technology paid off for these field conditions:

All of the fields with:

- A high average fertility level
- High fertility variability

All of the fields with:

- A medium average fertility level
- High fertility variability

Some of the fields with:

- A high average fertility level
- Medium fertility variability

Low average fertility	Medium average fertility	High average fertility
P = 30 lb. per acre	P = 50 lb. per acre	P = 70 lb. per acre
K = 200 lb. per acre	K = 300 lb. per acre	K = 400 lb. per acre

Variable rate technology did not pay off for any of the fields with low average fertility levels or low fertility variability.

In all, variable rate technology paid off for 30 percent of the field conditions examined. However, researchers found that economic benefits could increase significantly if application rates were based on more precise guidelines—rather than standard agronomic guidelines, which are not tailored to variable rate technologies.

If producers base their application rates on more precise guidelines, researchers projected that the variable rate technology would have paid off in approximately 60 percent of the field conditions examined. Also, keep in mind that this research was based on P and K application only. If variable rate technology is used for other purposes, such as N and pesticide application, the economic benefits go up.

Prepared with Carroll Goering, UI professor of agricultural engineering; Robert Hornbaker, farm management specialist, UI Extension; Mark Schluter, VRT coordinator/service manager, Illini FS, Inc., in Urbana, Illinois; and Wayne Smith, project manager, John Deere in East Moline, Illinois.

Arlen Ruestman

Cutting back with variable rates

Arlen Ruestman started grid sampling in 1982, testing his soil in 2-acre grids every four years. The land where he grid sampled was relatively flat and black and had been managed by a tenant who had been conscientious in maintaining fertility levels. That's why Ruestman was shocked when he received the soil test results and saw how much the fertility levels varied across each field.

The more variable the fertility levels, the more valuable variable rate technology becomes. So Ruestman eventually took the next step in managing fertility levels on his 1,600-acre farm near Toluca, Illinois. Since 1992, he has been applying phosphorus (P) and potassium (K) using site-specific technology, connected to a global positioning system (GPS).

By varying his P and K rates according to site-specific soil tests, Ruestman estimates that he has reduced his fertilizer costs by 20 to 25 percent when compared with even rates across the field.

In addition to being initially shocked by the variability of fertilizer levels on his farm, Ruestman says he had a similar reaction when he started using a GPS-based yield monitor in 1992 to check the variability of yields throughout his fields.

"What we have been finding has been pretty much echoed by others," he says. "We always knew there was a lot of yield variability in the fields, but we didn't know to what extent."

In 1995, for example, Ruestman says his corn averaged just under 200 bushels per acre, but he found some areas with yields as low as 120 bushels per acre and some as high as 270 bushels per acre. His soybeans averaged 55 bushels per acre, but the monitor revealed a range from the high 30s to just under 70 bushels.

"This variability actually raised more questions than it answered," Ruestman says. He is now looking for reasons to explain it, and the main suspects so far appear to be poor drainage in certain areas and differences in soil type.

"As we look at the yield maps and trends," he says, "the yield monitor is giving us a pretty good indication of where we might benefit from additional drainage. And every year of yield data that you add is that much better. But it will take better, more powerful software to handle these mountains of information."

Ruestman says his software can use the data collected to create maps that show how much the yields in different spots vary from the field average. His software can also create maps that show the difference between revenue and costs for specific areas of the field, taking into consideration fertilizer and pesticide costs and the price for corn or soybeans. Areas with lower profits would be candidates for hay production.

For producers interested in getting a start with GPS, Ruestman says you can go two different ways—start by grid soil sampling with GPS or start with a yield monitor.

"The consensus appears to be that the yield monitor is the better place to start," he says. "If you don't grid sample this year, you can always do it next year. But once a harvest goes by, there will never be another opportunity to map the yield of that crop. It's going to take multiple years of yield data before you start seeing trends. So the sooner you get started with yield monitoring, the better."

Ruestman says he hopes to eventually use variable rate technology to apply nitrogen, but the nitrogen controller he owns now is not accurate enough to use with GPS. In the meantime, he says GPS has paid off for him, although it's hard to put a dollar figure on the benefits of yield monitors. Says Ruestman: "I don't think we yet realize how valuable this data is."

Managing livestock waste effectively

Credit the ancient hero Hercules with being the first person to design a livestock waste management system, for according to legend he cleaned out the Augean Stables by diverting a river through them. Today, Hercules' strategy would not go over too well because the goal is to keep livestock waste and runoff as far as possible from rivers and streams.

When livestock waste washes into lakes and streams, it can raise nitrate concentrations to dangerous levels, produce algae blooms due to excessive phosphorus levels, cause fish kills, create noxious odors, increase water turbidity (cloudiness), and add any number of microbiological contaminants to the water (see the story on page 161.

The following chapters explain practical ways to make the best use of livestock waste while reducing the risks to yourself, your family, your livestock, and the environment.

Keep livestock out of water

Why fence them out?

Giving livestock free rein to water can do more than stir up mud. It can stir up a number of problems—from soil erosion to animal health hazards.

For instance, livestock contaminate the water directly with manure and urine, which teem with bacteria and viruses (see the accompanying sidebar "Microscopic mischief makers reside in livestock waste"). Livestock can also erode the bank, either by trampling it or by grazing away its protective cover. This increases the amount of sediment clogging and filling up both streams and ponds.

By using fencing to cut off the access of livestock to streams and ponds, you may see a number of benefits:

Protecting the health of your herd. Fencing will reduce your animals' contact with waterborne bacteria, which can cause bovine leptospirosis, mastitis, and other ailments. In addition, it will reduce the risk of leg injury, which can occur when livestock walk on crumbling banks.

Controlling soil erosion. The buffer zone of vegetation growing between the fence and stream provides erosion control, as does keeping livestock away from the streambank. In Ohio, for example, researchers measured erosion rates before and after they fenced cattle away from a stream and adjacent wooded area. They found that fencing cattle away from a stream cut soil erosion by 40 percent and reduced the amount of sediment reaching the stream by 50 percent over a five-year period, according to a report in the January/February 1996 issue of the *Journal of Soil and Water Conservation.*

Controlling the movement of pesticides and fertilizers. The vegetation between the fence and stream acts as a buffer, absorbing pesticides and nutrients before they wash into the water.

Improving fish habitat. Streamside vegetation provides protective cover for fish and adds organic matter to the stream, increasing the amount and diversity of aquatic life. Shrubs and trees along the stream provide shade, which makes for a cooler, healthier habitat for fish and other life.

Providing habitat for birds and small mammals. Over 80 kinds of birds use streamside vegetation for summer feeding or nesting.

Improving the landscape and neighbor relations. The wildflowers and other vegetation between the fence and stream increase the beauty of the landscape. In addition, solving environmental problems on your property will help neighbors downstream.

In keeping livestock out of streams and ponds, however, the two biggest questions you face are: "What kind of fencing do I use?" and "What are the best alternative sources of drinking water for the animals?"

Fencing options

Ordinary woven wire fences pose a problem. When a large storm strikes and the stream or pond overflows its banks, water may wash out your fence. There is less risk of washout with multistrand, high-tensile fences, which can be electrified.

For interior paddock fences, animals accustomed to electric fences can often be controlled by one strand of wire. Use $12^1/2$ gauge, galvanized, high-tensile steel wire wherever possible for interior or perimeter fences; and keep "temporary" fencing to a minimum because it is less durable and requires more maintenance.

The following are recommendations for additional electric fencing components:

Insulators. Use good-quality insulators, especially on steel posts. Cheap insulators cost more if you take their maintenance and aggravation into consideration.

Posts. Treated pine posts have the greatest strength and are probably better than steel t-posts for permanent fencing. You can build temporary paddock fences using such materials as PVC conduit posts and fiberglass.

Fence controllers. Decide on either a mains controller (120 volt AC) or a battery controller. The mains controller will cost less and deliver more bang for the buck. But if the pasture is far from the barn, sometimes a battery unit is the only way to go.

Be sure to protect the fence controller from lightning. Use a surge protector on the power cord to the mains controller. Use two 8-foot ground rods for the fencer ground and a set of three 8-foot rods for the lightning protection ground. Most fencing suppliers offer lightning arresters and choke kits that will help protect the controller under most conditions.

Place fencing as far from the stream as possible. The greater the distance, the greater the benefits. If you use electric fencing, the area directly below the fence may need to be mowed periodically to keep tall vegetation from shorting out the fence. You may not need to mow if you have cattle in adjacent pastures because cattle often graze directly under the fence, keeping it free of tall vegetation.

Most of the "weeds" that grow along the streambank are beneficial, but mowing may be needed occasionally to control certain plants. You can minimize problems by preparing the site properly when installing the fence. Plant desired grasses and seedlings.

Water sources

When providing water to livestock, you need to consider water volume, supply equipment, pressure tanks, electric power, and groundwater protection.

Water volume. Beef animals require about 9 gallons of water per 1,000 pounds per day in winter and up to 18 gallons per 1,000 pounds per day during summer. If you use a tank, it should hold about one day's water supply; the pumping system should be adequate to refill the tank in four hours.

Supply equipment: Surface-water source. If you draw livestock drinking water from a pond or other surface-water source, you can route it to a tank through a siphon. The siphon outlet must be lower than the level of the pond, and the line must be leakproof. A float valve on the tank is adequate for controlling the system. Use a floating inlet in the pond, and keep in mind that any screen on the inlet will drop the pressure and reduce flow.

Supply equipment: Groundwater source. If you draw livestock drinking water from a well, the simplest type of pump to use is a shallow-well suction pump. Theoretically, atmospheric pressure will allow a shallow-well suction pump to lift water from nearly 30 feet deep. But practically speaking, the limit is more like 15 to 20 feet.

Deep-well pumps are necessary where the groundwater is too deep for a shallow-well pump (more than 20 feet or so). For information on the kinds of deep-well pumps suitable for livestock watering applications, obtain a copy of the MidWest Plan Service's *Private Water Systems* handbook. For details on how to order a copy, see "For more information" on page 303.

Pressure tanks. Use a pressure tank in your water system because it reduces the cycling of the pump. Rapid, repeated cycling reduces the life of the pump motor and pumping efficiency. Size the pressure tank to supply 10 to 12 minutes of water.

Electric power. Getting electric power to the pump requires adequately sized wiring to limit voltage drop. Low voltage at the pump motor, caused by poor or undersized wiring, can cause the motor to overheat and fail. Wire sizes depend on full-load motor amps and the length of the wire circuit.

For details on how to determine wiring sizes, obtain the MidWest Plan Service's *Farm Buildings Wiring* handbook, the National Food and Energy Council's *Agricultural Wiring* handbook, or the *National Electric Code* handbook. To find out how to order copies of the *Farm Buildings Wiring* handbook, check "For more information" on page 303.

One other option is to use photovoltaic power (solar electric power) to pump the water. However, you would need a large water storage tank to carry you through overcast days when there is little sunlight for power.

Groundwater protection. Protect wells and groundwater from pollution by proper construction at the wellhead. Also, any tank or waterer supplied by well water should be fitted with a device that prevents backsiphoning of the tank water into the well in the event of a loss of pressure in the line. Most commercial float valves have an air gap or anti-backsiphoning valve, but it pays to check.

Stream crossing

If livestock and equipment need to cross the stream, your fencing plan should include crossings. These areas should be stabilized, usually with concrete, railroad ties, or rock, to minimize erosion. Hanging flood gates along the crossing will restrict livestock to a short stretch of stream, yet will swing out during high water.

Before constructing a crossing, check with your state environmental agency for information on regulations and permits.

Prepared with Ted Funk, farm structures specialist, and Ed Ballard, animal systems educator, UI Extension.

ALTERNATIVE WATER FOR CATTLE: A TEMPTING OPTION

You can lead a horse to water, as the saying goes, but you can *lure* a cow to a drinking trough.

Recent research from Virginia Polytechnic Institute and State University has shown that something as simple as providing an alternative water source—such as a trough—will significantly decrease the amount of time cattle spend in a stream. It will also cut the amount of pollutants that cattle add to the stream.

According to results released in 1996, when cattle were given the choice, they were observed to drink from a spring-fed water trough 92 percent of the time and only 8 percent from the stream. The presence of an alternative water source reduced the cattle's use of the stream for *all* activities (including drinking) by 58 percent.

Although simple electric fencing remains the best way to keep cattle away from a stream 100 percent of the time, this research underscores the impact of an alternative water source.

Researchers also found that by luring the cattle away from the stream, the concentration of pollutants in the stream went down as follows:

Fecal coliform bacteria: reduced by 51%

Fecal streptococci bacteria: reduced by 77%

Total nitrogen: reduced by 54%

Total suspended solids: reduced by 90%

Ammonium: reduced by 70%

Sediment-bound nitrogen: reduced by 68%

Total phosphorus: reduced by 81%

Sediment-bound phosphorus: reduced by 75%

Prepared with Michael Hirschi, soil and water specialist, and Ted Funk, farm structures specialist, UI Extension.

MICROSCOPIC MISCHIEF MAKERS RESIDE IN LIVESTOCK WASTE

Milwaukee microbes

In April 1993, some 400,000 Milwaukee residents—three out of every four people in the city—experienced acute gastrointestinal problems. The culprit: a protozoal parasite known as *Cryptosporidium parvum*, which had found its way into their drinking water.

Cryptosporidium parvum is one of several pathogens (disease-causing organisms) that young livestock shed in their waste—although it should be noted that authorities do not definitively know whether or not livestock waste was responsible for Milwaukee's water woes. The source of the *Cryptosporidium parvum* cysts was never pinpointed.

Nevertheless, the incident underscores the importance of keeping livestock waste out of surface water.

So how often do these microbes show up in livestock waste? According to research from Cornell University, *Cryptosporidium parvum* and *Giardia lamblia* (another protozoan parasite) have been found in 100 percent of the calves under six months of age on some farms. A calf infected with *Cryptosporidium parvum* may shed as many as 10 million infectious cysts per day in their feces.

Drinking water is treated (filtered and disinfected) to control many microbial troublemakers—protozoal parasites, viruses, and bacteria. In some cases, however, pathogens smaller than 1 micrometer can survive and make their way through filters, bypassing treatment processes. People also risk exposure to these pathogens if they accidentally swallow water while swimming in contaminated surface water or have open wounds that could contact contaminated water.

The best way to prevent microbial contamination is to use a multiple-barrier strategy—protecting the source of raw water from contamination, treating water, and monitoring the water entering and leaving the water distribution system. To protect water at its source, keep livestock at least 200 feet away from water, install buffer zones along lakes and streams, consider keeping livestock off the buffer zones, and control the runoff from livestock areas.

On the following page is a brief rundown on some of the pathogens that can be found in livestock waste and their effect on humans.

Pathogens in livestock waste

Protozoa

Pathogen	Disease	General symptoms
Cryptosporidium parvum	Cryptosporidiosis	Diarrhea, abdominal discomfort
Giardia lamblia	Giardiasis	Diarrhea, abdominal discomfort

Bacteria

Campylobacter jejeuni	Campylobacteriosis	Fever, abdominal pain, diarrhea
Shigella species	Shigellosis	Fever, diarrhea, bloody stools
Salmonella species	Salmonellosis	Mild gastroenteritis, acute diarrhea, and blood poisoning, depending on the *salmonella* strain

Viruses

Hepatitis non-A: waterborne	Hepatitis	Fever, chills, anorexia, abdominal discomfort, jaundice, dark urine
Norwalk, Rotavirus, and other similar viral agents	Viral gastroenteritis	Fever, headache, gastrointestinal discomfort

Prepared with Mel Bromberg, water and health specialist, and Michael Hirschi, soil and water specialist, UI Extension.

33 Divert runoff water

Keep clean water clean

It pays to keep clean water clean. For instance, it doesn't take long for a gutter system on your livestock buildings to more than pay for itself. If you do *not* put gutters on livestock buildings, you may have additional water running into your holding pond. This means your holding pond must have a greater capacity, increasing construction expenses. It also costs money to remove the additional dirty water whenever you dewater the holding pond.

If you have a 20-foot-wide roof without gutters, the cost to remove the additional dirty water is an estimated $1 per year for every foot of the building's length. Therefore, if you have a 100-foot-long building, you would face an expense of $100 per year just to remove the additional water entering the holding pond.

In addition to reducing the load on holding ponds or storage pits, diverting clean water around the lot prevents the excessive erosion of manure solids from the lot and increases the effectiveness of settling basins or other solid-liquid separation equipment. All of this makes environmental and economic sense.

Divert water from roofs

Prevent rainwater from entering the feedlot by using gutters and downspouts to handle water from building rooftops. The roof gutter should carry all water to one or both ends of the building. Select and install adequate downspouts and a pipe to carry this water away from the site. Ideally, the pipe should be underground, leading away from the building.

Keep in mind that standard roof gutters and downspouts are not adequate for runoff from large roofs. Also, if the water draining from a roof does not reach areas that are accessible to livestock, you may not need gutters and downspouts at all.

For information on sizing gutters and downspouts, refer to the MidWest Plan Service's *Livestock Waste Facilities* handbook. To find out how to order the handbook, refer to page 303.

Divert water around the feedlot

Divert water around the feedlot, buildings, or farmstead with terraces or channels—either paved or earthen. Earthen terraces and channels are more common because of their lower cost.

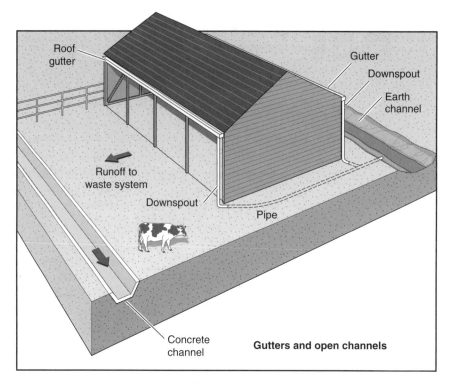

Roof gutter

Gutter

Downspout

Earth channel

Runoff to waste system

Downspout

Pipe

Concrete channel

Gutters and open channels

To prevent water from entering a feedlot, use gutters and downspouts to handle water coming from rooftops, and use terraces and channels to divert other water. Diverting clean water around the lot reduces the load on holding ponds or storage pits, prevents the excessive erosion of manure solids, and increases the effectiveness of settling basins or other solid-liquid separation equipment.

The most common earthen channels are grassed waterways with a roughly trapezoidal cross section. The channels are typically designed to handle water from a 10-year, 1-hour storm (the heaviest 1-hour rainfall that can be expected, on average, every 10 years).

For diversion channels to remain effective, you must maintain them. For example, periodically mow vegetation in the channel. If vegetation is allowed to grow too tall, the velocity of runoff water may become so slow that the channel overflows.

✔ CHECK IT OUT

For information on trapezoidal grassed waterways: page 78.
For more information on diversions: page 112.

Prepared with Ted Funk, farm structures specialist, UI Extension.

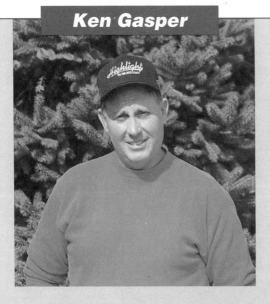

Composting manure reduces odor, phosphorus problems

A surprise awaited Ken Gasper when he returned from a vacation two years ago. His father and hired hand had finalized a decision to compost manure, and it's a decision that Gasper hasn't regretted. In fact, the Gaspers went full tilt with the system in 1996, putting all of the summer manure from the free stalls into the compost piles.

Gasper, who was named dairy farmer of the year in Michigan in 1992, composts manure on a 4-acre field behind the barn. Using a slinger spreader with a side discharge, the Gaspers apply manure in windrows that are 50 feet wide and about 30 to 40 rods long. After about a month, each pile forms a stack roughly 10 to 12 inches high.

During the summer, it takes about five to six weeks for the compost to fully cook. The result is an odorless compost product that Gasper applies to the fields or sells off the farm. Gasper's operation, located in Belding, Michigan (25 miles north of Grand Rapids), handles livestock waste from a herd of 120 cows.

Michigan has put an emphasis on composting manure partly because of high phosphorus levels in surface water—levels that encourage excessive algae growth in lakes and streams. In fact, Michigan's Right to Farm law recommends that no manure be applied to soils that have more than 300 pounds per acre of available phosphorus (according to the Bray P-1 test). When phosphorus exceeds that level, researchers have found a significantly greater risk that it will attach to soil and move with sediment into waterways.

Composting manure gets at this problem in a couple of ways, says Ted Loudon, agricultural engineer with Michigan State University. First, you can transport composted manure greater distances than other forms of manure. This reduces the temptation to make excessive manure applications on fields near the livestock facility—a practice that can boost phosphorus and nitrogen to unacceptable levels. Second, it is easier to transport composted manure off the farm entirely because the material contains less water and has less bulk.

Michigan State researchers projected that the annual net cost of composting manure for a 120-cow herd would be about $13,518. When you subtract the value of nutrients saved, the annual cost would be about $7,633. This is comparable to the daily haul system, which was about $12,870 annually ($7,907 once you subtract the value of nutrients saved).

When composting manure, stacks are covered with geotextile blankets, which shed water and allow gases to pass in and out of the pile. Gasper says he turns the piles every other week using a compost turner that he and another farmer purchased together.

To get carbon into the manure (an important part of the composting process), Gasper puts wood shavings and chopped straw in the alleyways of the free stalls—something his local vet had been encouraging him to do anyway. Gasper had been afraid that the shavings and straw would tempt the cows to lie down in the alleyways, but that hasn't been a problem.

According to Gasper, composted manure is odorless—an important consideration because new residential areas have been going up across the road from his farm.

"It's a way to stay out of trouble with the neighbors," he says.

While the compost piles handle manure from the free stalls, another innovative waste-management system takes care of milkhouse wastewater on the Gasper farm.

Previously, wastewater had been entering a ditch across the road and flowing toward the Flat River about a half mile away. Today, milkhouse wastewater enters a 2,000-gallon settling tank where the waste solids settle out. The wastewater then moves to another 2,000-gallon settling tank, equipped with an industrial sump pump that sends the water to a distribution tank.

From the distribution tank, the wastewater is pumped to one of four vegetated "cells"—20-foot by 50-foot grassed areas surrounded by 1-foot berms. The water is sprayed onto gravel and then trickles slowly into the vegetated cells where impurities are filtered out. A meter on the pump ensures that no more than 100 gallons of wastewater is applied to a cell at any one time.

In 1996, the Gaspers also completed a holding pond, which acts as a safety backup should the grassed filter system shut down.

"We decided to do our homework before someone *made* us do our homework," Gasper says. "This system may not be for everyone, but it would probably work for a lot of people who need to do something to keep wastewater out of streams."

Collect and store contaminated runoff

Provide direction

In addition to preventing clean water from entering an open feedlot, you need to handle the contaminated runoff coming from the lot itself. Using curbs, terraces, channels, dikes, pipes, and culverts, direct the contaminated runoff to an outlet that leads to either a settling tank or a settling basin.

If your open lot has only one outlet point, the job of collecting contaminated runoff is relatively straightforward. But if the lot slopes off in many directions, you may end up with many outlet points and a more complex system.

Settling tank

A settling tank is a stop-off point for contaminated livestock runoff on its way to a holding pond, lagoon, or infiltration area (such as a vegetative

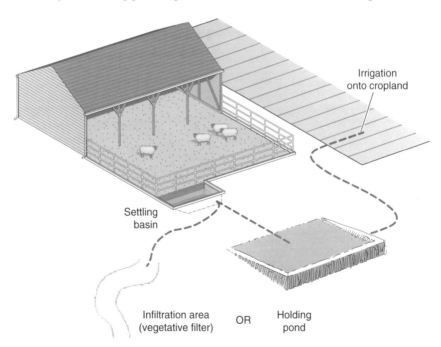

Irrigation onto cropland

Settling basin

Infiltration area (vegetative filter)   OR   Holding pond

To deal with contaminated runoff coming from a feedlot, direct it to either a settling tank or a settling basin. From the tank or basin, the contaminated runoff often flows to a holding pond, although in some situations you might be able to use a vegetative filter. A typical way to empty a holding pond is to pump out the water and apply it on the land.

filter). Solids settle to the bottom while some of the liquids (not all) move on. Because the tank stores some of the solids and liquids, it's a lot like a septic tank.

When sludge builds up, use a tank wagon or chopper pump to agitate the manure and clean out the tank—about one to two times per year. (Beware of the rapid build-up of toxic gases during agitation.) Some tanks need to be cleaned out more often, depending on the size of the tank, the area of the feedlot, and the intensity of the rainfall.

Settling basin

Like a settling tank, a settling basin captures runoff and allows liquids to slowly drain to a holding pond, lagoon, or infiltration area. Unlike a settling tank, however, a settling basin is designed to empty completely of liquids. The solids remain in the basin, drying out for later removal with a tractor and endloader. The best basin shapes are designed with a large surface area and shallow depth. The depth should be less than 3

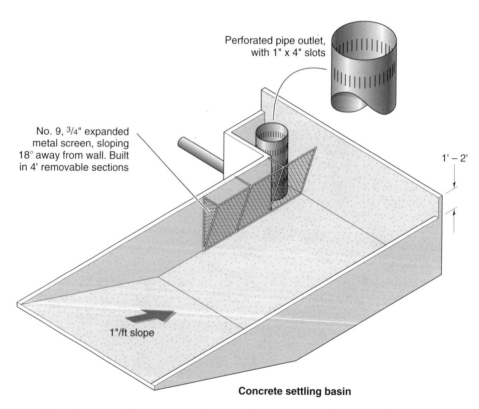

Perforated pipe outlet, with 1" x 4" slots

No. 9, 3/4" expanded metal screen, sloping 18° away from wall. Built in 4' removable sections

1' – 2'

1"/ft slope

Concrete settling basin

In humid areas, settling basins need concrete bottoms or must be completely concrete for equipment to enter and clean them out. The ideal basin shape is large and shallow.

feet deep if you intend to remove solids with conventional solid manure handling equipment.

In arid states, you may be able to get by with an earthen basin because basins dry out quickly. In humid areas, however, basins need concrete bottoms or must be completely concrete for equipment to enter and clean them out.

How often you need to clean out a settling basin depends on the size of the basin, the type of lot surface, the amount of manure on the lot surface, and the intensity of storms and runoff. In some cases, you may need to clean out the basin after each large storm, but it is usually adequate to clean it out two to six times per year—as long as the basin has been sized correctly. Designs vary greatly from state to state, but recommended capacities range from 5 to 10 cubic feet per 100 square feet of feedlot area.

Basin outlets come in many forms, two of the most common being (1) the perforated or slotted pipe riser; and (2) the porous spaced-plank dam. Most outlets clog periodically, so be sure to clean them out regularly.

Holding pond

After passing through a settling tank or basin, the contaminated runoff from a lot often enters a holding pond. The holding pond temporarily stores contaminated runoff water; it does not treat manure as a lagoon does.

The typical method for emptying a holding pond is to pump out the wastes and apply them on the land using drag-hose injection or some form of irrigation. Empty the holding pond before it is full and when field conditions allow.

CHECK IT OUT

For more information on manure application: page 185.

Livestock wastes should only be applied to farm ground that is readily tillable to reduce offensive odors. Do not empty the pond and apply wastes to the land when the soil is frozen, frosted, saturated, or snow covered; otherwise, the result may be excessive runoff on the soil surface and contamination of nearby surface water. In addition, livestock wastes should not be applied to permanent pasture or grassland unless there is no chance of an odor problem with neighbors.

Liquids stored in holding pond

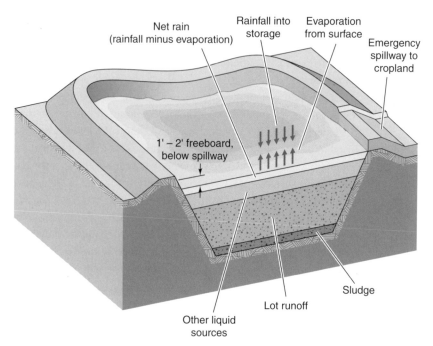

Net rain (rainfall minus evaporation)

Rainfall into storage

Evaporation from surface

Emergency spillway to cropland

1' – 2' freeboard, below spillway

Sludge

Lot runoff

Other liquid sources

A holding pond is designed to hold sludge, lot runoff, and other liquid sources, including rainfall.

Apply the livestock wastes at an appropriate agronomic rate and empty the holding pond completely when pumping.

Unless state regulations are more stringent, design your holding pond to contain the runoff from a 25-year, 24-hour rainfall (the heaviest 24-hour rainfall that can be expected, on average, every 25 years). To determine the required design capacity for your holding pond, you need to know the following information:

- How long you intend to store the contaminated runoff in the holding pond. The storage time may be up to a year, depending on local regulations and conditions.
- The size of the area draining into the holding pond
- The source of liquids (milkhouse wastes or animal washing water, for example)
- The amount of liquids, including rainfall, coming from the lot
- Evaporation and rainfall during the storage period. In dry areas, the volume of stored liquids is reduced by high evaporation; in wet areas, the pond must also be able to store the rain that falls directly into it.

Larger capacities give you more flexibility in deciding when to empty the pond. For details on how to estimate holding pond capacity, obtain a copy of the MidWest Plan Service's *Livestock Waste Facilities* handbook. To find out how to order the handbook, check the "For more information" section on page 303.

Vegetative filters

One alternative to a holding pond is a runoff field application system, which includes a vegetative filter. For details on vegetative filters, see Chapter 35.

Prepared with Ted Funk, farm structures specialist, UI Extension.

WHAT ABOUT SEMI-SOLID AND SOLID MANURE STORAGE?

Semi-solid manure

Semi-solid manure is manure with excess liquids drained off and some bedding added to increase solids content. To store semi-solids, use either an above-ground roofed structure or an outside facility with picket dams to drain off rainwater.

Outside facility with picket dam. A picket-type structure holds manure solids back but allows liquids to drain through. Liquid wastes should be directed to a holding pond, lagoon, or a vegetative infiltration area, using curbs or troughs.

Space the pickets so there is a $3/4$-inch space between each one. Vertical slots work much better than horizontal ones. You can use picket dams in earth storages or in the walls of bunker-type storages that have concrete or post-and-plank walls.

When the drainage structure is properly designed, water will run off the crusted surface of the manure and then flow around the edge in a channel formed between the manure and earth bank. The contaminated water, or leachate, then drains through the vertical slots of the picket dam.

The length of the picket dam is not as critical as where you locate it. Place a picket dam anywhere in the storage area where water will accumulate. To drain water from the loadout ramp, a picket dam must extend $2/3$ of the way up the length of the ramp.

When cleaning the manure storage area, remove any solids that have accumulated behind the pickets or in the vertical slots between the pickets.

Above-ground roofed storage. This system was developed for dairy comfort stall barns in high rainfall areas where large amounts of bedding are mixed with manure. However, with the new equipment available to handle semi-solid manure, some dairy producers are now building them for free-stall barn manure. Here are some key design points:

- The roof protects the collected manure from rainwater to keep it as dry as possible. As manure in storage dries, it will crust over, reducing odor and fly problems.

- Provide a concrete floor and a concrete footing down to 3 feet below existing grade.
- The walls can be 12- to 16-foot-high post-and-plank or concrete with an earth backfill.
- Translucent roof panels on the south slope will improve manure drying. But once the manure crusts over, the panels will not continue to affect drying.
- Provide a ventilation space between the top of the walls and the trussed roof.

Solid manure

Solid manure storage is possible when you add bedding to the manure until it contains enough solids to be stored in a pile. Although you may design the storage area to hold up to six months worth of manure, in reality you will want to clean it out every two months. In other words, this is a temporary storage solution.

With solid manure, you're looking for a storage area with a concrete floor, a retaining wall to increase storage volume, and adequate drainage. Unless the storage area is covered, it should be located on flat topography to reduce the likelihood of runoff reaching surface water.

Solid manure storage
Yard layout for sloping sites

Solid manure storage systems are a temporary solution. Even if you design the storage area to hold six months worth of manure, you will want to clean it out every two months.

Floors. Use a 4-inch concrete floor over 6 inches of coarse gravel or crushed rock (up to 1½-inch in size). On undisturbed or compacted soil, you can use 2 inches of sand in place of the gravel fill.

Retaining walls. The walls are usually concrete or post-and-plank. Provide one or two sturdy walls to buck against during unloading.

Drainage. To drain off liquids, you have two options:

- Slope the floor to one or both sides, with openings on the low side that lead to a gutter or surface drain.

- Provide floor drains with removable grills made of pressure-treated wood planks spaced about ¼-inch apart. Provide a gutter to carry away runoff.

Whichever option you choose, start stacking on the high side of the floor slope. Drained liquids must be channeled to a containment or treatment area, usually the same one used to handle feedlot runoff.

Solid manure storage
Stack slope and drainage

Manure stack

4" minimum rise
to divert runoff
away from stack

¼"/ft slope
towards drain

10' maximum
entrance

Drain

Gutter

To drain off liquids in solid manure storage, one option is to slope the floor to one or both sides. Openings on the low side should lead to a gutter or surface drain.

Prepared with Ted Funk, farm structures specialist, UI Extension.

35 Install a vegetative filter— if appropriate

Low cost, but limited

A vegetative filter provides a low-cost alternative to holding ponds on smaller operations. By handling contaminated runoff from open feedlots, a properly installed and maintained filter can remove a large amount of wastewater nutrients—in the range of 60 to 80 percent.

However, vegetative filter strips are much harder to design and maintain than holding ponds, and it can be difficult to ensure that the water leaving the filter is good quality. That's why some states, such as Illinois, do not allow vegetative filters on farms with over 300 animal units. Check with state regulations before considering this option.

A filter strip is not a stand-alone practice and should not be used as a substitute for other appropriate structural and management practices. It typically is used in combination with other structures, such as temporary liquid storage and almost always a solid removal structure such as a settling basin. After contaminated runoff from the feedlot passes through the settling basin to remove most of the manure solids, it moves to the filter where it is absorbed by vegetation, usually grass.

The most effective kind of filter is a broad, flat area with little slope, surrounded on the upslope sides by a berm or dike. In the past, some producers have used long, grassed, gently sloping channels; but channel systems are harder to build and maintain than broad, flat filters, so they are generally not recommended.

Designing a vegetative filter

Selecting the proper site is essential to ensure that the filter has uniform slopes along the path of the runoff water. Also, the earthwork required to create and maintain the slopes must be done carefully; mistakes in the earthwork are common reasons a filter strip fails, and they are the hardest problems to fix.

For assistance in designing a vegetative filter, work with the Natural Resources Conservation Service or the Cooperative Extension Service. They will help you determine key information, such as:

Size of the feedlot area. Measurements of the feedlot area should include all roofs that contribute runoff water and any areas that drain across the feedlot.

Rainfall. You need to know the amount of rain that will fall in a one-year, two-hour rainfall (the heaviest two-hour rainfall that can be expected, on average, each year). The filter should be designed to handle runoff from such a storm. Total runoff coming from the feedlot will be 90 percent of the rainfall.

Peak flow of runoff. In addition to total runoff, you need to know the "peak flow" of runoff—the greatest amount of runoff that can be expected to drain into your vegetative filter at any one time.

Available slopes and slope lengths. Determine the average slopes and slope lengths at potential locations for your vegetative filter. If you do not have any slopes that are long enough to handle the peak flow, you cannot install a vegetative filter.

Infiltration rate of soils. The rate at which runoff percolates through the soil is critical to sizing the filter. It determines the total capacity of the filter strip—the amount of runoff it will absorb, assuming a $1/2$-inch depth of runoff.

The primary way that a vegetative filter strip removes dissolved wastes is through infiltration into the soil. Unless infiltration occurs, dissolved wastes will not be removed.

The amount of nitrogen that will reach the filter strip. Knowing this information will help you determine the vegetation's capability of using nitrogen.

When designing and constructing a filter, always check the local design criteria. Also, check with your state Natural Resources Conservation Service or Cooperative Extension Service for seed mixture recommendations.

Maintaining the filter

To keep the filter operating effectively, follow these guidelines:

- Maintain the sheet flow of runoff over the entire width of the strip.
- Remove accumulated solids, especially around the distribution manifold. Also, level the distribution manifold.
- Scrape the feedlot regularly, especially during spring; direct runoff water from manure stacking facilities to the settling basin; and remove solids from the settling basin when 2 to 4 inches accumulate.
- Periodically test the soil of the vegetative filter to determine changes in phosphorus, potassium, and pH levels.
- Protect the filter from damage by farm equipment, traffic, and livestock. Fence out livestock to keep them off the filter.

- Promptly repair damage caused by erosion or equipment.
- Avoid damaging the filter with herbicides.
- Follow state regulations in harvesting forage on the filter. Harvesting may be necessary to maintain a good stand of vegetation. Many grass species should be harvested before they reach the reproductive stage to maintain strong vegetative growth.
- If you send "process-generated wastewater" (such as milking parlor waste) through the vegetative filter, do so periodically—no more than every few days. The vegetation needs rest periods—periods of drying—between applications. Therefore, a dairy operation will need a small storage area to keep parlor wastewater during these rest periods.

Prepared with Ted Funk, farm structures specialist, UI Extension.

36 Determine accurate manure application rates

Take a nutrient inventory

When applying manure to fields as fertilizer, accurate rates make sense from all angles. It's more economical, better for the crop, and better for the environment. Ensuring an accurate application rate involves four main tasks:

- Determine the nutrient content of the manure stored on your farm.
- Determine crop nutrient needs.
- Determine field application rates.
- Calibrate manure application equipment.

✓ **CHECK IT OUT**
For information on calibrating manure application equipment: page 182.

Determine the nutrient content of manure

The preferred way to determine the nutrient content of livestock manure is to have it tested. The less accurate method is to use tables that list standardized manure analyses—such as the tables on pages 180-181. These tables don't reflect how variable the actual nutrient content can be. (If you take samples of the same type of manure, but from different farms, nutrient content can vary by as much as 40 percent.) However, the tables do help you make comparisons between manure types, and they are useful in planning your facilities and land application areas.

The nutrient content of manure can vary according to the storage system, animal diet, and various other factors. Therefore, collect a series of samples from each manure storage system or feedlot and have them analyzed annually. It is also important to analyze samples whenever you make changes in the operation's management or feeding program.

A considerable amount of nitrogen can be lost if you don't collect and handle the sample correctly. So follow these guidelines for liquid and solid samples:

Liquid manure samples. Ideally, you should agitate liquid manures or mix them well before collecting a sample. Because agitating manure is often not practical just to collect a few samples, an alternative is to take samples from several areas within the lagoon or pit. Then combine them.

After mixing, fill a quart-sized plastic container (not a glass container) with a screw-on lid approximately two-thirds full. Close the lid tightly. Preserve the liquid sample immediately by freezing.

Caution: Gases released from agitated liquid manure can kill animals and people in a short time. Therefore, if you agitate manure before collecting a sample, open doors and curtains or windows and turn on all fans to provide adequate ventilation. Preferably, mix and obtain the sample when the building is empty of animals.

Solid manure samples. Obtain samples from several locations in the manure stack or on the feedlot. Combine the samples and place them in a gallon-size plastic bag. Twist and tie tightly, and for added safety, place the composite sample in a second bag. Freeze the sample; then ship.

Shipping samples. Before delivering the sample, label the container with your name, sample number, location, and date. For accurate analysis, keep the samples frozen or refrigerated en route. If this is not possible, package the sample in a strong, insulated container, such as a Styrofoam-lined cardboard box. Add ice to the container and ship the fastest way.

Some commercial laboratories provide sample containers, mailing boxes, and shipping instructions. So contact the laboratory for complete instructions before shipping.

Determine crop nutrient needs

Determine crop nutrient needs on a field-by-field basis. The fertilizer recommendation for a field will depend on the crop to be grown, anticipated yield goal, previous crop, and soil test results.

If you find that the manure contains more nutrients than needed on the fields where you intend to apply it, the excess nutrients can end up in surface water or groundwater. To prevent these problems, apply manure on additional fields.

Although alfalfa or soybean fields obviously do not need to have nitrogen (N) supplied, these crops could benefit from the phosphorus (P) and potassium (K) in manure—and they will still use the applied N. Therefore, you can consider them for manure applications, if necessary. But use caution on alfalfa and other forage legumes so you do not "burn" the crop's foliage.

Another option is to distribute the excess manure on off-farm locations, such as neighboring farms and tree nurseries.

Determine field application rates

Once you have determined the nutrient content of manure and the nutrient needs of crops, calculate the application rate for each field.

The rate can vary, depending on which nutrient you use as the basis for application.

Manure is relatively high in P and low in N compared to most crops' needs for those nutrients. Therefore, from an economic, environmental, and agronomic perspective, it usually makes more sense to base your application rate on the P content of manure. If you base the rate on N, you may end up with excessive levels of P in your soils.

Basing the rate on P generally means you have to add supplemental N fertilizer, but this easily fits into most systems.

For details on calculating application rates, obtain a copy of the *Livestock Waste Facilities* handbook. To find out how to order the handbook, check the "For more information" section on page 303.

Nutrients in solid manure
Approximate fertilizer value of manure from solid handling systems

Species	Bedding or litter	Dry matter	Ammonium nitrogen (N)	Total nitrogen (N)	Phosphorus (P₂O₅)	Potassium (K₂O)
		percent		pounds per ton of raw waste		
Swine	No	18	6	10	9	8
	Yes	18	5	8	7	7
Beef	No	15*	4	11	7	10
	No	52**	7	21	14	23
	Yes	50	8	21	18	26
Dairy	No	18	4	9	4	10
	Yes	21	5	9	4	10
Sheep	No	28	5	18	11	26
	Yes	28	5	14	9	25
Poultry	No	45	26	33	48	34
	Yes	75	36	56	45	34
	Deep pit	76	44	68	64	45
Turkey	No	22	17	27	20	17
	Yes	29	13	20	16	13
Horse	Yes	46	4	14	4	14

*Open concrete lot
**Open dirt lot

SOURCE: Reproduced with permission from *Livestock Waste Facilities* handbook, MWPS-18, 3rd edition, 1993. ©MidWest Plan Service, Ames, IA 50011-3080.

Nutrients in liquid manure
Approximate fertilizer value of manure from liquid handling systems

Species	Waste handling method	Dry matter	Ammonium nitrogen (N)	Total nitrogen (N)	Phosphorus (P_2O_5)	Potassium (K_2O)
		percent		pounds per 1,000 gallons of raw waste		
Swine	Liquid pit	4	26	36	27	22
	Lagoon*	1	3	4	2	4
Beef	Liquid pit	11	24	40	27	34
	Lagoon*	1	2	4	9	5
Dairy	Liquid pit	8	12	24	18	29
	Lagoon*	1	2.5	4	4	5
Veal calf	Liquid pit	3	19	24	25	51
Poultry	Liquid pit	13	64	80	36	96

*Includes lot runoff water.

SOURCE: Reproduced with permission from *Livestock Waste Facilities* handbook, MWPS-18, 3rd edition, 1993. ©MidWest Plan Service, Ames, IA 50011-3080.

Prepared with Ted Funk, farm structures specialist, and Robert Hoeft, soil fertility specialist, UI Extension.

37 Calibrate manure application equipment

Rates will vary

Manufacturers estimate how much manure a given spreader applies, but the actual rate will vary, even between the same models of equipment. Therefore, to get the most accurate idea of the rate at which your equipment applies manure, calibrate it.

Calibrating your manure application equipment takes less than an hour, but it's one of the best ways to avoid overapplication of fertilizer.

There are a variety of ways to determine your equipment's application rate. Your choice depends on the type of manure—liquid or solid—and the type of spreader. The accompanying chart, "Calibration methods," summarizes seven ways to calibrate your equipment.

Determining load size

For most of the calibration methods described in this chapter, you need to know the tank or spreader's load size, either in gallons or tons. Manufacturers often report two load-size ratings: a struck-level rating (if manure in the spreader is level) or a heaped rating (if solid manure in the spreader is heaped). The two types of ratings will be the same for closed tanks, but they will be different if you're using a box spreader and a circular or sloped-wall, open-top spreader. When in doubt, use the manufacturer's struck-level rating to estimate the spreader's capacity.

The plastic sheet method

Note that the "Calibration methods" table includes three different methods that use a plastic sheet. If you decide to calibrate your spreader using a plastic sheet, follow these steps:

1. Lay the plastic sheet in the field.
2. Start applying manure before you reach the sheet. Then drive over the sheet at the speed you would drive when applying manure.
3. Collect the sheet and pour manure into a bucket. If it's easier, you can put both the sheet and manure in the bucket.
4. Weigh the bucket, remembering to subtract the weight of the empty bucket (and the weight of the plastic sheet if you put it in the bucket too).
5. Repeat the procedure three times.

6. Determine the average weight of the three applications.

7. Determine the spreader application rate by making the appropriate calculation (see the "Calibration methods" table).

Adjusting the application rate

If, by calibrating, you find out that your spreader is applying manure at a rate that is too low or too high, change your travel speed. By increasing the travel speed of your spreader, you reduce the application rate and vice versa.

If you have a PTO-driven, beater-type spreader, keep the engine speed constant and change the application rate by making either of these adjustments:

- Changing the spreader delivery rate setting
- Changing the tractor gear ratio to alter the spreader's ground travel speed

To estimate how much a new travel speed will change the application rate, follow these two steps:

1. Multiply the spreader's application rate (determined during calibration) by the old travel speed.

2. Divide that number by the new travel speed. The result is the new application rate.

Whenever you change your travel speed, be sure to recalibrate the equipment.

Calibration methods
Some common ways to calculate the application rate of manure spreaders

Manure source	What you need to know	Calculations
Liquid manure in a tank	1. Tank load size (gallons of manure) 2. Acreage over which manure is spread at even rate	$\dfrac{\text{gallons}}{\text{acreage}} = \dfrac{\text{application rate}}{\text{(gallons per acre)}}$
Liquid manure in spreader: volume method	1. Spreader load size (gallons of manure) 2. Distance driven and width spread (feet)	$\dfrac{\text{gallons} \times 43{,}560}{\text{distance} \times \text{width}} = \dfrac{\text{application rate}}{\text{(gallons per acre)}}$
Liquid manure in spreader: weight method*	1. Spreader load size (pounds of manure) 2. Distance driven and width spread (feet)	$\dfrac{\text{pounds} \times 5{,}248}{\text{distance} \times \text{width}} = \dfrac{\text{application rate}}{\text{(gallons per acre)}}$
Solid manure in spreader: spreader volume method**	1. Spreader struck-level load size (bushels of manure) 2. Distance driven and width spread (feet)	$\dfrac{\text{bushels} \times 1{,}688}{\text{distance} \times \text{width}} = \dfrac{\text{application rate}}{\text{(tons per acre)}}$
Solid manure in spreader: plastic sheet weight method	1. Pounds of manure on the sheet after drive-over 2. Square footage of plastic sheet	$\dfrac{\text{pounds} \times 21.78}{\substack{\text{square footage}\\ \text{of plastic sheet}}} = \dfrac{\text{application rate}}{\text{(tons per acre)}}$
Shortcut method #1 with plastic sheet: for lighter application rates (use a 9' x 12' sheet)	1. Pounds of manure on the sheet after drive-over	$\text{pounds} \div 5 = \dfrac{\text{application rate}}{\text{(tons per acre)}}$
Shortcut method #2 with plastic sheet: for heavier application rates (use a 4'8" x 4'8" sheet) or 87" x 3' sheet)	1. Pounds of manure on the sheet after drive-over	$\substack{\text{pounds of manure}\\ \text{collected on}\\ \text{the sheet}} = \dfrac{\text{application rate}}{\text{(tons per acre)}}$

*The calculation for this method assumes that a gallon of manure will weigh a certain number of pounds. An average figure is used.

**The calculation for this method assumes that a bushel of manure will weigh a certain number of pounds. An average figure is used.

Prepared with Ted Funk, farm structures specialist, and Robert Hoeft, soil fertility specialist, UI Extension.

38 Apply manure wisely

Avoid excess

Applying manure to the land can save you money on fertilizer, maintain soil fertility, and improve the condition of your soil. It can improve tilth, increase water-holding capacity, improve aeration, reduce erosion, and create a healthy environment for beneficial organisms in the soil.

However, applying excessive amounts of manure is a waste of nutrients and can harm crop growth and reduce yields. In addition, excess nutrients can move with surface runoff, contaminating streams and other bodies of water.

The amount of nutrients lost in runoff depends, in part, on the type of manure application method used, application timing, and application rate.

Application methods

Surface application without plow-down or disking. This application method poses the greatest risk of nutrient losses, both through volatilization and surface runoff. Do not apply livestock manure on slopes that are frozen, snow-covered, or saturated because these conditions increase the threat of runoff. Also, never apply manure on slopes adjacent to lakes, rivers, or streams, nor within 100 feet of wells, springs, or sinkholes.

Surface application with plow-down or disking. If you till the soil after manure application, you reduce the chances that runoff will carry nutrients into surface-water supplies. But make sure that tillage does not reduce the protective cover of surface residue to levels that lead to severe soil erosion. Most nutrient losses occur within the first 24 hours after application, so incorporate manure as soon as possible after application.

Irrigation. Applying livestock manure through an irrigation system calls for careful management to prevent runoff, especially on fine-textured and tight soils, which may not be permeable enough to absorb the liquids quickly. One of the keys to reducing runoff is to avoid saturating the soil.

Injection. Knifing manure into the soil is the best way to prevent nutrient loss and protect surface-water supplies. It is also the best way to incorporate manure in conservation tillage systems because it disturbs a minimal amount of crop residue. The drawbacks are an increased investment in equipment and greater energy requirements. Injection also is slower than broadcasting manure on the soil surface. To be most effective, make sure the slots made in the soil by the injectors are closed after application.

Drag-hose injection. This system, which has become increasingly popular since it was introduced in the early 1990s, is essentially a combination of irrigation and injection. A flexible hose runs from a tractor-powered pump at the holding pond or pit to the field tractor; livestock manure is pumped through the manifold on a tool bar to soil-injection equipment.

Drag-hose injection eliminates the need to transport manure to the field in a tank—one of the drawbacks of ordinary injection systems. By injecting the manure, you also reduce the risk of runoff and odors. Soil compaction can be reduced because no tank is being pulled behind the injector tractor.

What about the effect of injection on crop growth?

Both research and farmer experience have shown that injecting manure can inhibit root growth in and around the manure zone during the first few weeks of crop growth. Under cool, wet, spring conditions, the accumulation of both ammonium and nitrite within the root zone appears to be the primary factor inhibiting root growth and, therefore, reducing crop growth.

However, research has also shown that this problem can be reduced and sometimes solved by shifting from a vertical (knife) to a horizontal (sweep) injection technique. In addition, studies have shown that including a nitrification inhibitor in the sweep application can result in yields equal to or greater than when commercial fertilizer was applied without manure.

Application timing

The ideal time: Spring. Apply manure as close as possible to the planting date so nutrients will be available to the plants. This reduces the chances of nutrient loss due to volatilization, denitrification, leaching, and surface runoff.

Summer application. You can apply manure in the summer on small-grain stubble, non-crop fields, or little-used pastures. However, do not spread manure on young stands of legume forage because legumes do not need nitrogen. Also, the nitrogen will stimulate competitive grasses and may introduce weeds. You can apply manure effectively on pure grass stands or to old legume-grass mixtures, although concentrated manure will sometimes "burn" foliage.

Fall application. Fall application means more nutrient loss, especially if manure isn't incorporated. So consider using a nitrification inhibitor to prevent nitrogen losses. In the fall, manure is best applied to fields that will be planted in winter grains or cover crops. If winter crops are not to be planted, apply manure to fields containing the most vegetation or crop residues. Sod fields to be plowed the next spring are also acceptable but not fields where corn silage was removed and a cover crop will not be planted.

Winter application. This is the least desirable time to apply manure. Never apply manure on frozen or snow-covered land because the frozen ground prevents water and manure from infiltrating the soil. The result is a greater risk of runoff, nutrient loss, and pollution.

CHECK IT OUT

For information on calculating accurate application rates: page 178.

Nitrogen losses during land application of manure
Percent of nitrogen applied that is lost within 4 days of application

Application method	Type of waste	Percent of nitrogen lost
Broadcast	Solid	15 to 30
	Liquid	10 to 25
Broadcast with immediate cultivation	Solid	1 to 5
	Liquid	1 to 5
Injection	Liquid	0 to 2
Drag-hose injection	Liquid	0 to 2
Sprinkler irrigation	Liquid	15 to 35

This table shows typical nitrogen losses due to volatilization—evaporation into the air. Remember, practices that reduce volatilization losses will also reduce surface runoff losses.

SOURCE: Adapted with permission from *Livestock Waste Facilities* handbook, MWPS-18, 3rd edition, 1993. ©MidWest Plan Service, Ames, IA 50011-3080.

Prepared with Ted Funk, farm structures specialist, UI Extension.

Reducing insecticide use

The changes in insecticide use have been fairly dramatic. In Iowa, for instance, university surveys have shown that the percentage of corn acres treated with insecticides dropped from 50 percent in 1979 to 35 percent in 1990. Meanwhile, the total pounds of active ingredient applied in Iowa slid from 7.1 million pounds in 1979 to 4.8 million pounds in 1990.

The trend has been the same throughout much of the Midwest, although insecticide use may be rising a little in east-central Illinois and west-central and northwestern Indiana, where producers have encountered western corn rootworm problems in rotated corn. Some of the credit for the overall drop in insecticide use goes to successful programs to monitor the black cutworm migration.

Spurred by an interest in cutting costs and reducing environmental risks, producers have added an array of nonchemical strategies to their pest-control arsenal. However, much remains to be done, especially in continuous corn, where many producers still do not scout for corn rootworms. This section is all about what can be done to cut back on chemicals, reduce surface-water contamination, and still keep insects below economic levels.

39 Scout fields for insects

Scouting: The better insurance policy

Many farmers apply soil insecticides as "rootworm insurance," but in a significant number of cases, scouting the previous year would have revealed that a treatment was unnecessary. According to University of Illinois research in 1991, for instance, many growers who participated in an on-farm research project actually lost money by needlessly applying a soil insecticide.

Accurate and timely scouting may prevent unnecessary treatments, and it helps you to identify potential problems before they become less manageable. Scouting allows you to plan a pest-management program that makes optimal use of the essential management tools.

When scouting, you will typically need to look for both crop injury and the insects. However, scouting techniques will vary considerably depending upon the insect and the crop involved. There is no quick and easy cookbook recipe that applies for all situations. That's why it is important to obtain a field crop scouting manual that provides information and photographs of insects, as well as details on what kind of injury to look for and what kind of scouting procedure to follow.

The University of Illinois offers such a guide—the *Field Crop Scouting Manual*. For details on how to obtain a copy, see "For more information" on page 304. This section also lists where you can obtain scouting equipment (see page 301).

While such manuals provide the details, the following are some general scouting guidelines.

Looking for injury on foliage and stalks

Examine plants next to each other, as long as disturbing one plant will not affect your observations of insects on adjacent plants.

In some cases, it will only be necessary to count the number of plants with or without injury. For many pests, the recommendation is to examine 100 plants (20 plants in five different parts of the field). Surveying 100 plants makes it convenient and quick to calculate the percentage of injured plants.

In other cases, particularly in soybeans, you will also need to note the severity of the injury. In soybeans, this is most commonly done by determining the amount of defoliation. But keep in mind that until you acquire a lot of experience, defoliation is usually overestimated.

If it is necessary to dissect the aboveground parts of plants to look for injury or insects, a knife with a hooked blade (such as a linoleum blade) works well.

Looking for insects on foliage or stalks

When looking for insects, you can count them in a variety of ways.

Number of insects per plant. Example: In field corn, consider treatment

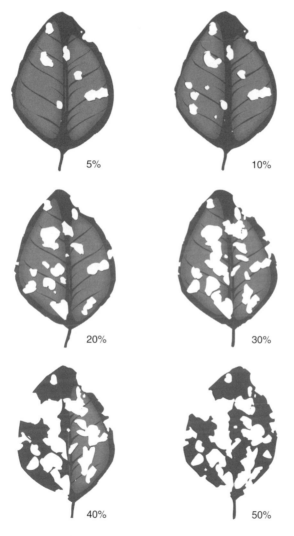

Levels of soybean leaflet defoliation

Above are levels of soybean defoliation by a green cloverworm larva. You can use this illustration to help calibrate your estimates of defoliation.

if you count five or more corn rootworm beetles per plant, pollination is not complete, and you observe silk clipping.

Number of insects per foot of crop row. Example: In soybeans before bloom, consider treatment if you count five or more bean leaf beetles per foot of row and defoliation reaches 30 percent.

Number of insects per sweep. Example: In alfalfa, 6 to 12 inches in height, consider treatment if you count one leafhopper per sweep with a net.

Number of insects per square foot or yard. Example: If you count more than seven grasshoppers per square yard in corn, treatment may be warranted.

Looking for insects or injury underground

Scouting approaches:

- The most common approach is to remove soil around the root system of a single plant. Take as many samples per field as time will allow and determine the average number of insects per plant. After digging up the soil with a knife, garden trowel, shovel, or army "trenching tool," place insects on a plastic sheet. Black plastic, 2 feet by 2 feet and stapled to two plaster laths, is a good choice; light-colored soil insects show up readily against the black plastic. Also, you can place insect-infested soil on the plastic and then stir it and search until you locate all insects.

- Another strategy is to dig a trench along the row and count the average number of insects per foot of row. This method works well for wireworms or white grubs. A tile spade is a good tool for this kind of digging.

- If you need to examine the surface of roots for insect injury, carry roots out of the field to a source of water. Wash the roots to expose the damage and use a knife to look for insects inside the roots. Soaking roots in buckets of water works very well to remove soil and, in the process, insects will float on the surface of the water.

The beat cloth

When scouting for soybean insects, one of the most common techniques is to use a beat or ground cloth. Follow this procedure:

1. Spread out the beat cloth so it completely covers the ground between two rows of soybeans. The cloth should be 2 feet long and wide enough to stretch between the two rows.

2. Pull the soybean canopy over the cloth and shake and beat leaves vigorously to dislodge insects.

3. After the insects are dislodged, push the canopy back and count the insects on the cloth.

The sweep net

Scouts use a sweep net most often in solid stands of plants—such as al-falfa or drilled soybeans. When you swing the canvas net through the foliage, insects become dislodged and fall into it (see illustration). After you make the recommended number of sweeps, determine the average number of insects per sweep.

Pictured above is the "sweeps across" method. To capture insects, swing the net from side to side with a pendulum-like motion. The top three frames show one sweep, while the bottom frame depicts a second sweep.

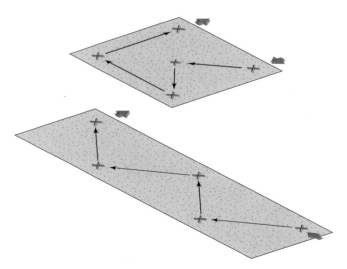

Pattern 1. *If you expect to find pests uniformly across a field, select sampling sites that are also evenly distributed. In a square field, sample the center and the four corners. In a rectangular field, you might want to make a zigzag pattern.*

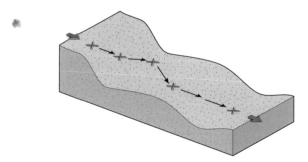

Pattern 2. *If pests tend to concentrate in particular areas, such as high or low spots, examine those spots more carefully than other areas. That way, you can determine the extent and severity of damage.*

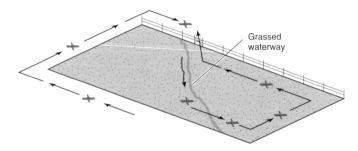

Pattern 3. *If pests first invade a field at the borders (as stalkborers and grasshoppers often do), scout along the fence lines and along any waterways that run into the field.*

Scouting procedures

When entering a field to scout, follow these basic procedures:

1. Make sure you have the proper equipment.
2. Identify the field on a scouting report form by the field number, location, or other characteristics.
3. Record the date, time of day, and weather conditions.
4. Record the stage of growth of the crop.
5. Record general soil and crop conditions.
6. Sample the field in the pattern prescribed for the particular problem (see illustrations of patterns 1 through 3 on page 194).
7. Record the species and number of insects found.

Scouting patterns

As a general rule, you should enter the field about 50 paces beyond the end rows before making counts. Avoid border rows unless you are scouting for a specific type of insect that may attack these areas first.

There are three basic patterns for pest infestations in a field. That's why there are also three basic patterns for scouting (see illustrations). Keep in mind that it may be necessary to combine two or more patterns.

Traps

In some cases, you can effectively monitor insect populations by luring them to traps. Most commonly, the traps are baited with one of two types of synthetic "pheromones":

Sex pheromones: chemicals used by insects to attract mates.

Aggregation pheromones: chemicals used to attract insects to a food or nesting site.

An advantage of attractant-baited traps is that they may capture insects that are present at densities too low to detect easily in other ways. This can be important if you're trying to detect "exotic" pests as soon as they enter an area. Also, traps baited with a pheromone lure will capture only insects attracted to that specific pheromone. This simplifies the identification and counting of insects.

One of the most successful trapping programs, conducted in several states, uses a sexual lure to trap male black cutworm moths as they migrate into an area. A coordinated force of cooperators sets out the traps, making it possible to estimate the time and severity of "first cutting" damage by black cutworm larvae. This alerts producers to when they should scout for cutworm larvae.

Prepared with Michael Gray, field crops entomology specialist, UI Extension.

Adding profit through scouting

Jim Wilkinson's farm near Oxford, Indiana, lies right in the middle of the "Triangle of Death." This is the tongue-in-cheek description that Wilkinson gives to the expanding region where western corn rootworms have been causing serious damage since the early 1990s— a triangle that stretches from Kankakee, Illinois, to Logansport, Indiana, to Vincennes, Indiana.

In his battle with the western corn rootworm, Wilkinson finds scouting to be a crucial element. "Scouting is by far the smartest way to go," he says. "It's the quickest way to add $10 to $15 per acre of profit to your bottom line."

Wilkinson says he starts scouting a few days after planting, keeping a careful eye on crop emergence and taking steps to identify why certain plants are not coming up. In late July, he starts scouting once a week for western rootworm, and he continues to do so until about the first week of September.

Scouting saves in two ways. It makes it possible for Wilkinson to avoid unnecessary insecticide applications, and it boosts production in areas that he discovers are seriously infested. The economic benefits have been documented by Purdue University on-farm research.

In 1995, Wilkinson planted a 13-acre test plot in first-year corn, leaving a single untreated row every eight to 10 rows apart. Researchers found that the untreated rows had about 35 percent lower yields than the treated rows.

Although this yield impact demonstrates the economic importance of scouting and treating for such problems, Purdue researchers stress caution when applying these findings to all first-year corn fields. This trial showed the effect of rootworm damage in one high-risk, first-year corn field during a single growing season; what's more, the growing season was marked by abnormal conditions that put moisture and temperature stress on the crop.

In addition to scouting, Wilkinson combats western corn rootworms with genetic warfare. He carefully analyzes the genetic differences among different corn varieties, looking for hybrids that provide a greater root mass. University of Illinois research has shown that during dry years, varieties that regrow a greater root mass after rootworm injury tend to yield better than other varieties.

Two of Wilkinson's fields have been included in a multi-county project, in which Purdue researchers are examining many variables that affect the risk of corn rootworm damage—including the hybrid selected. In 1997, Purdue researchers also hope to compare the regeneration of roots with different hybrids in a demonstration plot on Wilkinson's farm.

If Wilkinson can find and use varieties with good root regeneration, one possible outcome of this work may be that he can reduce rates or eliminate soil insecticide use for low to moderate infestation levels of rootworms.

Although western corn rootworm is by far the most serious pest that Wilkinson faces, he says he also keeps a sharp eye out for Japanese beetles, and he puts out a pheromone trap to monitor the flights of cutworm moths.

Wilkinson has been scouting in earnest since 1988, which was also when he switched his 700 acres to conservation tillage.

"Good stand establishment is crucial with conservation tillage," he points out. "Scouting helps me to identify the problem when it's just starting, and that's important to getting a good stand. That's why I'm a fanatic about scouting."

40 Base decisions on the economic thresholds for insects

Avoiding a costly error

Economic thresholds may not be perfect, but they can help you avoid an expensive mistake—paying more money to control an insect problem than you would have lost if you did nothing. By helping to avoid unnecessary pesticide applications, economic thresholds keep money in your wallet and minimize environmental problems.

An economic threshold, or action threshold, is the point at which you need to take action to prevent a pest population from reaching an economically damaging level. The economic threshold is always slightly less than the economic injury level (EIL)—the level at which a pest population is high enough to cause significant crop damage. The EIL is the point when the cost of crop damage by a pest *equals* the cost to control the pest population.

Specific economic thresholds have been developed for many insect pests. Sometimes, these thresholds are expressed as numbers of insects—the average number of bean leaf beetles per foot of row, for instance. Other times, economic thresholds are expressed as a level of injury—the percentage of soybean pods injured within a field.

Pest control guides

Keep in mind, however, that economic thresholds are flexible guides, not recommendations carved in stone. One problem is that most currently used thresholds are rather simplistic. They do not take into consideration what happens when there are multiple pests in a field, and they can be affected by many economic and environmental factors.

Crop value. As the price paid for a crop increases, the economic threshold decreases.

Cost of control. As the cost of control increases, the economic threshold increases.

Crop stress. As the amount of stress on a crop increases, the economic threshold may decrease. For instance, if a crop is already under stress from weeds, disease, lack of moisture, or lack of fertility, insect control may be economically justified even if the insect population is below the threshold.

Although many economic thresholds available today do not take these factors into consideration, a growing number of them do. A case in point: Many states have developed excellent, comprehensive worksheets that help you determine economic thresholds for European corn borers. To obtain copies of these worksheets, contact the nearest Cooperative Extension Service office.

If a comprehensive threshold hasn't been developed yet for a particular pest, don't be discouraged from using the more limited, but available, threshold. Less comprehensive thresholds still serve as helpful guides.

Know your pests

To make use of economic thresholds, it helps to understand how the populations of different insects change over time. It helps to know an insect's feeding habits and the conditions under which it thrives. And it helps to know whether an insect is an occasional or perennial pest.

Occasional pests usually do not cause economic damage during average years. It takes certain environmental conditions to boost their population above average and pose a threat. For example, the normal population of spider mites usually does not pose a threat to soybeans. But if weather is hot and dry, spider mite numbers go up and economic damage can result.

Perennial pests tend to cause damage almost every year, so they must be carefully monitored and controlled if thresholds are exceeded.

New directions

You may also want to monitor the progress of new research that could incorporate environmental concerns into economic thresholds. Researchers at Iowa State University and the University of Nebraska asked thousands of farmers how much they were willing to spend per acre to protect their groundwater, wildlife, beneficial insects, and other natural resources from insecticide contamination.

The result was the creation of economic thresholds that include environmental costs. If you add in the environmental costs of an insecticide application, you will have to accept more crop loss before you begin chemical control of the pests. But, in the long run, you could be protecting lakes, streams, and other resources.

Considering the environment when calculating economic thresholds has not been commonly accepted, but years ago the economic thresholds that are popular today seemed just as far off on the horizon.

CHECK IT OUT

For more information on economic thresholds that consider the environment: page 248.

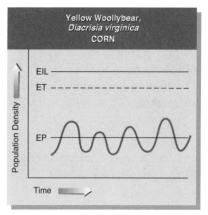

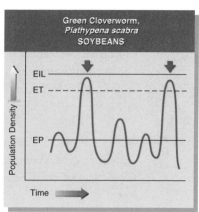

Nonpests. *The average population density, or equilibrium position (EP), of nonpests is well below the economic threshold. These pests never reach a population level high enough to cause an economic loss.*

Occasional pests. *Occasional pests are only a problem when environmental conditions are favorable for an increase in population. That's when population levels exceed the economic threshold. Most agricultural pests are occasional pests.*

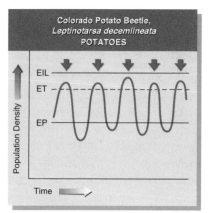

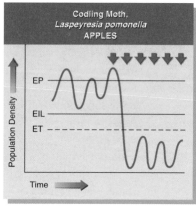

Perennial pests. *The average population density of perennial pests is only slightly below the economic injury level. As a result, perennial pests exceed the economic threshold regularly. Agricultural pests that fall into this category require a carefully designed integrated pest management program.*

Severe pests. *This is the most difficult category of pests to manage. For these pests, the average population density is above the economic injury level. Routine pesticide applications are often necessary to produce marketable crops.*

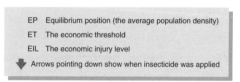

Threshold information

The accompanying table describes the economic thresholds for the most common insect pests of corn, soybeans, and alfalfa. For more detailed information on thresholds for particular crop pests, see the *Field Crop Scouting Manual*, available from the University of Illinois. To find out how to order the manual, see "For more information" on page 304. Also, you can obtain more information on thresholds by contacting your nearest Cooperative Extension Service office.

Economic thresholds for select pests

Field corn

Armyworm

Seedling corn: Control is justified when 25 percent of the plants are being damaged.

After pollen shed: Control is justified when armyworms are eating leaves above ear level.

Corn rootworm

To protect pollination, treat if there are 5 or more beetles per plant, pollination is not complete, and you observe silk clipping. To protect plants from root injury the following season, consider treatment when beetles reach these thresholds:

Average number of plants per acre	Average number of beetles per plant	
	Continuous corn	First-year corn
14,000	1.4	1.0
16,000	1.3	0.9
18,000	1.1	0.8
20,000	1.0	0.7
22,000	0.9	0.6
24,000	0.8	0.6
26,000	0.8	0.5
28,000	0.7	0.5

Corn leaf aphid

Apply during late whorl to early tassel when 50 percent of the plants have light to moderate infestations (50 to 400 aphids per plant) and plants are under drought stress. If soil moisture is adequate, treatment may be warranted if there are more than 400 aphids per plant.

Cutworms

Apply a postemergence rescue treatment when 3 percent or more of the plants are cut and larvae are still present.

European
corn borer,
first or second generation

Contact your Cooperative Extension Service office for worksheets to determine whether treatment is needed.

Grasshoppers

Treatment may be warranted when there are 7 or more grasshoppers per square yard in the field. After pollen shed, control is justified when grasshoppers are feeding on leaves above ear level. Densities of 15 to 20 per square yard along roadsides and fencerows may indicate a potential economic infestation of nearby row crops.

Japanese beetle

A treatment may be necessary during the silking period to protect silks if you find 3 or more beetles per ear and pollination is not complete.

Wireworms

Treat at planting if crop history or bait stations (or both) indicate a potential for wireworm damage. To minimize potential adverse effects to wildlife, incorporate insecticide granules or apply the insecticide in-furrow (if labeled) and shut off insecticide units in turn rows. If you find an average of 1 or more wireworms per bait station, an insecticide may be justified. For details on setting up bait stations, see page 215.

Soybeans

Bean leaf beetle

Seedlings: An insecticide treatment for seedling soybeans is rarely justified. Densities of 16 per foot of row in the early seedling stage or 39 per foot at stage V2+ are necessary for economic injury.

Before bloom: Treat when defoliation reaches 30 percent and there are 5 or more beetles per foot of row.

Bloom to pod fill: Treat when defoliation reaches 20 percent and there are 16 or more beetles per foot of row.

Seed maturation: Treat when 5 to 10 percent of the pods are damaged, the leaves are green, and there are 10 or more beetles per foot of row.

Grasshoppers

Treat when migration into fields begins and defoliation or pod feeding reaches economic levels.

Economic levels for defoliation: when defoliation reaches 30 percent before bloom and 20 percent between bloom and pod fill.

Economic levels for pod damage: when 5 to 10 percent of the pods are damaged.

Japanese beetle adults

Treat when defoliation reaches 20 percent during bloom and pod fill.

Spider mites

Treat when you note 20 to 25 percent discoloration before pod set or 10 to 15 percent discoloration after pod set.

Stink bugs

Treat when adult bugs or large nymphs reach 1 per foot of row during pod fill.

Alfalfa

Alfalfa weevil
(spring treatment
for larvae)

Consider treatment if 25 to 50 percent of the tips are being skeletonized, and there are 3 or more larvae per stem. Do not apply sprays during bloom. Instead, cut and remove the hay. Two treatments may be necessary on the first cutting. Control may also be warranted after cutting when larvae and adults are feeding on more than 50 percent of the crowns and regrowth is prevented for three to six days.

Alfalfa weevil adults

Control may be warranted after cutting when larvae and adults are feeding on more than 50 percent of the crowns and regrowth is prevented for three to six days.

Potato leafhoppers

Treatment may be justified at these combinations of alfalfa height and leafhopper numbers:

Alfalfa height in inches	Leafhoppers per sweep
0 to 3	0.2
3 to 6	0.5
6 to 12	1.0
12 or taller	2.0

Prepared with Michael Gray, field crops entomology specialist, UI Extension.

41 Use insect-resistant crop varieties

Thorns and tough roots

Plants have many natural mechanisms to keep insects at bay: repellent or toxic chemicals, thorns, hairs, and tough roots and stems.

Seed companies try to tap into these mechanisms by developing crop varieties that are resistant to certain insects and diseases, while still producing a good yield. But like everything else, there are pros and cons in using resistant varieties.

The pros

- Resistant crop varieties will not interfere with other pest-management techniques such as crop rotation or, if needed, an insecticide application.
- They are usually the same price or only slightly more expensive than other seeds.
- They may reduce the need for certain insecticide treatments, reducing costs and protecting water quality.

The cons

- Resistant varieties are usually only resistant to one or a limited number of pests.
- When resistant crops are being developed, some positive traits (such as high yield) may be inadvertently lost while other traits are strengthened.
- Some resistant varieties spend more of their resources protecting themselves; subsequently, their yields may drop.
- If resistant varieties are widespread and insect densities are high, insects may develop new strains that are not affected by the plant's defenses.

New technologies

Conventional crop breeding and variety development represent a form of "genetic engineering." But new techniques in genetic engineering now allow the transfer of genes from one species to another, which could result in the quicker development of pest-resistant varieties.

More dramatically, researchers recently used gene transfer techniques to develop crop varieties that contain a microbial insecticide inside the plant; they have produced corn plants that contain the *Bacillus thuringiensis (Bt)* toxin for European corn borer control. *Bt* is a bacterium that is toxic to some insects, but not to people or animals, and has been used effectively as a rescue insecticide on plant foliage for the control of first-generation corn borer.

While these new techniques offer the possibility of dramatic advances in host plant resistance, there are some potential problems. If corn varieties containing a *Bt* toxin are used extensively, European corn borer populations may develop resistance to this specific insecticidal compound. Applying *Bt* as a foliar spray can also lead to the development of resistant borers, but the risk is greater if *Bt* is part of each plant because the selection pressure is much greater for resistance to occur.

To slow down the corn borers' development of resistance to *Bt*, maintain "refuges"—areas where the corn borers are not exposed to the *Bt* toxin. If any corn borers should survive in the *Bt*-corn fields, you will want to increase the odds that these surviving moths will mate with moths emerging from the refuges. A refuge includes all corn fields without *Bt* corn, as well as fields with other plant species on which corn borers can develop.

It's still not known how close these refuges must be located to *Bt* corn or how much corn should be used as a refuge. Throughout most of the Midwest, you will need to maintain at least 20 to 25 percent of your fields in non-*Bt*-corn to delay the onset of resistance to *Bt* by corn borers.

Such potential pitfalls do not necessarily overshadow the advantages of corn that contains *Bt*, but they need to be considered as new technologies develop.

What's available

The following is a table of some pests that are affected by resistant crops.

For additional information, contact your integrated pest management or crop systems educator with the Cooperative Extension Service or a seed dealer.

Corn

European corn borer

- Screening trials conducted by seed companies since the 1960s have selected varieties less susceptible to infestation, stalk breakage, and yield reduction. However, the factors that increase resistance have not always been clearly identified.

- In some varieties, high levels of the plant chemical DIMBOA in young corn plants will kill first-generation corn borers. Other unidentified factors reduce tunneling by second-generation borers.

- From 1986 through 1989, researchers at the University of Missouri found that 90 percent of the hybrids produced by the seed industry have some resistance to whorl leaf feeding and 75 percent have some resistance to sheath and collar feeding.

- Gene transfer techniques have been used to produce corn hybrids that contain a gene taken from the bacterium *Bacillus thuringiensis* (*Bt*). The *Bt* gene produces a protein that is toxic to certain caterpillars, including the European corn borer. The presence of this *Bt* toxin provides season-long protection against European corn borer in some *Bt* hybrids.

Corn rootworms

- Varieties with larger root masses and greater regrowth of roots may show greater "standability" or reduced lodging.

- Contemporary data on varietal differences in rooting habits or rootworm resistance are not well known or widely available. Ongoing research at the University of Illinois began in 1993 and is looking at how well 12 popular corn hybrids respond to rootworm injury. Researchers in this investigation are measuring the amount of root regeneration that occurs after larval injury to the root systems.

Varieties resistant to different insects, cont.

Soybeans

Potato leafhopper

- Varieties that are pubescent, or "hairy," generally deter feeding by potato leafhoppers.

Spider mites

- In variety trials conducted in 1988 (during a severe outbreak of the twospotted spider mite), the variety Burlison was the least damaged. However, its performance under rigorous screening for resistance to spider mites has not been evaluated.

Bean leaf beetle and Mexican bean beetle

- Hairiness may deter pod-feeding beetles.

- An experimental Maturity Group III germ line, resistant to foliage feeders in general, has been identified in breeding programs at Purdue University. However, this germ line is low-yielding, and resistance factors have not yet been incorporated into agronomically acceptable commercial varieties.

Wheat

Hessian fly

- Twenty different genes that build resistance into plants have been identified. But only five of them have been used in commercial varieties. Also, many of these resistant traits have been overcome by new biotypes of the fly. Efforts to use other resistance genes in wheat varieties are ongoing.

- When a wheat variety is not resistant to Hessian flies, other strategies become especially important—residue destruction, crop rotation, and strict adherence to fly-free planting dates.

Alfalfa

Aphids (spotted alfalfa, pea, and blue alfalfa aphids)

- A plant's physical characteristics, especially hairiness, interfere with aphids' ability to feed.
- Alfalfa resists the blue alfalfa aphid mainly by developing tolerance to injury.

Potato leafhopper

- Plant "hairiness" interferes with feeding and egg-laying.
- Saponins and other plant chemicals may convey "nonpreference." Nonpreference means the insect will not select the plant as a source of food or as an egg-laying site.
- The hardening of plant stems may reduce egg-laying by potato leafhoppers.

Alfalfa weevil

- Heavy terminal growth and axillary branching helps the plant develop tolerance to insect injury.
- No truly resistant varieties are available.

Prepared with Michael Gray, field crops entomology specialist, UI Extension.

42 Use crop rotation and plant diversity to control insects

How effective are rotations?

Crop rotations do not solve all insect problems—or even most of the problems. But rotations can work reasonably well for pests that are relatively nonmobile and feed on specific crops. In these cases, rotations most effectively control pests that overwinter in the soil as eggs or partially grown larvae. By rotating to a different crop, you prepare a surprise for these insects when they become active in the spring. They discover that their food source is gone.

Although crop rotations cannot solve all problems, they help manage some of the worst pests, such as northern and western corn rootworms. It should be noted, however, that a corn-soybean rotation couldn't prevent western corn rootworms from causing considerable root injury in rotated corn (first-year corn) in east-central Illinois and western Indiana during 1995. Current speculation suggests that the rigorous rotation of corn and soybeans triggered the development of a new strain of western corn rootworms that lays eggs in soybeans as well as in corn.

Insecticide use for rootworms is greater than for any other insect pest in the Corn Belt. Therefore, by managing corn rootworms culturally, you greatly reduce insecticide use, save money, and protect the environment.

Targeting pests

The key to crop rotation is to determine which pests you are most concerned about and then rotate your crops accordingly. In making choices, note that if a rotation cycle includes legumes, it can help build or maintain soil structure and fertility.

The table on pages 212-213 describes common rotation patterns and their effect on insects.

Constraints on rotations

In addition to the potential for reduced insecticide use, crop rotations generally increase yield and profit. However, there are situations in which crop rotations are not environmentally or economically desirable; it all depends on the soil, contour of the land, and climate. For example:

- Highly erodible rolling land may be more suitable for continuous corn because corn stubble is more effective for erosion control than soybean stubble. Although planting a winter cover crop might help to hold soil in place after soybean harvest, establishing a cover crop before winter is not always possible in some areas.

- Farmers who raise hogs or cattle may require supplies of feed corn that can be met most economically by growing corn on the majority of their land.

Diversity through stripcropping

As rotations demonstrate, crop diversity can disrupt insect life cycles. Another way to increase plant diversity is through intercropping, the practice of growing two or more crops simultaneously in one field. Intercropping comes in many forms, but for field crops in the Midwest, the most practical form is stripcropping—alternating multiple rows of crops (usually four or more rows per strip).

Stripcropping can result in a more balanced insect population with an increase in beneficial insects and parasitoids. Mixed crop stands also can make it more difficult for pests to locate their host plants.

However, exactly how much impact diversified systems have on insect populations and yields is the subject of debate. A review of 150 different studies of insect populations on farms with increased diversity came up with these results:

- 53 percent of 198 plant-eating insects encountered in these studies were less abundant than in conventional systems.
- 18 percent of the insect pests were more abundant in diversified systems.
- 9 percent of the insects were equally numerous in diversified and conventional systems.
- 20 percent of the insects increased in some studies and decreased in others.

Nineteen of the 150 studies also compared yields between the diversified and conventional systems. Four studies found greater yields with the diversified system, nine studies found lower yields with the diversified system, and six studies found variable yields.

Because of the yield results, this review indicates that the economic benefits of diversification remain unclear.

✓ CHECK IT OUT

For more information on crop rotations and yields: page 50.
For more information on stripcropping: page 95

Effects of crop rotation on insects

Rotation	Insects managed	Problem insects
Continuous corn (not truly a rotation)	Wireworms and white grubs are less of a problem for two reasons: (a) They are controlled by soil insecticides used to control rootworms; and (b) adults prefer to deposit eggs in other crops.	Western and northern corn rootworms often occur at damaging levels whenever corn is planted after corn. This problem outweighs the benefits of reducing wireworms and white grubs.
Corn after soybeans	Western and northern corn rootworms are controlled.* Wireworms and white grubs usually do not build up to damaging levels in a corn-soybean rotation.	Black cutworms are slightly more common in corn after soybeans than in corn after corn. A bigger problem is that cutworm moths like to lay eggs in weedy fields in March and April. These fields are most likely to suffer cutworm damage later.
Corn after wheat	Western and northern corn rootworms typically are managed by any rotation that disrupts corn after corn.*	Armyworms, wireworms, and white grubs may infest wheat and then cause economic damage to corn, especially in a no-till system.
Corn after alfalfa (or clover or other hay)	Western and northern corn rootworms typically are managed by any rotation that disrupts corn after corn.*	Wireworms and cutworms are more common (but still sporadic) in corn after legumes and other perennial crops. Grape colaspis may cause economic damage to corn after red clover.
Corn after sod or set-aside	Western and northern corn rootworms typically are managed by any rotation that disrupts corn after corn.*	Wireworms, white grubs, corn billbugs, cutworms, armyworms, and sod webworms are more common.

Rotation	Insects managed	Problem insects
Continuous soybeans (not truly a rotation)	None	Grape colaspis, as well as diseases and nematodes, are more common.
Continuous wheat (not truly a rotation)	None	Hessian fly infestations may build up if fly-free dates are not observed and resistant crop varieties are not used.

*Injury by western corn rootworm larvae was severe in rotated corn (first-year corn) throughout east-central Illinois and western Indiana in 1995.

Prepared with Michael Gray, field crops entomology specialist, UI Extension.

43 Spot-treat insect infestations when possible

Distribution patterns

Some common insect pests can be managed without treating an entire field with insecticide. Knowing the distribution patterns of the pests in your fields can help you determine whether you should spray the whole field or just certain spots.

Stalk borers, wireworms, grasshoppers, and twospotted spider mites are pests that may be managed by using a spot treatment.

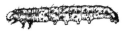

Stalk borers

Stalk borers often lay eggs during late summer in fencerows, grass conservation lanes, or grassy terraces. When corn is planted next to these areas during the following spring, there is a risk that stalk borer larvae will move from the grassy areas and infest the crop.

By using sprays along the field edges, larvae may be killed as they move from weeds to young corn plants. If you miss this chance, and if the stalk borer larvae do infest the small corn plants, it is usually too late to do anything except consider replanting the infested area of the field.

If you must replant, and if you cannot disk under the injured plants, consider an insecticide as soon as the plants begin to spike through the soil. This treatment should prevent larvae from infesting the most recently planted corn.

Also, controlling weed and grass growth in and around your fields can help minimize stalk borer populations by reducing the number of available egg-laying sites.

Wireworms

A very small percentage of cornfields in the Midwest are affected annually by wireworms. Consequently, concern over potential wireworm damage does not justify the widespread use of soil insecticides on first-year cornfields planted after soybeans.

Wireworms tend to cluster in bottomlands, low spots, or other unique areas in fields. The greatest potential for a wireworm infestation is in fields in which small grain or grasses have been grown for two or three years.

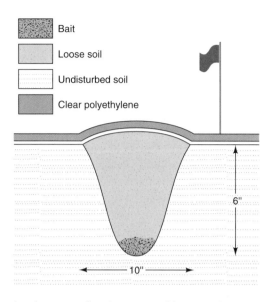

Bait

Loose soil

Undisturbed soil

Clear polyethylene

6"

10"

To determine the extent of a wireworm problem, set wireworm traps one to two weeks before planting corn. Here are the steps:

1. Mix 1 cup wheat and 1 cup shelled corn as the bait.

2. Bury the bait 4 to 6 inches deep. Cover with loose soil and an 18-inch, clear plastic sheet that will collect heat and speed germination of the bait.

3. Mark each station with a flag or stake.

4. Come back in 10 to 14 days and count the number of wireworms in the traps.

If you find one or more wireworms in each trap, you may have to treat the entire field. But if some traps are empty and others have several wireworms, you may be able to limit your treatment to the areas where you found the infested traps.

To determine if you should spot-treat or treat the entire field for wireworms, set bait stations two to three weeks before planting corn. Distribute the bait stations evenly to obtain representative samples from the entire field. To find out how to set a bait station, refer to the accompanying illustration.

If you find one or more wireworms in each trap, you may have to treat the entire field. But if some traps are empty and others have several wireworms, you may be able to limit your treatment to the areas where you found the infested traps.

Attempts to control wireworms with an insecticide rescue treatment after the damage appears are not successful. Therefore, if you find wireworms in bait stations, consider an insecticide at planting.

Grasshoppers

The primary grasshopper species in most of the Midwest lays eggs in late summer and fall in noncrop areas, such as roadsides, fencerows, and field edges. After the eggs hatch in spring, grasshopper nymphs feed in noncrop areas for roughly 40 to 60 days.

This is the time when grasshoppers can be managed easily by spot-treating the noncrop areas. At this stage, the grasshoppers are not very mobile since they lack fully developed wings.

These young grasshoppers will feed harmlessly in noncrop areas during the spring and early summer. But if populations reach 15 to 20 per square yard, consider spraying the noncrop areas and border rows because the grasshoppers may soon move into your fields.

If you don't get the grasshoppers early enough to prevent them from invading your field, wait until populations in the field have reached the economic threshold before spraying. In warm, humid weather, fungal and bacterial diseases may develop among the grasshoppers, which can help reduce their numbers and even make chemical treatment unnecessary.

CHECK IT OUT
For more information on economic thresholds: page 198.

Twospotted spider mites

Spider mites complete a generation in only one to three weeks, depending on environmental conditions. This short life cycle allows spider mite densities to build up rapidly in hot, dry weather.

Spider mites usually overwinter in grassy areas in field margins. When their numbers build up during hot, dry weather, they may move from these border areas into the field edges. Therefore, spot-treating border rows and other infested areas before the spider mites move farther into a field often is the best way to handle them. In periods of prolonged drought, such as in 1988, treating the entire field may eventually be necessary even if you previously used spot treatments.

Keep in mind that mite damage may not show up immediately. If you find a damaged area, you should also examine plants from other areas to determine if mites are present. If they are, consider spraying the area surrounding the damaged plants to make sure the infestation does not spread.

Prepared with Michael Gray, field crops entomology specialist, UI Extension.

44 Conserve beneficial insects

Predators and parasites

Some bugs are on your side. They are known as beneficial insects, and they fall into a variety of categories, two of which are predators and parasites.

Predators hunt and feed on pests. Common examples include praying mantids, lady beetles, and green lacewings.

Parasites hatch inside or on a pest, and then they eat the pest as they grow. Many parasites are tiny wasps that don't sting humans but lay their eggs inside other insects.

Some companies sell predators or parasites for release in the field, but often they are expensive and ineffective. Many questions remain unanswered about when to release them and how many to release.

Your best bet for now is to *conserve* the beneficial insects already in your field. Keeping these bugs alive may help to keep pest problems at an acceptable level so you can reduce insecticide use.

There are no easy answers for keeping beneficial insects alive, but the guidelines listed below should be a good start. Then you can find out what works best on your land.

Five steps to conserving beneficial insects

1. *Recognize the difference between pests and beneficial insects.* To decide whether you need to take control measures, you must be able to distinguish a pest from a beneficial insect. For assistance and information on identifying beneficial insects, contact the nearest Cooperative Extension Service office.

2. *Minimize insecticide applications.* Many insecticides are nonspecific, which means they kill all insects, including the ones you want to keep. Also, many beneficial insects take longer to return to treated fields than do pests.

   Therefore, try to reduce insecticide use by rotating crops, altering planting and harvesting dates, and using resistant crop varieties. Set realistic yield goals and use economic thresholds. Then apply insecticides only if the threshold has been exceeded.

3. *Use selective insecticides and apply them sparingly.* The ideal insecticide would be one that kills only the particular pest you have tar-

geted. But most insecticides are not this selective. Nevertheless, shop carefully and you may find an insecticide that is more directly aimed at your pest problem.

If possible, use spot-treatment methods. When it is necessary to apply insecticides on an entire field, apply only when pest levels exceed the economic threshold. In addition, use the most accurate application methods whenever you can.

CHECK IT OUT

For information about spot treatments: page 214.
For details about economic thresholds: page 198.

4. *Maintain the habitat of beneficial insects.* Beneficial insects are often slow to colonize a field. The best way to make sure they are nearby is to maintain their natural habitats. You can do this by leaving crop residue on the ground and preserving woodlots, windbreaks, fencerows, and unmowed grassy ditch banks and waterways.

Maintaining standing crops also improves the survival chances of beneficial insects. For instance, harvesting alternate strips of alfalfa on a schedule that allows several days of regrowth before the remaining strips are cut helps to preserve beneficial insects in alfalfa. If the entire crop is harvested at once, beneficial insects either leave the field or die.

Increasing crop diversity also increases the population of beneficial insects.

5. *Provide pollen, nectar sources, or artificial food.* Adults of some natural enemies need to feed on pollen and nectar. Plants with very small flowers (such as some clovers and Queen Anne's lace) and some flowering weeds in and around the fields may help keep a diversity of insect life in your fields.

In addition, artificial food supplements that contain yeast, whey proteins, and sugars can attract or increase the numbers of adult lacewings, lady beetles, and syrphid flies.

Important considerations

Although the first three points mentioned above are excellent ideas for any field management, the last two must be thought through carefully.

Beneficial insects

Big-eyed bug

Common damsel bug

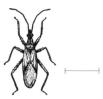

Chinese praying mantid

*Egg case
with newly hatched nymphs*

*Adult
Actual size: about 3 to 4 inches*

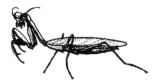

Common green lacewing

Egg

Larva ("aphid lion")

Adult

Convergent lady beetle

Larva

Pupa

Adult

Ground beetle

Minute pirate bug
Actual size: the size of a dash

⊢———⊣ Indicates actual size of adult insect

Predatory mite

Adult and egg
Actual size: the size of a period

Rove beetle

Some important lady beetles

Spotted lady beetle

Twospotted lady beetle

Seven spotted lady beetle

Twice-stabbed lady beetle

Spined soldier bug, feeding on a Mexican bean beetle pupa

Adult

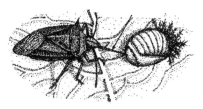

Syrphid fly

Larva   *Adult*

Trichogramma wasp

Adult
Actual size: the size of a period

⊢——⊣ Indicates actual size of adult insect

Maintaining habitats and providing artificial food do more than just attract beneficial insects. These strategies can attract pests as well. So you must carefully examine your yield goals and farming methods to determine whether you can afford a wide range of insects competing in your field.

Also, keep in mind that although it is important to bring pest populations below economic thresholds, it is not necessary to *completely* eradicate pests. In fact, leaving some pests alive will help maintain the populations of beneficial insects. If you eradicate all pests, then your beneficial insects will leave in search of other food sources.

Limitations

In many cases, conserving beneficial insects will provide natural control of insect pests. But natural control does have its limitations.

- Predators and parasites work slowly. With insecticides, farmers see quick results. In contrast, it may take many seasons for beneficial insect populations to build up.
- When pests become few and far between, the natural enemies leave the field in search of more prey. So you are always left with a moderate number of pests still in the field.

Despite the limitations, maintaining and cultivating natural enemies is not difficult. And it could save you some money on insecticides.

Prepared with Rick Weinzierl, entomology specialist, UI Extension.

Reducing herbicide use

Herbicide use took its most significant drop throughout the Midwest in the mid-1980s. For instance, the amount of active ingredient applied in Illinois slid from a peak of 65 million pounds in 1982 to 47 million pounds in 1988, according to a series of five pesticide use surveys conducted in the state between 1978 and 1990.

The *percentage* of acres treated with herbicides has actually remained level over the years, but producers are becoming much more efficient and selective in their use of herbicides on those acres. Specialists attribute the dramatic decline in total pounds of herbicide applied to several factors: the introduction of new herbicides that are effective at much lower rates; the reduction in the labeled rates of many older herbicides, such as atrazine; better management; and efforts to cut expenses.

The following chapters cover some of the ways to get by with the least amount of herbicide and still get the job done. These ideas will help you put more money in your pocket, less product on the land, and protect water supplies in the process.

45 Scout for weeds and know their economic thresholds

Early-season weed scouting

Scouting for weeds keeps you on top of shifting weed pressures and makes it easier to spot-treat for weed problems. The result may be less chemical use and less risk that weeds will develop resistance to certain herbicides. The following are some key elements of weed scouting:

- Scout weeds early (7 to 20 days after planting) to determine whether a herbicide application is needed. Scout periodically for four to six weeks.
- Sample enough areas to get an accurate count of the different weeds present throughout the field.
- Identify and record the location of all weed species found. If a weed cannot be identified, samples can be sent to a local or state laboratory.
- Record the approximate height and growth stage of both the weeds and the crop.
- In all sample areas, calculate the severity of the problem by counting the number of weeds per 10 feet of row for large infestations or every 100 feet of row for smaller infestations. (The accompanying economic threshold charts are based on weed counts per every 100 feet of row.)
- Draw a weed map for each field early in the season. This map will be useful for monitoring changes in weed infestations from year to year. It should include notes on: the locations of perennial weeds; severe infestations of annual weeds; differences in weed populations in various areas of the field; weeds located in fence rows, near the edges of the field, and along waterways; and physical descriptions of the field itself. The accuracy of the map is important, so it may take several scouting trips through the field to create a thorough map.
- Along with weed condition reports, early soil moisture observations are important. Adequate moisture is necessary for effective weed control with most soil-applied herbicides.

Economic thresholds

After you assess a weed problem through scouting, consider the economic threshold, which compares the cost of weed control with the expected yield loss due to weeds. Economic thresholds help you determine whether there is a return on your weed-control investment, and they may help you avoid an unnecessary chemical application.

There are some limitations to the widespread adoption of economic thresholds for weeds—one of them being the landlord/tenant relationship. If landowners feel that tenants are not controlling weeds satisfactorily, they may not rent to those tenants in the future. However, both the landlord and tenant need to be sensitive to the potential for making unnecessary herbicide applications.

Another limitation is that economic threshold programs may not address weed seed production. If a new weed problem is just beginning on a farm, it may not be appropriate to rely solely on economic threshold data. For example, if only a few shattercane plants are found in a field, they might not reach an economic threshold this year, but it would still be important to remove these plants before the problem has a chance to spread. As more research is conducted on weed seed production and germination, economic thresholds will be adjusted to allow for seed production.

Economic thresholds for weeds may be most useful after some form of primary weed control has been done. Growers could then decide if the level of weed control in a given field is acceptable or if additional weed management practices are economically justified.

Determining the threshold

There are seven basic steps in determining an economic threshold for weeds. If you must make *separate* herbicide treatments for grasses and broadleaf weeds, run through the seven steps twice—first for the broadleaf treatment and a second time for the grass treatment. However, if one herbicide treatment will handle both broadleaves and grasses in your field, you only need to make one calculation. You can combine the figures for broadleaves and grasses.

Step 1. Estimate the potential yield for the field, assuming weed-free conditions. Use the previous field history and prevailing conditions to help you.

Step 2. Determine weed densities in the field for each type of broadleaf weed and each type of grass by scouting the field 7 to 20 days after planting. For broadleaf weeds, count or estimate the number of weeds per 100 feet of row. For grasses, count or estimate the number of weeds or weed *clumps* per 100 feet of row.

Step 3. After you know the average number of each type of weed in the field, refer to the two accompanying tables—one for broadleaf weeds and the other for grasses. These charts will tell you the percentage of yield loss you can expect with different weed densities. If you are looking at the effect of more than one weed species, determine the effect of each weed species separately. Then add the different percentages of yield loss together.

Step 4. Multiply the percentage of expected loss from the weeds by your expected yield. This will tell you what yield loss to expect *without* additional weed control.

Step 5. Determine the cost of yield loss without additional weed control by multiplying the expected yield loss by the expected cash grain price per bushel.

Step 6. Determine the cost of weed treatment, including wages, fuel, herbicide, and additives.

Step 7. Subtract the cost of herbicide treatment from the cost of yield loss to determine whether weed treatment results in a net economic return or a net loss. A positive figure indicates a probable net economic gain from the use of herbicide.

Grasses: Determining percent yield loss

	Corn Percent yield loss						Soybeans Percent yield loss					
	1	2	4	6	8	10	1	2	4	6	8	10
Weed	—— number of weeds or weed clumps per 100 feet of row* ——											
Giant foxtail (5 to 8 stems per clump)	10	20	50	100	150	200	5	10	17	25	32	40
Shattercane (2 to 3 stems per clump)	6	12	25	50	75	100	2	5	8	11	14	17
Volunteer corn (up to 10 stems							1	2	3	4	5	6

NOTE: Yield losses due to weeds will vary between fields and across years. The figures in these weed competition tables should be considered *estimates* to help make weed management decisions.

*Grass seedlings may tiller soon after emergence. Therefore, it is often easier to count the number of grass clumps (rather than the number of single weeds) per 100 feet of row.

Broadleaf weeds: Determining percent yield loss

Weed	Corn Percent yield loss						Soybeans Percent yield loss					
	1	2	4	6	8	10	1	2	4	6	8	10
	number of weeds per 100 feet of row											
Cocklebur	4	8	16	28	34	40	1	2	4	6	8	10
Giant ragweed	4	8	16	28	34	40	1	2	4	6	8	10
Jimsonweed	10	20	40	60	70	80	2	4	6	10	15	20
Lambsquarters	12	25	50	100	125	150	2	4	6	10	15	20
Morningglory	6	12	25	50	75	100	8	16	24	32	40	50
Pigweed	12	25	50	100	125	150	2	4	6	10	15	20
Smartweed	10	20	40	60	70	80	2	4	6	10	15	20
Velvetleaf	6	12	25	50	75	100	8	16	24	32	40	50

Examples

Corn: You scout a field and find an average of 28 cocklebur and 50 pigweed per 100 feet of corn row. According to the chart, the cocklebur will cause a 6-percent yield loss, whereas the pigweed will cause a 4-percent loss. By adding the two yield losses together, you get a total loss of 10 percent.

Expected yield: 150 bu/A

Yield loss: 10%

Expected loss: 150 bu/A x 10% = 15 bu/A

Expected cost of loss: 15 bu/A x $2/bu = $30/A

Average treatment cost: $10/A

Net gain: $30 - $10 = $20/A

Verdict: Treat the crop.

Soybeans: You scout a field and find an average of 8 giant ragweed, 25 velvetleaf, and 10 giant foxtail clumps per 100 feet of row. This translates into a potential yield loss of 8 percent, 4 percent, and 2 percent, respectively. Adding these values, you get an expected yield loss of 12 percent from the broadleaf weeds and 2 percent from the grasses. With available herbicides, broadleaves and grasses would have to be treated in *separate* applications, so you should make two separate calculations.

Broadleaf weeds

Expected yield: 40 bu/A

Yield loss: 12%

Expected loss: 40 bu/A x 12% = 4.8 bu/A

Expected cost of loss: 4.8 bu/A x $5/bu = $24/A

Average treatment cost: $12/A

Net gain: $24 - $12 = $12/A

Verdict: Treat the crop for broadleaf weeds.

Grasses

Expected yield: 40 bu/A

Yield loss: 2%

Expected loss: 40 bu/A x 2% = 0.8 bu/A

Expected cost of loss: 0.8 bu/A x $5/bu = $4/A

Average treatment cost: $10/A

Net loss: $4 - $10 = -$6/A

Verdict: Do not treat the crop for grass weeds.

Important points

- If a weed is *not* listed on these charts, use data from a listed weed that has similar growth habits (size of plant, rate of growth, life cycle, time of emergence, and other characteristics).

- Weeds that begin growth four to six weeks after crop emergence typically do not result in crop losses. If the crop fails to develop a complete canopy because of adverse conditions, however, late-emerging weeds can cause losses.

- Conditions that slow crop growth and keep the canopy from closing quickly give weeds the edge. Under these conditions, weeds will have a greater impact on crop losses.

- Certain weeds, such as black nightshade in soybeans, may not always cause economic damage but can still hinder harvesting. Consider this when deciding whether to control weeds.

Final weed survey

Before harvest, make a final weed survey. Although it will be too late for most weed management options, you can plan the cropping system and weed control program for each field for next season.

To conduct a final survey, walk through the field and record observations along the entire route, being sure to cover parts of each area of the field. Also, record observations along the edge of the field, or where unusual conditions exist (such as along waterways or in low, poorly drained areas). Rank weed species from the most to the least commonly found and draw another weed map.

For additional information on scouting, check out the *Field Crop Scouting Manual*, available from the University of Illinois. For details on how to obtain a copy, see "For more information" on page 304.

Prepared with David Pike, pesticides specialist, and George Czapar, integrated pest management educator, UI Extension.

46 Fine-tune your weed control program to cut back on herbicides

A two-pronged approach

There are two basic ways to approach the ultimate goal of cutting back on herbicides.

- Reduce the application rate. Many herbicide labels give a range of recommended application rates, so try to get by with the lower rate.
- Cut back on total chemical use by targeting the treatments in various ways.

The following ideas put these two approaches into practice.

Are rate reductions realistic?

If weeds are small and you treat early, you can sometimes cut back to the lowest recommended herbicide rate—as long as you know your soil, weed problem, herbicide, and equipment. Reducing rates may also require more time in planting and cultivation. For example:

- Reduced rates of herbicides work best if applied early when weeds are 1 to 3 inches high, 14 to 21 days after planting.
- Any late-emerging weeds may be shaded out by the crop, assuming proper seedbed preparation, high quality seed, and uniform planting (in other words, a competitive crop).
- For weeds that still emerge, try two timely cultivations—the first 14 days after spraying and the second in another 10 to 14 days.

Some producers have had success using less than the recommended rates, but be aware that you may assume liability if herbicides do not adequately control weeds.

Use herbicides that require lower rates

A less risky way to reduce herbicide application rates is to select some of the more recent products that recommend extremely low rates. Instead of requiring rates that range from 1 to 2 pounds per acre, the improved chemistry of many new herbicides makes them effective when applied at rates as low as 1 ounce per acre or even $\frac{1}{8}$ ounce per acre.

The major drawback to these herbicides is that many of them use the same mode of action to kill weeds. Therefore, if you use the same herbicides year after year, resistance may develop in some weed populations.

Spot-treat with postemergence products

Many of the newer herbicides are postemergence products, which means they are the result of improved chemistry and more intensive screening. They are often less toxic and have less potential to damage the environment. Postemergence products also allow you to treat specific problem areas instead of treating the entire field. The result: less total product applied, less risk to water, and reduced costs.

For example, irregular, localized infestations of weeds can be spot-treated with postemergence herbicides. "Bean buggies" and rope-wick applicators are ideal for maximizing control with this approach. New technology may also make it possible to spot-treat using electronic sensing devices that locate weeds and trigger the spray.

A 1995 University of Illinois study offers some idea of the impact that postemergence applications can have on water quality. Researchers used a computer model to compare different methods for applying atrazine over a 30-year period in a central Illinois watershed. They projected that postemergence applications, when compared to early preplant applications, would significantly reduce the number of times that atrazine levels exceeded the maximum contaminant level (MCL) in a nearby public water supply.

The researchers also projected that farmers could reduce MCL violations by using atrazine at reduced rates in blends with other herbicides, and by limiting atrazine applications to land that is not highly erodible.

Consider adjuvants

Adjuvants improve the performance of postemergence herbicides, so using certain adjuvants could make it possible to reduce herbicide rates. It all depends on the adjuvant used, the weed species and size, and climatic conditions. Most adjuvants fall into one of four classes:

Surfactants increase spray coverage and penetration.

Crop-oil concentrates increase penetration of the spray through the cuticle (waxy layer) of the leaves. Because of this quality, crop-oil concentrates work best to improve the control of "waxy" weeds, such as lambsquarters.

Liquid fertilizers (28-0-0 and 10-34-0) increase the control of velvetleaf. When you're applying contact herbicides, liquid fertilizers often are used in place of surfactants and crop-oil concentrates. But when you're using systemic herbicides, it's usually better to *add* the liquid fertilizer to the surfactant or crop-oil concentrate.

Methylated seed oils are relatively new products. They are similar to crop-oil concentrates and are as effective—sometimes more effective.

Some herbicides will require specific adjuvants, so double-check the label.

Know the impact of environmental conditions

In addition to being affected by spray adjuvants, postemergence herbicides perform differently under different environmental conditions. High temperatures and humidity may make it possible to apply herbicides at the lower recommended rates. But weeds that develop under droughty conditions may need a higher rate. Also, heavy dew can cause the spray to run off when you add a surfactant.

Know the impact of crop rotation

Crop rotation makes it possible to include crops that require less herbicide—forage legumes, for instance. But even if you have no plans to include a forage legume such as alfalfa or clover in your rotation, crop rotation can make an important difference in herbicide selection. For instance, most of the newer herbicides that can be applied at very low rates are soybean herbicides. So a corn-soybean rotation offers more potential for reducing herbicide use than continuous corn.

Consider split applications

Split applications may be more effective than single-pass applications, allowing you to reduce rates.

Split applications make it easier to control both early emerging weeds (lambsquarters, smartweed, and ragweed) and late-emerging weeds (cocklebur and morningglory). However, extra trips over the field are costly in time, fuel, and equipment wear.

Use herbicides in combination

When you use herbicides in combination, you can often cut back to 30 or 50 percent of the rate that is required when the herbicides are used alone.

Using herbicides in combination usually will not reduce your *total* load of herbicides, but it does make it possible to reduce the rate of a problem herbicide. If you want to reduce the rate of atrazine, for instance, use it in combination with another herbicide.

Herbicide combinations also reduce crop injury, carryover, or the potential for herbicide resistance.

Prepared with Marshal McGlamery, weed science specialist, and George Czapar, integrated pest management educator, UI Extension; and Loyd Wax, USDA/ARS research agronomist.

Reduced rates, one step at a time

Steve, Fred, and Tim Berning don't just jump into things. When they first started no-till farming in 1982, they did it in stages, steadily working their way up to 100 percent no-till by 1992. Now they are taking the same careful approach with reduced rate applications of herbicides.

Steve Berning says they first became interested in reduced rates when they looked at an Ohio State University Extension test plot on a nearby farm in 1993. Impressed with what they saw, the Bernings became part of an Ohio State reduced rate study in 1994—a project that was funded with farmer check-off dollars through the Ohio Soybean Council. They applied $1/4$, $1/2$, and full rates of herbicides to a 5-acre soybean plot on their farm near Minster, Ohio, and they found no difference in weed control or yields among any of the rates.

With this first success, the Bernings felt comfortable taking their trial run to the next level—reduced rates on a full 35-acre field in 1995. Once again, their re-sults were impressive (see the chart on page 235). However, weed pressure forced them to follow their burndown application with two $1/4$-rate applications, rather than what they had planned: a burndown application followed by just one $1/4$-rate application.

"If we had sprayed our burndown closer to planting, we might have gotten by with only one $1/4$-rate spray," Berning says. "But rain followed our burndown, delaying our planting. As a result, weeds were tall enough to justify a second $1/4$-rate spray."

This flexibility is one of the pluses of the reduced rate approach, he adds. If the first $1/4$-rate application doesn't do the job, you can always follow with a second application of $1/4$ or $1/2$ rate. In addition, if you misidentify a weed, you can always change chemicals and follow with a second application.

As for savings, Berning estimates that they cut costs by about $10 to $15 per acre with the two $1/4$-rate applications in 1995. They didn't cut their costs exactly in half because they still apply adjuvants at full rate, and they had an estimated $3-per-acre cost for each pass across the field with the sprayer.

Reduced rates also provided the environmental protection they were looking for, especially since some of their land is only 300 yards away from the edge of Lake Loramie. The lake has a state park at one end; it is used primarily for fishing and boating—with some swimming.

Timing is critical with reduced rates, Berning notes. You must catch the weeds when they are less than 1 inch tall, which means you have a window of opportunity of about two days to get into the field with the sprayer.

"If you miss this window, you can go in with a half rate instead," he says.

Another key is narrow rows, Berning continues. The crop canopy needs to be up as quickly as possible, shading out the weeds. The Bernings drill their beans because it provides a more extensive canopy, giving better weed control than 15-inch-row beans.

Then there is scouting. According to Berning, a reduced rate program calls for more aggressive management, which means scouting for weeds. "We scout two to three times per week after planting," he says. "We want to hit it as close as possible to when the weeds emerge."

On the horizon, the Bernings are looking at the possibility of reduced rates in corn and have already agreed to a 5-acre test plot with Ohio State. To get the extensive crop canopy that helps to cut off sunlight to the weeds, the test plot will feature ultra-narrow, 15-inch corn rows.

Also, because of the importance of timing, they are considering selling their tractor-pulled sprayer because they can only reach 6 mph before the boom starts bouncing too much. With a self-propelled sprayer or a truck sprayer, they will be able to reach 12 to 15 mph and cover more ground.

But what about the product liability risks in cases of poor weed control? Going below the labeled rate means that the chemical manufacturer will not stand behind the product.

"This has not been a problem," Berning says. "Reduced rate has given us good control, so we're not concerned."

1995 reduced rate demonstration
The Berning farm, Shelby County, Ohio

Herbicide rate	Application timing	Giant foxtail	Common lambsquarter	Soybean yield
% of labeled rate	*days after planting*	*———% weed control———*		*bushels per acre*
25% + 25%	4 + 19	99	100	57
50%	12	99	100	57
100%	19	99	100	57

47 Manage crops to compete aggressively with weeds

Standing up to weeds

When your plants thrive, weeds suffer. So anything you can do to help the crop compete aggressively with weeds will reduce your need for herbicides. Here are a few ideas.

Narrow-row soybeans

As many growers have demonstrated over the years on their farms, planting crops such as soybeans in narrow rows makes them much more competitive with weeds than planting them in rows 30 or 40 inches wide. The narrow rows allow soybeans to shade their competitors earlier in the season, reducing weed growth. By providing more surface cover, narrow rows also reduce soil erosion.

However, if weeds do establish themselves in narrow-row soybeans and if control is necessary, you will not be able to cultivate mechanically. You will have to rely on herbicides. Therefore, going with narrow-row planting takes careful planning and consideration of the weed species present.

More oats

Planting oats at 3 bushels per acre, rather than at 1.5 bushels per acre, makes this crop much more competitive with weeds. But the higher planting rate is not useful if you are planting a legume companion. In this case, the higher planting rate would compete with the legume, slow the legume's growth, and perhaps reduce the legume stand.

Planting dates

Adjusting your planting dates can be an important way to reduce weed damage, but you need to consider the type of weeds you're up against.

In general, if you're dealing with early-germinating weeds, such as lambsquarters or foxtail, give yourself enough time to control these weeds before planting. You may want to plant these fields last. Just keep in mind that delaying planting too long can lead to yield loss in corn and soybeans.

If you're dealing with late-emerging weeds, such as johnsongrass, pigweed, shattercane, or crabgrass, plant these fields first. An early planting will give your crop a head start on such weeds.

If you plant forage crops early enough, herbicides may not be necessary at all.

Other management pointers

- Note that the most important time for weed control in corn and soybeans is the first five or six weeks after planting.
- Plant early-germinating hybrids that have good vigor.
- Fertilize to get the crop vigorously growing.
- Use clean seed (quality, weed-free seed).

Prepared with Marshal McGlamery, weed science specialist, UI Extension, and Loyd Wax, USDA/ARS research agronomist.

48 Don't assume that no-till requires more herbicide

Common assumptions

Time and time again, you've probably heard two of the most common assumptions about no-till:

- Weed problems increase.
- Increased herbicide use is needed to make up for the reduction in tillage.

The first assumption is sometimes justified because some weeds can proliferate with no-till—weeds such as fall panicum, marestail (horseweed), hemp dogbane, and common milkweed. However, certain weeds, such as velvetleaf, actually may become less of a problem with no-till.

The second assumption (you have to use more herbicide) often does not hold true. University weed scientists have developed successful no-till systems using herbicides that can give both burndown and residual control with little or no increase in herbicide use. However, some labels may suggest slightly increased rates for no-till, compared with conventional tillage.

In some cases, you may be able to *decrease* herbicide use in no-till by taking advantage of certain cover crops or mulches. But it may be necessary to use more combinations of herbicides—a knockdown herbicide to control existing vegetation, and preemergence or postemergence herbicide to control later-germininating weeds. If cultivation is ruled out, additional postemergence treatments may sometimes be needed.

The following are some general guidelines for weed control in no-till situations.

No-till corn after soybeans

In university studies, no-till corn planted after soybeans has produced excellent yields with good weed control from commonly used herbicides—and generally with little or no increase in herbicide rates or costs (see chart on page 241).

No-till corn after corn

With continuous corn, a mulch of corn residue can gradually build up to improve moisture retention and help control some weeds. But other weeds, such as fall panicum, may increase. Fall panicum's small seeds can filter through the residue to the moist microclimate below, where

Effect of tillage systems on giant foxtail in untreated corn

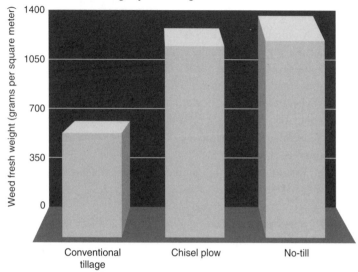

SOURCE: "Influence of Tillage Systems on Giant Foxtail and Velvetleaf Density and Control in Corn," by Douglas D. Buhler and Tommy C. Daniel, *Weed Science*, Vol. 36, pp. 642-647, 1988.

Effect of tillage systems on velvetleaf in untreated corn

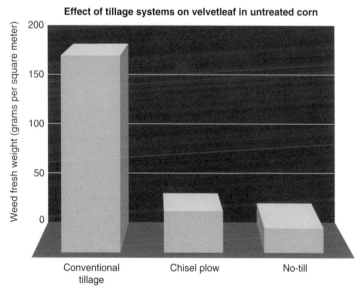

SOURCE: "Influence of Tillage Systems on Giant Foxtail and Velvetleaf Density and Control in Corn," by Douglas D. Buhler and Tommy C. Daniel, *Weed Science*, Vol. 36, pp. 642-647, 1988.

Weed populations change as tillage systems change. As a general rule, grasses will increase as tillage is reduced, but large-seeded broadleaves will decrease. For example, a 1988 Wisconsin study demonstrated that giant foxtail (a grass) increased with less tillage, while velvetleaf (a large-seeded broadleaf) decreased with conservation tillage. Large seeds must be covered to germinate. Because they are not uniformly covered in reduced tillage situations, especially in no-till, they are generally less of a problem.

they germinate. Although controlling fall panicum can be challenging in continuous corn, it can be done.

Continuous corn may be justified in some areas, but a crop rotation, accompanied by a tillage rotation, provides more opportunities to control some weeds. Grasses such as fall panicum, wirestem muhly, johnsongrass, and shattercane are usually easier to control with herbicides for soybeans. However, newer postemergence herbicides for corn offer good control of many grasses, particularly johnsongrass and shattercane. In addition, new herbicide resistant/tolerant crops offer even more herbicide options.

Rotating both crops and herbicides also helps prevent the development of herbicide-resistant weeds.

No-till soybeans after corn

Improved seeding equipment, such as no-till drills, and an increasing arsenal of herbicides for soybeans make no-till soybeans an economically viable option. Consider an early burndown of grass and broadleaf weeds, as well as residual control with preemergence herbicides. Postemergence treatments can be used as needed.

Although the activity of postemergence herbicides is generally greater during warmer weather, you can apply some of these compounds for early burndown; then you can use additional postemergence treatments later if they are needed.

No-till corn in sod

If you have small-seeded legumes and/or grasses for hay or pasture, you have an opportunity for no-till when you rotate back to corn.

No-till corn in sod can work, but not always as successfully as you might like. While some farmers would like to harvest a crop of hay in the spring before no-tilling corn in sod, the removal of moisture by the forage crop can create a moisture shortage for the corn, especially in a dry year. Therefore, it is best to kill the sod in the fall. Another alternative is to kill the sod early in the spring and not try to harvest the hay.

If you do harvest the hay, allow sufficient regrowth for the herbicide to be effective. In a wet spring, no-till planting in sod may allow earlier field operations.

No-till soybeans in sod

Legume sod. There is some advantage to planting corn, rather than soybeans, in legume sod; you can take advantage of the nitrogen. However, soybeans can be successfully grown no-till after clover or alfalfa if the forages have been killed prior to planting.

No-till corn after soybeans
Yields and weed control, Urbana, Illinois, 1993

Treatment	Giant foxtail	Fall panicum	Pennsylvania smartweed	Velvetleaf	Corn yield
	——— percentage of weeds controlled ———				bu/acre
Bicep II	97	95	100	77	198
Bullet	100	96	100	89	195
Extrazine	100	96	100	93	206
Frontier + Marksman	94	96	100	93	215
Roundup + 2,4-D/Accent + Beacon	98	97	100	87	211
Surpass + atrazine	95	93	100	97	196
Untreated check	0	0	0	0	120

Illinois agronomists have referred to these results as their anti-myth research. Many people believe that no-till requires more herbicide at higher cost. But in this research, herbicide rates were the same as would be used with a conventional tillage system. For most treatments, crop-oil concentrate was added at a cost of $1 per acre to improve herbicide performance. Treatments were designed to provide burndown of early weeds as well as extended control.

No-till soybeans after corn
Yields and herbicide costs, Urbana, Illinois, 1993

Treatment	Cost of herbicide and adjuvant per acre	Cost of application per acre	Yield	Net return per acre
			bu/acre	
Roundup + 2,4-D/Classic + Pinnacle + Assure II	$28.00	$6.50	76	$240.00
Poast Plus + 2,4-D/Galaxy/Poast Plus	33.00	9.75	71	205.00
Canopy (5 oz.) + Pursuit (2 oz.)/Select	35.00	6.50	70	199.00
Canopy (5 oz.) + Command (1.5 pt.)	27.00	3.25	70	208.00
Canopy (7 oz.)/Assure II	26.00	6.50	68	198.00
Roundup + 2,4-D + Pursuit Plus	34.00	3.25	68	194.00
Roundup + 2,4-D + Dual (1 pt.)/Pursuit	37.00	6.50	66	173.00
Metribuzin + 2,4-D/Fusion	26.00	6.50	62	157.00
Untreated check	0.00	0.00	31	5.00

This study explored ways to reduce the cost of weed control for no-till soybeans. Results indicate that you can get good weed control, yields, and net returns for less than $30 per acre for herbicide and adjuvants. In some situations, however, a cost a little above $30 per acre, with two or three trips through the field, may be necessary to get good weed control and good crop tolerance with little or no carryover. The cost of herbicides and adjuvants was based on 1993 prices. A cost of $3.25 was used for each spray application, and $6 was used for the price of soybeans. The charge for other costs, including land, labor, management, fertilizer, seed, planting, and harvest, was $180 per acre.

Do not plant soybeans in clover or alfalfa that is not adequately controlled because selective postemergence treatments to kill these legumes in soybeans have not been adequately developed. If a little biennial sweet clover survives in soybeans, it may die naturally.

Grass sod. Planting no-till soybeans in grass sod is possible, but research indicates that it may not be as successful as some other no-till options.

Small-grain cover crops

To prepare for no-till corn or soybeans, it may be necessary to kill a cover crop of wheat or rye that was seeded to reduce erosion. Or you may want to kill a wheat stand that has been significantly thinned by ice, lack of snow cover, or standing water.

For no-till corn, applying atrazine alone may be enough to control wheat or rye, but applying modest rates of a nonselective burndown herbicide is usually preferable.

For no-till soybeans, burndown plus preemergence residual herbicides can be effective.

What about cultivation?

To some farmers, using any form of cultivation means you no longer have a no-till system. But other no-tillers don't have a problem with using some cultivation as needed. The drawback is that cultivation buries crop residue, reduces moisture conservation, and can create ridges and furrows that may increase water runoff on sloping fields.

CHECK IT OUT

For information on cultivator selection: page 244.

When cultivating in a residue-covered field, the key is to avoid clogging the machinery. Specially designed cultivators available today can handle residue. But if you have the common, sweep-type cultivator, you may need to make modifications. Conventional cultivators usually are equipped with five sweeps per row, so you may have to remove a couple of the sweeps to provide enough clearance for the residue to flow.

University studies indicate that for soils with good tilth the main purpose for cultivation is to control weeds. Therefore, if your herbicides are providing good weed control, there may be little or no benefit from cultivation.

Prepared with Ellery Knake, weed science specialist, and John Siemens, power and machinery specialist, UI Extension; and Loyd Wax, USDA/ARS research agronomist.

49 Band herbicides and cultivate

Does cultivation pay off?

Some farmers see cultivation as a way to cut herbicide costs, improve profits, and protect water from contamination by herbicides. But much of the need for cultivation depends on whether you broadcast herbicides or apply them in bands (narrow strips, usually over the rows).

Broadcasting herbicides. When herbicides are broadcast-applied, studies have generally shown that cultivation may increase yields on soils that form a tight surface crust by improving soil aeration and water infiltration. On most soils, however, cultivation does not improve yields when herbicides are broadcast and weeds are adequately controlled.

Although the yield boost is not there, cultivation may still provide an opportunity to reduce application rates when broadcasting herbicides.

Banding herbicides. When you apply herbicides in a band over the rows, you need to use the cultivator to control weeds between the rows. Although the yield data are mixed, certain studies suggest that the combination of banding and cultivation may give yields a small boost. Iowa State University research, for example, has shown that corn yields went up slightly when banding plus cultivation was compared with broadcast applications without cultivation.

In addition to the potential yield increase, banding means the use of less chemical because the application is made only over the rows. Not only does this reduce the potential for water contamination, some researchers say that it can reduce expenses. They say the reduction in herbicide more than makes up for the cost of additional cultivation.

How does cultivation affect erosion?

University of Illinois studies indicate that cultivation can reduce erosion initially by increasing water infiltration and significantly reducing surface runoff. However, once runoff begins, the soil loosened by cultivation can erode down the slope.

Over the long run, cultivation loosens the surface soil and decreases the amount of surface residue, so you can expect soil erosion to increase.

The risks

Cultivation is a time-consuming practice. If you do not cultivate carefully, at the right time, or with properly adjusted equipment, you can bury the plants with soil, prune the crop's roots, bend and break some plants, or compact the soil. If you depend solely on cultivation to control weeds, you can control weeds in the row only when they are small; what's more, rainy weather could delay cultivation during a critical time.

If you band herbicides, timely cultivation of the area between the rows is important for acceptable weed control. Rain can prevent you from keeping to this schedule, allowing weeds to take hold and compete with the crop for moisture, light, and nutrients. In addition, rain immediately *after* cultivation can sometimes provide the right amount of moisture for weeds to take root again.

Selecting row cultivators

When choosing a cultivator for the job, consider these options:

S-tine or Danish tine. This cultivator, usually equipped with five tines per row, is designed to operate at shallow depths and high speed in tilled soil with low residue cover.

C-shank (multiple shanks per row). The multiple c-shank cultivator has good soil penetration, is usually operated at a slow speed (2 to 4 mph), and will clog when used in heavy residue. It is equipped with three to five shanks with sweeps per row and can be equipped with weeding disks. Various sweep shapes and sizes are available.

C-shank (single shank per row). The single-shank cultivator works with conservation tillage because a coulter to cut the residue is mounted in front of each shank. Each row assembly consists of a shank with a sweep 16 to 24 inches wide and two weeding disk blades (or disk hillers).

The weeding disk blades are positioned near the crop row and set to move soil toward or away from the row. Although the disk blades can be used to help build ridges, most ridging cultivators include ridging wings mounted on the c-shank, which is positioned in the middle of the row.

Rolling cultivator. The rolling cultivator uses two "spider" gangs on each row assembly. It will operate in high amounts of residue without clogging and can penetrate hard soils.

The rotary hoe

A rotary hoe consists of staggered, spiderlike wheels, spaced about 4 inches apart. The rotary hoe is a fast, economical way to control small weeds and break a surface crust to improve crop emergence.

The operating speed is usually 6 to 10 mph, and the draft requirement is low. Rotary hoes, especially those with self-cleaning abilities, can be used in most conservation tillage systems.

Prepared with John Siemens, power and machinery specialist, and Marshal McGlamery, weed science specialist, UI Extension; and Loyd Wax, USDA/ARS research agronomist.

50 Control weeds with cover crops

What works best

Cover crops are often planted to reduce soil erosion during the winter and early spring. If you manage cover crops properly, they may also help reduce weed populations. How much weed-control benefit you get from cover crops depends on many factors, such as rainfall, temperature, soil characteristics, and the growth and thickness of the stand. Before beginning a cover-crop program, experiment with different management techniques and crop species to find out what works best on your farm.

In the Midwest, the cover crops with the best potential for controlling weeds are rye, wheat, and spring oats. Each of these crops has advantages and drawbacks.

CHECK IT OUT
For more information on cover crops: page 46.

Rye and wheat

Some studies have shown that after rye and wheat are killed, they release chemicals that may reduce weed growth. If you kill them a few weeks before planting corn or soybeans in the residue, rye and wheat could help you fight weeds.

Other researchers are not sure that the chemicals in rye or wheat effectively control weeds. What's more, some point out that the chemical released to fight weed growth can also hurt corn. But most agree that planting in the heavy residue left by these grasses will reduce weed germination and growth and will provide good mulch for your next crop.

One drawback is that rye and wheat take water from the soil. If it is a dry summer and you kill these crops too late, your cash crop could suffer from lack of moisture. It is also important to monitor rye and wheat stubble for insect pests such as armyworms.

Oats

Oats planted in the fall can also reduce weed growth when crops are planted in its residue. But the protection is not as effective as with rye and wheat. The oats usually die over the winter and don't leave as much residue at planting time.

An oats cover crop can still help you, however, because the residue provides shade and mulch. Also, because the oats usually don't survive the winter, you don't have to worry that they will deprive your next crop of soil moisture. Another advantage is that you do not have the expense of a knockdown herbicide to control the oats cover crop.

Prepared with Bill Simmons, soil and water management specialist, and George Czapar, integrated pest management educator, UI Extension; and Don Bullock, UI associate professor of crop production.

Selecting pesticides

There are many factors to consider in the pesticide selection process—cost, effectiveness, past experience with the product, compatibility with your soil type and tillage system, carryover potential, and convenience, to name just a few. Today, however, many farmers have added yet another ingredient to the mix—the environmental cost.

The chapters in this section focus on two of the most important environmental considerations when selecting a pesticide: the toxicity of the chemical and its potential to move with runoff water. To get an even more complete environmental perspective on a particular chemical, you also need to consider the pesticide's potential to leach through the soil and threaten groundwater, as well as any potential threats to nontarget species.

By using pesticides that are more likely to stay in their place, you have more chemical to do the job and you reduce leaching and runoff losses. In other words, making sound choices makes sense, both economically and environmentally.

51 Select the least-toxic pesticide

Real concern

In 1988, Iowa State University's farm and rural life poll asked over 2,000 farm operators to list the agricultural issues that most concerned them. As it turned out, four of the nine top issues they selected related to the hazards of using pesticides and other farm chemicals.

So the question is not whether producers are concerned about pesticides. The question is exactly how to work these concerns into the pesticide selection process.

Right now, pesticide selection boils down to evaluating chemicals according to effectiveness and economics, but researchers are trying to come up with systematic ways to add environment into the equation. One of the most complete sets of ideas comes from Iowa State University and the University of Nebraska, where researchers have come up with economic injury levels that take into consideration environmental costs. They are called environmental economic injury levels.

Environmental economic injury levels

An economic injury level (EIL) is the point at which the cost of controlling the pest equals the benefits of controlling the pest. EILs are used to set economic threshold levels—levels at which producers should take action to control various pests. The idea is to take action a little before pest levels reach the EIL.

However, EILs consider only the material and application costs of the pesticide—not environmental costs. To come up with EILs that consider environmental damage, researchers surveyed 8,000 field crop producers in Illinois, Iowa, Nebraska, and Ohio, asking them to rank how concerned they were about each of eight environmental categories: surface water, groundwater, aquatic organisms, birds, mammals, beneficial insects, acute (short-term) effects in humans, and chronic (long-term) effects in humans. They also asked producers how much they would be willing to spend or accept in yield losses to avoid different levels of risk from an insecticide application.

Next, the Nebraska and Iowa researchers identified how much risk various insecticides pose in the eight environmental categories. The risk levels were based on a variety of physical and biological properties of the chemicals, such as persistence in the environment, toxicity, and solubility.

Environmental risks and costs
For one application of field crop insecticides

| Trade name | Chemical name | The risk to... | | | | | | | | Environmental cost |
		Surface water	Ground-water	Aquatic life	Birds	Mammals	Beneficial insects	Humans (acute)*	Humans (chronic)**	
										$ per acre
Ambush	Permethrin	High	Low	High	Low	Low	High	Low	Low	8.25
Asana	Esfenvalerate	High	Low	High	Medium	Medium	High	Medium	Low	9.34
Counter	Terbufos	Medium	Low	High	High	High	Medium	High	Low	9.79
Cygon	Dimethoate	Low	Medium	High	High	Low	Medium	Low	Medium	8.53
Diazinon	Diazinon	Medium	Medium	High	High	Low	Medium	Low	Low	8.95
Dipel	Bacillus thuringiensis	None	Low	Low	None	None	None	None	Low	2.25
Dyfonate	Fonofos	High	Medium	High	High	High	High	High	Medium	11.52
Furadan	Carbofuran	Low	High	High	High	High	High	High	Low	10.76
Lannate	Methomyl	Medium	High	High	High	High	High	High	Low	11.14
Lorsban	Chlorpyrifos	High	Low	High	High	Medium	High	Medium	Medium	10.18
Malathion	Malathion	Low	Low	Medium	Low	Low	Low	Low	Low	6.14
Orthene	Acephate	Low	Low	Low	Medium	Low	Low	Low	Low	6.14
Penncap-M	Methyl parathion	Medium	Low	High	High	Low	Medium	Low	Medium	8.51
Pounce	Permethrin	High	Low	High	Low	Low	High	Low	Low	8.25
Sevin	Carbaryl	Medium	Low	High	Medium	Medium	Medium	Medium	Low	8.41
Temik	Aldicarb	Low	High	High	High	High	High	High	Low	10.76
Thimet	Phorate	High	Low	High	High	High	High	High	Low	10.72

None = No risk.   *High = High risk.*   *Medium = Medium risk.*   *Low = Low risk.*

*Acute risk is the health risk posed by a single dose or exposure to a chemical.

**Chronic risk is the long-term health risk posed by repeated doses or exposures over time.

NOTE: These are *relative* risks. A low risk means that the chemical poses low risk when compared to other pesticides; it does not mean the chemical is low in toxicity. All pesticides should be handled with caution.

Using all of this information, researchers then calculated the environmental cost of using each insecticide. Examples of the risks and environmental costs are listed in the chart on page 249.

Using environmental EILs

To illustrate how to incorporate environmental cost into a conventional EIL, let's compare four insecticides that might be used for first-generation European corn borers in the early whorl stage of corn. Three of the insecticides are conventional insecticides (carbofuran, chlorpyrifos, and permethrin), and one of them is a microbial insecticide (*Bacillus thuringiensis*).

The environmental EIL
First generation European corn borers
Early whorl stage of corn

Trade name	Common name	Insecticide cost	Environmental cost	Total cost	Conventional EIL	Environmental EIL
		$ per acre			*larvae per plant*	
Dipel	*Bacillus thuringiensis*	10.35	2.25	12.60	1.28	1.56
Furadan	carbofuran	14.65	10.76	25.41	1.40	2.42
Lorsban	chlorpyrifos	12.70	10.18	22.88	1.21	2.18
Pounce	permethrin	11.57	8.25	19.82	1.10	1.89

The accompanying chart shows the insecticide cost, the environmental cost, and the total cost of each insecticide. It also shows the conventional economic injury level (which is based on the insecticide cost, effectiveness, and other factors) and the environmental EIL (which is based on the total cost and other factors).

The surface-water connection

Environmental EILs take into consideration a wide range of risks posed by pesticides. If you would like to focus solely on the risk that pesticides pose to surface water, see Chapters 52 and 53.

Prepared with Wendy Wintersteen, interim director, Extension to Agriculture and Natural Resources, Iowa State University; Leon Higley, associate professor of entomology, University of Nebraska; and Rick Weinzierl, entomology specialist, UI Extension.

EARTHWORMS AND PESTICIDES: CONSIDER TOXICITY LEVELS

Consider the earthworm

The ancient philosopher Aristotle knew what he was talking about when he dubbed earthworms "the intestines of the earth." He was one of the first to point out the important role worms play in life of the soil. Consider just some of the impressive work that they perform:

Creating soil. Worms consume organic matter and mix it with minerals, resulting in new soil clusters.

Turning over large amounts of soil. Worms bring up soil from the deeper strata to the surface.

Maintaining soil aeration and drainage. Worms create cracks, crevices, and burrows, which aerate the soil and provide pathways through which water drains and roots can grow.

Converting nutrients. Earthworms are the key organisms in the breakdown of organic matter, converting nutrients into a form readily available to plants.

With such an impressive record, it makes sense to do what you can to avoid killing earthworm populations on your farm. This means trying to select pesticides that are not as toxic to worms.

Which pesticides are toxic?

Although most pesticides are not toxic to earthworms, some can be deadly. Here are the specifics.

Herbicides. Most herbicides do not have a direct effect on earthworms. Herbicides are more likely to have an indirect effect by reducing weeds and other vegetation, which provide organic matter for the worms to feed upon.

Fungicides. Carbamate-based fungicides, such as benomyl, can be extremely toxic. Otherwise, fungicides have little effect on earthworms.

Insecticides. Insecticides vary in their toxicities to earthworms. The following chart categorizes some commonly used insecticides in terms of their toxicity to earthworms, grouping them in four categories that range from slightly toxic to extremely toxic.

Insecticide toxicity to earthworms

Trade name	Chemical name	Relative toxicity to earthworms
Ambush	Permethrin	Insufficient evidence*
Counter	Terbufos	Moderately toxic
Dyfonate	Fonofos	Moderately toxic
Diazinon	Diazinon	Slightly toxic
Furadan	Carbofuran	Very toxic
Lindane	Lindane	Insufficient evidence**
Lorsban	Chlorpyrifos	Very toxic
Lannate	Methomyl	Extremely toxic
Malathion	Malathion	Slightly toxic
Orthene	Acephate	Insufficient evidence**
Penncap-M	Methyl parathion	Insufficient evidence*
Pounce	Permethrin	Insufficient evidence*
Sevin	Carbaryl	Extremely toxic
Temik	Aldicarb	Extremely toxic
Thimet	Phorate	Extremely toxic

*Probably nontoxic at normal exposure rates.

**Probably toxic at normal exposure rates.

Slightly toxic: The chemical is reasonably safe to use without harming worms.

Moderately toxic: Use with caution.

Very toxic: To preserve earthworms, avoid this chemical.

Extremely toxic: To preserve earthworms, avoid this chemical.

SOURCE: "The Effects of Toxic Chemicals on Earthworms," by Clive A. Edwards and Patrick J. Bohlen, *Reviews of Environmental Contamination and Toxicology*, Vol. 125, Springer-Verlag New York, Inc., 1992.

Prepared with Clive Edwards, entomologist, The Ohio State University.

52 Determine your soil's potential for runoff

The soil connection

Hitting your target with pesticides is one thing. Making sure that the pesticide *remains* on or near the target is another.

The risk that your pesticide will move off-target in runoff water depends on its chemical characteristics, as well as the application rate. However, soil type also plays a part and should not be ignored in the pesticide selection and application process. If your soil is highly susceptible to surface runoff, you will want to take extra care in evaluating the risk of surface runoff posed by your pesticide (see Chapter 53).

The risk of runoff has a lot to do with the internal drainage of the soil and how easily the soil is compacted.

Soil qualities that affect internal drainage

Internal soil drainage is a measure of the rate of water moving through the soil profile.

If water moves through a soil slowly, the soil can become saturated. The result: Water begins to accumulate on the surface. When water cannot seep down fast enough, it will either pond on level ground or start running off on sloping surfaces.

Water doesn't move as freely through the small pores of a fine-textured soil as it does through the large pores of a coarse, sandy soil. But keep in mind that other factors also come into play, such as the water table (the highest level of groundwater).

Soil can be very permeable but still poorly drained if the water table is high. When the water table is high, the water moving through the soil has nowhere to go. As a result, the water table may rise and eventually the soil becomes saturated—filled with water to the surface. Increased runoff results.

Soil qualities that affect compaction

Compaction restricts the movement of water down through the soil, and this can increase ponding and surface runoff.

The proportion of sand, silt, and clay in a soil greatly affects how easy it is to compact. Moderately coarse-textured sands, with enough organic matter to help provide structure, are most resistant to compaction. In addition, many loam, silt loam, and silty clay loam soils are relatively resistant to compaction.

Generally, the higher the clay content of a soil, the more prone the soil is to compaction, particularly if organic matter content is low. Fine-textured soils (such as clays) have a greater proportion of pore space than coarser soils, but the pores in the soil are very small and the clay particles hold the water tightly.

Leaving crop residue on the soil surface is one way to improve infiltration and slow runoff on clay soils.

Soil runoff ratings

To get a handle on how these and other factors work together to affect pesticide losses in runoff water, check with your USDA Natural Resources Conservation Service (NRCS) office. The NRCS has analyzed the characteristics of each soil type to determine its potential for surface runoff. It places all soil types into one of three categories:

- High potential for runoff
- Intermediate potential for runoff
- Low potential for runoff

CHECK IT OUT

For more information on soil compaction: page 74.
For information on how conservation tillage affects pesticide runoff: page 26.

Prepared with Michael Hirschi, soil and water specialist, George Czapar, integrated pesticide management specialist, and John Siemens, power and machinery specialist, UI Extension.

53 Determine your pesticide's potential for runoff

Two paths

Pesticides can make their way into lakes, rivers, and streams in two basic ways. They can dissolve in runoff water and move with the water as it flows across the surface. Or they can hitch a ride with eroding soil by "adsorbing," or attaching, to soil particles. If the soil washes into waterways, so will the "piggybacked" pesticide.

So how do you know if a pesticide is likely to move, either by dissolving in runoff or by attaching to soil? It depends on specific physical and chemical characteristics—soil adsorption, water solubility, and persistence.

Soil adsorption (K_{oc})

"K_{oc}" is a measurement of a pesticide's tendency to attach to soil particles. A high K_{oc} value (greater than 1,000) means the pesticide can attach tightly to soil and is less likely to move, except with eroding soil particles.

Pesticides with low K_{oc} values (less than 300 to 500) are not as likely to attach to soil particles. Therefore, they tend to move in runoff water.

As examples, Treflan and Prowl have high K_{oc} values, which means they attach tightly to soil particles and can move with eroding sediment.

Pesticides can reach surface water by dissolving in runoff water and then moving across the soil surface. They can also adsorb, or attach, to soil particles and then move with eroding soil.

Atrazine and Bladex have moderate K_{oc} values, which means they move primarily with runoff water.

Water solubility

Solubility is a chemical's tendency to dissolve in water. The higher the solubility, the greater the risk of the chemical dissolving in and moving with runoff.

In general, pesticides with a solubility of 1 part per million (ppm) or less tend to remain on the soil surface—where they might move with eroding soil. Pesticides with solubilities greater than 30 ppm are more likely to move in runoff water or leach into groundwater, although a lot depends on whether the chemical tightly bonds with soil.

Persistence (half-life)

Another factor you need to consider is how long the pesticide will remain in the environment—a quality known as "persistence."

Scientists measure persistence by half-life days—the number of days that it takes for the pesticide to break down into one-half of its previous concentration. In general, the longer the half-life, the longer the pesticide will remain in the environment.

A pesticide with a half-life greater than 21 days is more likely to persist long enough to move with runoff or eroding soil.

Consider all three factors

Soil adsorption, solubility, and persistence should be considered together. If you look at one of these factors alone, you might get a false picture of a pesticide's likelihood to move with runoff. It's the *interaction* of the three factors together that determines how a pesticide will behave in the environment.

For example, paraquat is very soluble in water; therefore, you might expect that it would dissolve in water and move with runoff. In reality, though, it isn't likely to move with runoff water because it is so tightly attached to clay particles. With a high K_{oc} of 100,000, paraquat will not release its hold once it becomes attached to soil particles.

The chart on pages 258-259 provides approximate values for these three key pesticide properties. The actual values may vary considerably, depending on specific soil and environmental factors.

This chart can help you to compare chemicals, and it can give you an idea of what you need to concentrate on to keep pesticides from leaving your fields. If your pesticide attaches to soil particles, you need to control soil movement; if your pesticide moves in runoff water, you need to control the flow of water.

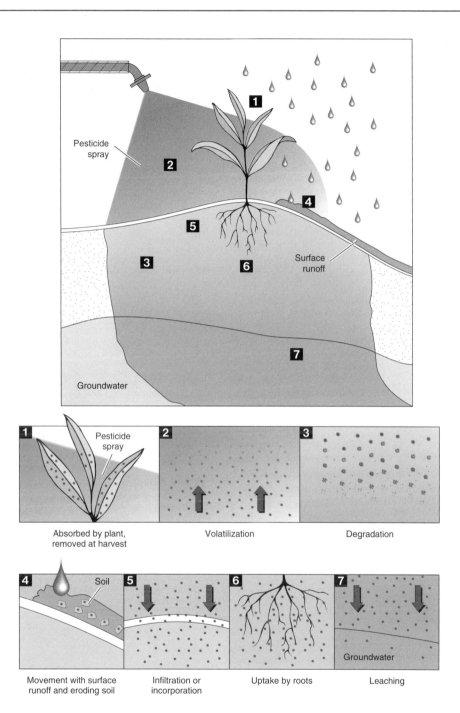

When a pesticide is applied, it can enter the plant, change into a gas (volatilize), break down into compounds that are usually less toxic (degrade), attach to soil particles and move with eroding soil, or dissolve in water and move with surface runoff. It can also move through the soil layer, where it can be taken up by roots, continue to break down, or possibly leach deeper.

Pesticide characteristics that affect runoff potential

Herbicides

Trade name	Chemical name	K_{oc} (soil adsorption index)	Water solubility (parts per million)	Soil half-life (days)
AAtrex	Atrazine	100	33	60
Ally	Metsulfuron	35	9,500	120
Assure	Quizalofop	510	0.31	60
Balan	Benifin	9,000	0.1	40
Banvel	Dicamba	2	500,000	14
Basagran	Bentazon	35	2,300,000	20
Bladex	Cyanazine	190	170	14
Blazer	Acifluorfen	139	250,000	30
Buctril	Bromoxynil	190	0.08	5
Butyrac 200	2,4-DB	20	709,000	10
Classic	Chlorimuron	110	1,200	40
Cobra	Lactofen	10,000	0.1	3
Command	Clomazone	274	1,100	24
Dual	Metolachlor	200	530	20
Eptam	EPTC	280	375	30
Eradicane	EPTC	280	375	30
Fusilade 2000	Fluazifop	3,000	2	20
Gramoxone Extra	Paraquat	100,000	1,000,000	500
Lasso	Alachlor	170	240	15
Lexone	Metribuzin	41	1,220	30
Lorox	Linuron	370	75	60
Many names	2,4-D amine salts	20	796,000	10
Many names	2,4-D ester	1,000	1	10
Micro Tech	Alachlor	170	240	15
Option II	Fenoxaprop	53,700	0.9	5
Pinnacle	Thifensulfuron	45	2,400	12
Poast Plus	Sethoxydim	100	4,390	10
Princep	Simazine	138	6.2	75
Prowl	Pendimethalin	24,300	0.275	90
Pursuit	Imazethapyr	100	11,000	90
Ramrod	Propachlor	80	613	6
Reflex	Fomesafen	50	600,000	180
Roundup	Glyphosate	24,000	900,000	47
Scepter	Imazaquin	20	60	60
Sencor	Metribuzin	41	1,220	30
Sonalan	Ethalfluralin	4,000	0.3	60
Stinger	Clopyralid	1.4	300,000	30
Sutan+	Butylate	126	46	12
Treflan	Trifluralin	7,000	0.3	60

Insecticides

Trade name	Chemical name	K_{oc} (soil adsorption index)	Water solubility (parts per million)	Soil half-life (days)
Ambush	Permethrin	86,600	0.2	32
Asana	Esfenvalerate	5,300	0.002	35
Counter	Terbufos	3,000	5	5
Cygon	Dimethoate	8	25,000	7
Diazinon	Diazinon	500	40	40
Dyfonate	Fonofos	532	13	45
Furadan	Carbofuran	22	351	50
Lannate	Methomyl	72	58,000	33
Larvin	Thiodicarb	100	19	7
Lindane	Lindane	1,100	7	400
Lorsban	Chlorpyrifos	6,070	2	30
Malathion	Malathion	1,800	145	1
Orthene	Acephate	2	818,000	3
Penncap-M	Methyl parathion	5,100	60	5
Pounce	Permethrin	86,000	0.2	32
Sevin	Carbaryl	200	114	10
Tempo	Cyfluthrin	100,000	0.002	30
Thimet	Phorate	2,000	22	90

NOTE: These values can vary, depending on soil and environmental factors.

SOURCE: Adapted from *Pesticides: Surface Runoff, Leaching, and Exposure Concerns* by R.L. Becker, D. Herzfeld, K.R. Ostlie, and E.J. Stamm-Katovich, Minnesota Extension Service, University of Minnesota.

Prepared with George Czapar, integrated pest management educator, Bill Simmons, soil and water management specialist, and Michael Hirschi, soil and water specialist, UI Extension.

Mark and Janice Hinze

Using software to select herbicides

When it comes to herbicide recommendations, Mark Hinze has gone from "shooting from the hip" to "shooting from the laptop."

Hinze, a crop consultant in central Nebraska, uses WeedSOFT, a weed management computer program that gives producers a clear picture of their weed-control options, from both an environmental and economic perspective. Gone are the days in which, as he puts it, crop consultants would shoot from the hip by basing recommendations on rough estimates of weed pressure and economic impacts.

WeedSOFT, a program developed by the University of Nebraska, offers considerably more precision as it takes into consideration an array of factors: anticipated crop selling price; crop cultivar; row spacing; method of herbicide application; herbicide costs; proximity to surface water; water table depth; crop or weed stage; weed species and density; soil type, residue, pH, moisture, and erodibility; annual precipitation; and next year's crop.

After entering this information, Hinze says the program can provide literally dozens of herbicide options, which can be ranked according to which ones will provide the highest yield or the greatest net gain per acre.

By providing information about your soil, proximity to surface water, and groundwater depth, you can even find out the environmental impact of various herbicides.

WeedSOFT will also project what kind of weed control you can expect with various application rates, including rates that are below the labeled rate.

Hinze, along with his wife and business coordinator, Janice, have been using the Nebraska program since it first appeared in 1990. Each of their three pickup trucks is equipped with a computer, which can make on-the-spot estimates of how a producer will fare with or without making a particular herbicide application.

WeedSOFT consists of three independent modules. The heart of the program is ADVISOR, which offers a detailed analysis of the herbicide options, including some environmental concerns such as label restrictions. The second module is WeedVIEW, a visual catalog of more than 35 weed species. The third module is EnviroFX, which can be used to call up environmental information on particular herbicide mixes.

WeedSOFT is more refined in its groundwater information than it is in surface-water data, says Dave Mortensen, a University of Nebraska associate professor of weed ecology and co-leader of the WeedSOFT project. However, the latest version, which was available in the winter of 1996-97, has boosted the amount of information on surface-water quality.

In the latest version, Nebraska producers can call up digitized images of their farmstead, which were provided by the Natural Resources Conservation Service. They can then access information about their land's soil type, topography, and depth to groundwater.

WeedSOFT is aimed at Nebraska farmers and even breaks down some of the corn data according to conditions in the western and eastern halves of the state. But Mortensen says the basic model could be adapted to other states. With this in mind, the Nebraska team has begun to work with other midwestern states to coordinate efforts.

"A lot of other states would like to have this but don't have the resources to start from scratch," Mortensen says. "Therefore, efforts are underway to make such a decision aid available in other states. Because herbicide efficacy and the effects of weed competition vary with the climate, localized data would be required to modify the program."

Mortensen and his co-leader, Extension specialist Alex Martin, work closely with a programmer and team of specialists to continually refine the program. In turn, this team meets with producers and crop consultants to gather ideas for improvements. The result is an updated version of WeedSOFT each year.

"WeedSOFT gives us another tool to quantify our decision-making process," says Hinze. "It gives us a handle on exactly how much the weeds are costing producers. It takes the environmental and economic information and puts it out on the table. There's nothing else like it."

For information on WeedSOFT, call (402)472-1544 or write to: WeedSOFT, P.O. Box 830915, Lincoln, NE 68583-0915.

Handling pesticides safely and efficiently

It's not always easy to put pesticides in their place. Even when the target is stationary, pesticides are not.

Some pesticides are more likely to attach to soil particles and organic matter and then move with eroding soil. Pesticides that are more soluble are more likely to dissolve in water and leach down into drain tiles, which can then carry them to streams and creeks. What's more, some of the pesticide may volatilize, or evaporate, into the air, while some may be taken up by plant roots, absorbed by plant leaves, ingested by insects and worms, or broken down by sunlight or microorganisms in the soil.

All of these processes can make it difficult to keep pesticides on target. But advances in technology are making the job easier. The chapters in this section focus on some keys to handling pesticides with accuracy and safety. They also cover ways to deal with pesticide that remains in the container and spray tank after the job is done. For your health and for the environment, this chemical residue also needs to be put in its place.

54 Calibrate your sprayer

A top-paying job

University studies have shown that about one out of every four sprayers is miscalibrated by more than 10 percent, which can mean overapplication or underapplication, greater risk to water or lack of pest control, and wasted money. Assuming that pesticide application costs you $25 per acre, overapplying chemicals by 10 percent would mean a loss of $2.50 per acre—or $2,500 for a 1,000-acre farm.

That $2,500 would remain in your pocket if you spent a few hours calibrating your sprayer equipment. That makes calibrating equipment an awfully good-paying job.

Check the calibration of your spray equipment every few days during the season or whenever you change the pesticides being applied. New nozzles do not lessen the need to calibrate because some nozzles "wear in," which means they will increase their flow rate most rapidly during the first few hours of use. Checking a new nozzle for accuracy before you begin spraying is a good safeguard against misapplication.

You can easily calibrate spraying equipment yourself, or you might want to take advantage of the free calibration services being offered by some chemical suppliers. If you do the calibration yourself, use the following procedure.

Calibration

Step 1. Determine your sprayer's ground speed in miles per hour, according to existing field conditions. Do not rely on ordinary speedometers as an accurate measure of speed because slippage and variation in tire sizes can result in speedometer errors of 30 percent or more. For details on how to measure the actual ground speed, see the accompanying sidebar.

Step 2. Determine the "effective sprayed width" in inches for each nozzle. The effective sprayed width will be different for different spray methods:

- For broadcast spraying, the effective sprayed width equals the distance between nozzles.

- For band spraying, the effective sprayed width equals the band width.

- For row-crop application, such as spraying from drop pipes, bander kits, or directed spraying, the effective sprayed width equals the row spacing (or band width) divided by the number of nozzles per row (or band).

Step 3. Calculate your nozzle's required flow rate in gallons per minute. Use the following equation:

$$GPM = \frac{GPA \times MPH \times W}{5,940}$$

GPM is the nozzle's required flow rate in gallons per minute.
GPA is the application rate in gallons per acre.
MPH is the ground speed in miles per hour.
W is the effective sprayed width in inches.
5,940 is a constant used to convert gallons per acre, miles per hour, and inches to gallons per minute.

Step 4. Check whether the nozzles are delivering the required flow rate. The common way to do this is to use a stopwatch and a special container marked in ounces. By spraying into the container and timing the process with the stopwatch, you can determine the number of ounces per minute that the nozzle delivers.

An easier, more efficient way to check nozzle flow rates is to obtain a nozzle flow rate tester, an inexpensive item that can be purchased from some spray equipment suppliers. A flow rate tester is a vertical, plastic

The easiest, most efficient way to check nozzle flow rates is to purchase a nozzle flow-rate tester. It will tell you how many gallons per minute the nozzle is delivering.

meter that you simply place under the nozzle and use to take a quick reading. It will tell you how many gallons per minute the nozzle is delivering.

It's okay if the flow rate varies from the required flow rate, as long as you know that and adjust for it. However, the flow rate for different nozzles should not vary from each other by more than 5 to 10 percent.

Step 5. Be sure you operate spray nozzles within the recommended pressure range. This is important because as spray pressures increase or decrease, flow rates change. (See the nozzle catalog to determine what spray pressure the manufacturer recommends.) Keep in mind that the range of recommended operating pressures refers to pressure *at the nozzle tip*. Because of pressure loss in the line and at check valves, the main pressure gauge at the controls may need to read much higher.

When you have calibrated your sprayer, be sure to operate it in the field at the application rate and ground speed that you selected and at the pressure you determined in Step 5. After spraying a known number of acres, check the liquid level in the tank to make sure your application rate is correct.

Check the nozzle flow rate frequently and adjust the pressure to compensate for small changes in nozzle output, which can result from nozzle wear. If the output is different from that of a new nozzle by 10 percent or

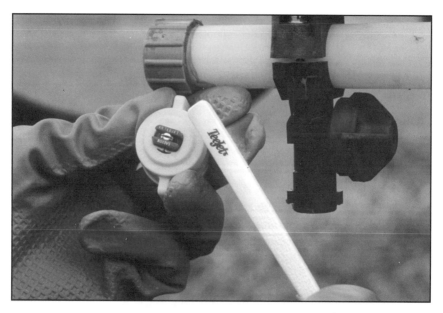

To make sure your nozzles give out an even spray pattern, clean them regularly with a soft brush rather than with abrasive objects such as a knife or wire. An even spray pattern means more effective pest control and less concentration of chemical in strips.

more, replace the nozzle tips and recalibrate. Also, replace the nozzle tips when the spray pattern becomes uneven.

Electronic spray control systems

An electronic spray control system gives you added confidence that your sprayer is properly calibrated. If you input the application rate, speed, and nozzle spacing for each application, the system's monitor can verify the sprayer's accuracy. Some systems can also make adjustments for speed changes. However, an electronic system does not lessen the need to physically calibrate your sprayer, as outlined in this chapter. You still need to put the correct parameters into the electronic spray control systems, and that means calibrating your sprayer.

Prepared with Robert Wolf, pesticide applicator training specialist, UI Extension.

HOW TO MEASURE GROUND SPEED

Speedometer-based systems are unreliable ways to measure ground speed because they do not take wheel slippage in soft areas of the field into consideration. A more accurate way to determine ground speed is to purchase wheel kits that use magnetic sensors on a wheel. Radar and sonar are also accurate methods for measuring ground speed, although they are more expensive than wheel kits.

Keep in mind that even if you use a wheel kit, radar, or sonar, it's important to check these devices for accuracy. It's also important to check ground speed in the field, not on the road or in a lot.

To measure ground speed, follow these steps:

Step 1. Lay out a test course in a field that has similar surface conditions as the field to be sprayed. Suggested distances for your test course are 200 feet for speeds up to 5 mph, 400 feet for speeds from 5 to 10 mph, and at least 500 feet for speeds greater than 10 mph. Longer distances improve the accuracy of the measured speed.

Step 2. At the engine throttle setting and gear that you plan to use while spraying with a loaded sprayer, determine how many seconds it takes you to travel the distance on your test course. Do this again going the other direction. Then add the two travel times and divide by two. This will give you an average travel time.

Step 3. To determine your ground speed, you need to use two numbers. To get the first number, multiply the distance of the test course (in feet) by 60. To get the second number, multiply the travel time (in seconds) by 88. Then divide the first number by the second number. Here is what the equation looks like:

$$\text{Ground speed (mph)} = \frac{D \times 60}{T \times 88}$$

D is the distance of the test course in feet.

T is the average travel time in seconds.

NOTE: For this equation, 1 mph = 88 feet traveled in 60 seconds.

Step 4. Once you decide on a particular ground speed, record the throttle setting and gear used.

Example: You measure a 200-foot course. The first pass takes 22 seconds, and the return trip takes 24 seconds. You add the two travel times and divide by 2. This gives you the average travel time—23 seconds. Knowing the average travel time and distance of the test course, you are ready to use the equation.

$$Ground\ speed\ (mph) = \frac{200 \times 60}{23 \times 88}$$

Calculations

200 x 60 = 12,000

23 x 88 = 2,024

12,000 ÷ 2,024 = 5.9

Ground speed = 5.9 mph

Prepared with Robert Wolf, pesticide applicator training specialist, UI Extension.

55 Consider direct injection and closed handling systems

Why direct injection?

Direct injection offers more precise pesticide application, allows you to change rates on the go, and makes it easy to spot-treat. What's more, you don't have to tank-mix chemicals, and there is no leftover mix.

The key to a direct injection system is that it keeps the pure chemicals separate from the carrier tank. Chemicals are injected into the main sprayer line where they are mixed with carrier and then applied through conventional nozzles.

Direct injection units can be equipped with multiple containers to hold different pesticides. (The number of containers depends on the equipment.) With a flip of the switch, you can move from one pesticide to another on the go, and some systems allow you to apply multiple

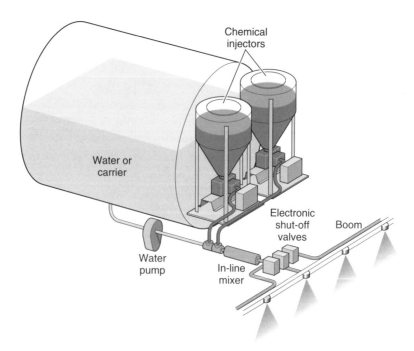

The direct injection system allows you to mix chemicals with water or carrier in the spray boom, not in the tank. That way, you can apply different pesticides to different areas of the field—rather than applying a pesticide mix on the entire field. Direct injection units come with multiple containers to hold different pesticides.
(Illustration adapted with permission of Raven Industries, Inc.)

chemicals at a time. With such features, you can apply pesticides to only the areas that need them, not to the entire field, thus reducing your total chemical use.

Because the spray tank with this system contains only water or some other carrier, you don't have to worry that the residues of one pesticide will interact with the next chemical you put into the tank. Also, direct injection may eliminate the need to mix chemicals, so pesticide compatibility problems may be reduced.

When you are done spraying the field, simply remove the container, make sure it is properly marked, and store it until the next use. By using the same container for the same pesticide, you don't have to worry about leftover chemical, reducing your chances of spilling and exposure. There is no leftover rinsate to deal with and no need to flush or clean the entire rig.

What's available?

Direct injection equipment is available to both the farm-sized market and the commercial applicator market. The type of mixing that occurs in the equipment depends on whether the pesticide is injected before or after the carrier pump. There are two basic systems:

- Pumps that inject the chemical into the spray boom or near the spray nozzle. They use an in-line mixer to properly mix the chemical.
- Pumps that inject the chemical on the suction side of the carrier spray pump. The pump is used to mix the chemicals.

Try to keep the chemical injection line as short as possible. The longer the line, the more potential there is for waste at cleaning time.

Direct injection also works in conjunction with electronic spray controllers. Electronic controllers, which may or may not be computer-based, are designed to automatically compensate for changes in speed and application rates on the go. They offer an even greater precision in pesticide placement. On-line printers are also available to produce a permanent record of what chemicals you used and where you applied them.

Any limitations?

Early direct injection systems had several limitations, including a lag time before the chemical reached the nozzles and improper mixing of the chemical before spraying. In addition, the units were not adapted for wettable powder formulations. However, many of these problems have been solved. Improved metering pump systems have reduced the chemical lag time, in-line mixers have resulted in more uniform mixing, and the addition of agitation devices to mix wettable powders allows the use of a wide variety of formulations.

Considerations and questions

You need to answer several questions before purchasing and installing a direct injection system.

- How many chemicals will need to be injected at one time? Each chemical requires a separate pump and returnable storage container.
- Will any of the injected chemicals need to be mixed? If so, you may need to purchase special agitation devices.
- What chemical carrying capacity will meet your needs? Most companies offer several tank sizes.
- What is the range of your application rates? You need to know this to install a pump that is the right size.
- What types of carrier materials will be used?

Closed handling systems

Direct injection has sometimes been described as a closed handling system, but that is not entirely accurate. With a true closed handling system, the operator has virtually no contact with the chemical as it is loaded into the sprayer. In theory, this could be done with direct injection if you could connect a product's original container to the injection unit. But because of the wide variety of container shapes, sizes, and openings, a direct injection unit cannot accommodate all containers. Therefore, you still may have to transfer chemical from the original container to the injection containers.

True closed handling systems, however, can reduce your exposure to chemicals by 99 percent, according to one study. They also go a long way to reduce the risk of spills during mixing and loading, thus providing environmental protection as well as personal protection.

Closed handling systems come in three basic forms:

Special containers that attach to the applicator. With this system, you can attach insecticide containers directly to the planter so they drain directly into the planter box. A University of Illinois demonstration, conducted in conjunction with *Successful Farming* magazine, found a dramatic reduction in a farmer's exposure to pesticides when using such a system.

Hoses with "drylock" connectors. With drylock connectors, these hoses virtually eliminate leaks and spills as chemical is pumped from a bulk or mini-bulk container into the spray tank. In addition, many of the pumps with these transferring devices are equipped with an electronic meter, which measures out the precise amount of chemical moving into the spray tank. The meter also keeps a running total of all chemical used.

Water-soluble packages. Many chemicals now come in water-soluble bags, which dissolve in the spray tank within minutes. They eliminate pesticide container disposal problems, provide premeasured quantities of chemicals, and reduce exposure to chemicals.

Prepared with Robert Wolf, pesticide applicator training specialist, UI Extension.

Targeting sprays: Just what the doctor ordered

Jerry Nibarger says that sometimes he feels more like a pharmacist than a farmer when he's mixing pesticide sprays.

"It used to be that you measured in gallons of chemical, but now we mix in ounces," says this farmer from Chillicothe, Missouri. "And it used to be that you went for broad coverage of the crop. Today, everything is much more precise."

It's spraying by prescription. But by targeting sprays with greater precision, the payoff is reduced chemical costs, more effective control, and a reduced risk that pesticides will run off into the Grand River, which adjoins some of Nibarger's land.

One of the newest pieces of equipment that Jerry and Diane Nibarger have been using to target sprays is an electrostatic particle sprayer, which they tested for the manufacturer on two plots in 1996. The electrostatic particle sprayer carries a transformer that charges the spray solution with 40,000 volts. By giving the solution a negative charge, the droplets become attracted to the plants, which carry a positive charge. The result is better spray coverage on the plant and possibly reduced chemical rates. It also means less drift because the droplets are looking for something with which to ground.

"We had been getting about 40 percent coverage at best with traditional equipment," Nibarger says, "but the electrostatic particle sprayer gives 75 to 80 percent coverage, according to the manufacturer. It's done an extremely good job of covering the plant."

The electrostatic particle sprayer is an idea that has been tried before—with less positive results. In previous attempts, Nibarger says, the solution was charged either in the main tank or at the boom tips, and neither worked well. With the new system, the solution is charged in an isolation tank, which is insulated from the rest of the machine.

The Nibargers also take the low-volume approach to spraying on their 1,000-acre farm, as well as in their custom application service, which covers more than 10,000 acres per year. Instead of using 10 to 20 gallons of water per acre with the pesticide mix, they use 5 to 7$\frac{1}{2}$ gallons per acre. It's a "hotter" mix, but he says the reduction in water means less runoff and less risk to nearby surface water.

To get the flexibility they want with droplet size, the Nibargers use an extended range flat-fan nozzle. When the crop is under a lot of stress and they need more complete coverage, they go for the finer droplets. But under windy conditions, when the risk of drifting is greatest, they go with the larger droplets and they reduce the pressure.

In addition, the Nibargers use ceramic spray tips, which cost almost twice as much as stainless steel tips. However, the investment has more than paid for itself.

"We had a lot of wear with stainless steel tips," Nibarger points out. "In fact, with stainless steel tips, we were wearing out a set in just one season. But our ceramic tips have not yet shown any wear, although we have broken some. We have been using ceramic tips for four years now and the spray pattern and volume are remaining consistent."

With the ceramic tips, Nibarger says they have much more confidence that the tips at the end of the boom will be putting out basically the same rate of chemical as the tips in the center. But just to make sure that all of the tips are putting out the optimum gallons per minute, the Nibargers check them every 50 machine hours.

As he puts it, "Doing so makes my job as an applicator so much better."

56 | Observe setback zones

Atrazine and setbacks

Atrazine, first registered for use in 1958, has long reigned as one of the most popular herbicides in the Midwest. But atrazine began to take some heat in the 1980s when it started showing up in certain community water supplies, sometimes at levels exceeding health standards.

The result was a manufacturer-initiated change in the label that affected all atrazine-containing products manufactured after August 1, 1992. The new label eliminated some uses, called for reduced application rates, and required the establishment of setback zones—areas around wells, streams, lakes, and tile inlets where atrazine cannot be mixed, loaded, or applied.

Setback zones are not required by pesticide labels other than atrazine and cyanazine (as of 1997). But they still make a lot of sense whenever you are using chemicals that are particularly susceptible to surface runoff. (Chapter 53 helps you determine which pesticides have a high potential for moving with surface runoff).

To give you an idea how much of a setback makes sense for chemicals that have a high runoff potential, consider the following requirements for mixing, loading, or applying atrazine. These are currently the best available setback guidelines.

Also, remember that these are *minimum* setback zones for atrazine. The larger the setback, the more effective it will be.

Mixing/loading setbacks

Atrazine may not be mixed or loaded within 50 feet of any perennial or intermittent stream, natural or impounded lake, sinkhole, or well. (Perennial or intermittent streams are defined on page 278.)

Application setbacks

Setback requirements for applying atrazine vary according to the type of water source being protected. The following setback distances are required around surface-water sources.

Perennial or intermittent streams. Atrazine cannot be applied within 66 feet of the points where field runoff enters perennial or intermittent streams or rivers. In addition, if the 66-foot setback is on highly erodible land, the setback zone must be planted to a crop or seeded with grass or another suitable cover crop.

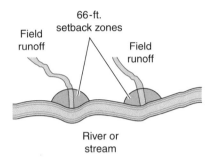

But what if field runoff *doesn't* enter the stream at a specific point? What if runoff flows uniformly over a wide area of the streambank? In these cases, you will have to establish a setback strip alongside the stream.

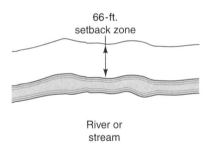

Channelized streams. Channelized streams are waterways that have been straightened or modified in some way. If a naturally flowing stream has a channelized section in the middle of it, the entire stream is subject to the same setback requirements as perennial or intermittent streams.

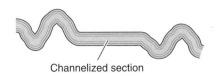

However, if the channelized section is at the *beginning* of the stream, only the naturally flowing portion of the stream is subject to setback requirements.

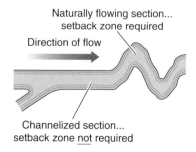

Naturally flowing section...
setback zone required

Direction of flow

Channelized section...
setback zone <u>not</u> required

Lakes or reservoirs. Atrazine cannot be applied within 200 feet of natural or impounded lakes or reservoirs.

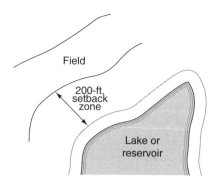

Field

200-ft
setback
zone

Lake or
reservoir

What are perennial and intermittent streams?

When the atrazine label talks about "perennial" streams, it is referring to streams that flow in a natural surface channel all year or for most of the year. This includes most rivers and larger streams.

By "intermittent" steams, the label is referring to streams that flow only during certain periods of the year. This includes "ephemeral streams," which flow only for a short period of time, such as during a rainstorm. Some intermittent and ephemeral streams may not show on a U.S. Geological Survey or USDA Natural Resources Conservation Service (NRCS) map, but they are still covered by atrazine setback requirements.

Special cases

Ditches and grassed waterways. Most ditches and grassed waterways are exempt from atrazine setback requirements. However, a setback zone is necessary if a ditch or grassed waterway discharges water within 50 feet of a well or sinkhole, within 66 feet of a perennial or intermittent stream or river, or within 200 feet of a natural or impounded lake or reservoir.

Establish the setback zone where water from the grassed waterway or ditch enters the well, sinkhole, stream, lake, or reservoir.

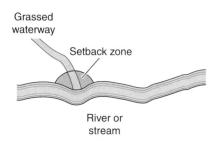

Farm ponds. Natural or constructed farm ponds are exempt from atrazine setback requirements if they meet *all three* of these conditions:

- The pond is located entirely on your property.
- The pond is not used for drinking water by humans.
- Overflow water from the pond does not travel to a stream, lake, or other surface-water impoundment through a clear, traceable, concentrated water course.

In most cases, if the pond doesn't meet any one of these conditions, it is treated as if it were a natural or impounded lake or reservoir, and requires a 200-foot setback.

If the pond meets the first two conditions but not the third, contact the NRCS, Farm Service Agency, or Cooperative Extension Service for assistance. These agencies can help you determine what kind of setback is necessary, according to your field conditions.

Tile surface-water inlets. Field runoff enters subsurface drainage tile through standpipes and other tile surface-water inlets. Subsurface tile, in turn, directs runoff to outlets that sometimes discharge directly into a lake, stream, or river. Atrazine setbacks are required if the outlet discharges within 50 feet of a well or sinkhole, within 66 feet of a perennial or intermittent stream or river, or within 200 feet of a natural or impounded lake or reservoir.

Establish setback zones around each tile surface-water inlet. The size of the setback depends on whether the tile discharges into a sinkhole, well, stream, or lake.

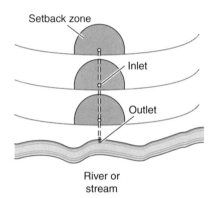

Setback zone

Inlet

Outlet

River or
stream

However, there are a couple of exceptions to this requirement, approved by the EPA in 1997. Applying atrazine within the setback zone is permitted in two instances on *terraced fields* with standpipes and tiled outlets:

- If you immediately incorporate the atrazine into the soil to a depth of 2 to 3 inches in the area drained by the tile inlet.
- If you use no-till or other high crop residue management practices in the area drained by the tile inlet. (By "high crop residue management," the label means that little or no crop residue is destroyed during or after harvest.)

Prepared with Warren Goetsch, chief, Bureau of Environmental Programs, Illinois Department of Agriculture; and George Czapar, integrated pest management educator, UI Extension.

57 Rinse and dispose of chemical containers safely

Empty is not empty

Appearances are deceiving. Empty pesticide containers are not really empty because as much as 2 to 4 ounces of the chemical may remain inside an unrinsed container. That's why an unrinsed container remains an unsafe container and cannot legally be disposed of anywhere but in a hazardous waste landfill.

Rinse containers immediately after emptying them. Otherwise, chemical could dry and cake on the inside, making the container harder to rinse. Also, take special care when rinsing suspension formulas. They tend to settle and harden in the container so you may need to do extra rinsing.

Although the technology is constantly changing and improving, there are currently three basic ways to make sure a liquid pesticide container is properly rinsed: the triple-rinse procedure, the jet-spray system, and the jug-rinsing system.

With proper rinsing, your container can be disposed of in most landfills or other disposal sites.

Triple rinsing

To triple-rinse a container:

1. Empty the container into the spray tank and let it drain for 30 seconds.
2. If the container is designed to hold less than 5 gallons of pesticide, fill it about one-fourth full with clean water. If the container is designed to hold 5 gallons of pesticide or more, fill it one-fifth full with clean water.
3. Shake or swirl the container vigorously to rinse all inside surfaces.
4. Empty rinsate into the spray tank and let it drain for 30 seconds.
5. Repeat the procedure two more times.
6. Puncture the bottom so the container cannot be reused.

Jet spray

Speed is the advantage of jet spraying, or "pressure rinsing," as it is also called. According to Southern Illinois University research, it takes about 2 minutes and 40 seconds to triple-rinse a container. It takes about 65 seconds to rinse a container with jet sprays.

A special pressure rinse nozzle is required to jet-spray, but it can be easily attached to your pumping equipment.

With the jet-spray system, an applicator thrusts a pressure-rinse nozzle through the bottom of a pesticide container. As the container is rinsed (usually for 60 seconds), the rinsate drains into the spray tank.

To jet-spray:

1. Drain the container into the spray tank.
2. While the container is still on the tank, puncture the bottom of the container with the pressure rinse nozzle; then rinse for 60 seconds. The rinsate will drain directly into your spray tank.
3. Allow time to drain; then remove your clean container.

Jug rinsing

With jug rinsing, you do not puncture the container. Instead, you place the jug over a specially designed nozzle, which rinses it with a pressurized stream of fresh water. This system saves time when compared to jet spraying because it takes only 30 seconds to rinse a container. Jug rinsing is also safer because it eliminates the jet-spray puncturing device, which has injured some farmers. However, you should still puncture the bottom so the container cannot be reused.

What to do with container rinse water

Do not dump pesticide container rinse water on the ground. Empty all rinsate into your spray tank and apply it to your fields, *as long as you do not exceed label rates.* If you cannot apply the rinse water without exceeding rates, store it in a rinsate drum for later use as mix water in the spray tank mix.

Disposing of containers

Always follow label directions for disposal and do not reuse pesticide containers for other purposes. What you can do with your containers depends on whether you have liquid formulation containers, bags, or boxes.

Liquid formulation containers. When pesticide containers have been properly rinsed, they are considered nonhazardous material. In most cases, you can dispose of them in a sanitary landfill. Most cases. Not all cases.

Some waste disposal operators will not accept pesticide containers. They do not want to take the risk that the containers were *not* rinsed. But there are a couple of things you can do to make the containers more acceptable.

- Be sure the containers appear as clean as possible.
- Puncture the containers on both ends.

Bags and boxes. Open bagged and boxed chemicals at both ends so the landfill operator can see that they are completely empty.

Disposal alternatives

Keep in mind that there are ways to avoid the disposal dilemma entirely. Here are three options.

Disposable packages. Some packages are designed to dissolve in the tank.

Recycling. Certain areas have recycling programs for pesticide containers. For example, recycling programs in Illinois, Iowa, and other states handle containers that have been pressure-rinsed by farmers. The plastic jugs are collected at county landfills, inspected, and shredded. The plastic chips are then used to create new pesticide containers.

Check with your local agrichemical dealer or state Department of Agriculture for the availability of programs in your area.

Reusable containers. Reusable containers are usually only an option for applicators who use large volumes of pesticide. These "mini-bulk" containers typically hold 15 gallons or more and can be refilled numerous times. Bulk handling of pesticides can also reduce spills and physical contact with the chemicals. You need a separate container for each chemical.

What about burying and burning containers?

The threat to groundwater makes it illegal to bury pesticide containers or other pesticide wastes in some states, including Illinois. Take the rinsed containers to a licensed sanitary landfill instead.

In some areas, it is also illegal to burn pesticide containers or other pesticide wastes. Some pesticides and their containers produce toxic fumes when burned, which may be carried great distances in the smoke. If you live in a state where burning paper containers is allowed (with certain restrictions) and you decide to do it, stay out of the smoke and burn only on the ground where the chemical was applied.

Prepared with Robert Wolf, pesticide applicator training specialist, UI Extension.

58 Dispose of excess chemical safely

Solutions

Excess pesticide solution calls for solutions of a different kind. It calls for practical ideas on how to handle the following material.

Haulback tank mixes. This refers to unused pesticide mixtures left over from spraying operations. Pesticide mixtures may be left over for many reasons: miscalculations, misinformation, or interruptions in the spraying by weather or mechanical breakdown.

Rinse water. This is wastewater generated when you clean residues on the inside of spray tanks or nurse tanks. You need to rinse tanks at the end of each day and whenever you change pesticides, especially when spraying a crop that cannot tolerate the pesticide residues from the previous spraying.

Handling haulback tank mixes

Dealing with haulback tank mixes starts early on in the game. Know the exact area to be treated, calibrate your sprayer, and mix only as much pesticide as you will need. These steps eliminate a lot of disposal and storage worries.

No matter how well you plan, though, you may still end up with excess chemical solution after spraying. If this is the case, apply the remaining solution to a field *as long as it is in accordance with the label.*

Another option is to transfer a full or partial sprayer tank of material to a holding tank. Store the mixture for use at the first opportunity and keep a thorough record of the pesticide concentration in the holding tank. That way, you can consider the effect of this pesticide when making up a new tank solution.

Handling rinse water

When sprayers are empty, they usually still contain anywhere from 2 to 10 gallons (or more) of field-strength spray that cannot be forced out of the boom nozzles. So always flush out your spray tank at the end of the day or whenever you switch to another chemical. One way to do this is shown in the illustration on page 286. Attach a separate tank of clean water to your main spray tank so you can rinse out the tank when the spraying is done.

The rinsate from this procedure can be sprayed on the field as long as you don't exceed label rates.

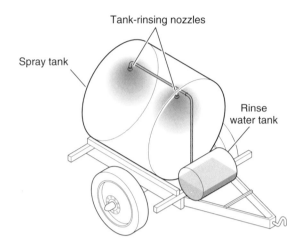

Tank-rinsing nozzles

Spray tank

Rinse
water tank

*Attaching a separate tank of clean water to your main spray tank is an easy,
efficient way to flush out your spray tank at the end of the day or whenever you
switch to another chemical.*

If spraying on the field is not possible, store the rinsate in a holding
tank. The best way to do this is to rinse your spray tank or pesticide
containers on a rinse pad (see Chapter 59). Sumps would then direct the
rinsate to the appropriate holding tank. You should have one rinsate
holding tank for the corn herbicides and another for the soybean herbicides.

The next time you use the same type of chemical, you can use the
appropriate stored rinsate as part of the carrier or mix water. The chemical concentration in the rinsate should be negligible as long as the recycled rinsate does not make up more than 5 to 10 percent of the next
spray mix.

One last point

Consult the pesticide label for suggestions on how to clean the equipment. Some pesticides require cleaning solutions such as ammonia and
water or detergents and water, rather than water alone. However, beware
of potential interactions between cleaning solutions. For example, mixing ammonia and bleach is dangerous because it produces toxic fumes.
So follow directions carefully. Commercial cleaning agents are also
available.

Prepared with Robert Wolf, pesticide applicator training specialist, UI Extension.

59 Construct a rinse pad

Concrete reasons

The most obvious reason for installing a rinse pad is to prevent pesticides from moving off site through leakage or spills. This is important because of both the environmental and financial costs. Some insurance companies do not cover the cost of cleaning up a chemical spill unless it is specifically mentioned in the policy.

A rinse pad reduces legal liability and the chances of being penalized if a chemical spill occurs. It also allows you to recapture and recycle rinse water. In addition, some dealers will not deliver bulk fertilizer or chemicals unless you have a rinse pad.

Design ideas

There are many ways to design a rinse pad, but the best of them follow common guidelines.

- Locate the pad away from surface water and wells.
- Construct the pad from watertight concrete.

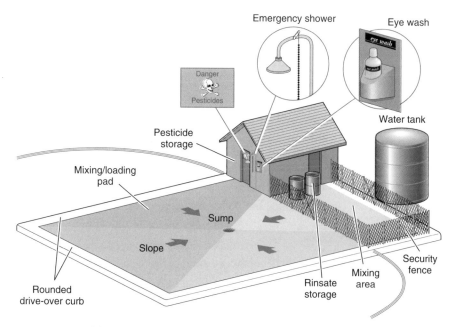

Rinse pad for a small-scale, drive-across facility

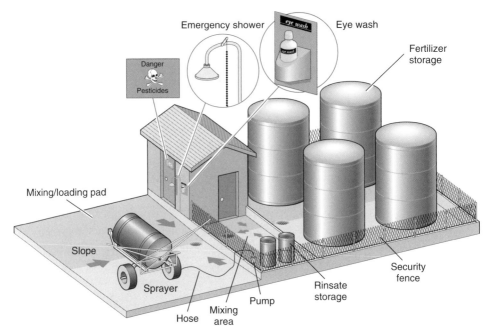

Emergency shower eye wash Eye wash

Danger ☠ Pesticides

Fertilizer storage

Mixing/loading pad

Slope

Sprayer

Hose   Mixing area   Pump

Rinsate storage

Security fence

Rinse pad for a medium-sized facility

- Make sure the pad is large enough to hold your largest application vehicle.
- Design the pad so it slopes to the center and contains floor drains that lead to sumps. Sumps collect spills and rinse water, and they transfer the liquid to above-ground rinsate tanks.
- If possible, do not locate the pad in an area where mixing and loading have been done in the past. Constructing a pad in such an area might seal soil that is contaminated. If the pad must be located in an area where mixing and loading have been done, test the soil for contamination at several depths. If the test shows residual pesticide in the soil, remove the contaminated layer of soil before installing the concrete pad. This will help you avoid liability problems in the future.
- Locate pumps and piping above ground and within the rinse-pad area.
- Make sure there is a level area for storage tanks at the back of the pad.
- Enclose the storage tanks with a low, concrete dike. Dikes should be big enough to contain an amount that is at least 10 percent greater than the volume held by the largest rinse-water tank. That way, the dike will be able to contain a serious leak.

- Store the various rinsates of incompatible chemicals in separate containers.

- Label rinsate storage tanks carefully so you don't mix incompatible chemicals.

- Be sure rinsate tanks are small enough to encourage the rapid reuse of rinsate material.

- Mount rinsate storage tanks 3 to 5 inches above the concrete floor. This allows you to spot leaks more easily.

- Keep undiluted fertilizers in a different containment area than undiluted pesticides. Each area should have a separate sump as well. You can divide fertilizers from pesticides with a concrete subdividing wall.

- For security and safety, enclose the undiluted chemicals with a fence and locked gate. If chemicals need to be protected from weather, keep them in a weatherproof shed.

Special note

These guidelines are aimed at small- and medium-sized farms. In certain states, some large farms are required to meet specific regulations. Before constructing any rinse pad, large or small, check with your Cooperative Extension Service office, state Department of Agriculture, or environmental agency to find out about state requirements.

Prepared with Robert Wolf, pesticide applicator training specialist, UI Extension.

60 Dispose of other farm waste safely

Sources of waste

How's this for a nightmare? For the past 40 years, local folks have dumped trash on the property of an Illinois farmer. Now, not only does this farmer need to figure out how to make them stop, he needs to spend $5,000 to $10,000 to clean the mess or risk possible fines up to $50,000.

As this example illustrates, there's more to hazardous waste on a farm besides pesticides. In fact, a typical farm contains many other forms of waste that not only risk possible financial burdens but may pose a threat to your health and to surface water.

In addition to pesticides, the two main sources of hazardous waste that you should be concerned about are from farm equipment and from paints and solvents. For example, a hazard can arise when you leave old equipment on your land so you can salvage parts from it. Quite often, the batteries and oil are left to rot in these abandoned vehicles. Lead-acid batteries can contain 18 pounds of toxic metals and 1 gallon of corrosive, lead-contaminated acids. If the equipment corrodes, these chemicals can contaminate soil and may find their way into nearby surface water.

Farm equipment

Motor oil. The used oil from a single oil change can seriously contaminate a *million gallons* of fresh water—enough water to supply fifty people for one year. Used motor oil contains several organic chemicals and metals. Although most waste oil is produced by automobiles and industry, farmers still have reason to be concerned. A typical farmer buys an average of 50 gallons of motor oil each year.

Used oil should never be mixed with *any* farm chemicals under any circumstances. Some states have banned the disposal of used oil in landfills, so your best option is to recycle your oil. Contact common recycling sites such as local oil distributors, auto repair stations, and commercial recycling services; or call the Cooperative Extension Service to find recyclers in your area. When storing oil before recycling, be sure it is in a sealed container such as a steel drum or plastic jug. Make sure the container is clean.

Some states allow you to burn used oil in a used-oil fired space heater—but only under certain conditions. Check with the state environmental agency to find out when this is allowed.

Oil filters. An oil filter, even after being drained overnight, still contains significant amounts of motor oil. The best option is to "hot-drain" filters by puncturing the dome end and draining them overnight (12 hours). Oil should be drained when the air temperature is 60°F or higher.

After hot-draining the filter, place it in a sealable plastic bag, a coffee can with lid, or another leakproof container. Some states have banned oil filters from landfills, so you may have to take them to a hazardous waste collection site. If a hazardous waste collection site is not close enough, check with local oil distributors or an auto repair station. They may accept filters for free or for a modest charge.

Antifreeze. Antifreeze can be very dangerous because its sweet taste attracts animals and small children. Five tablespoons of antifreeze can kill a 25-pound dog.

Because of personal and environmental risks, do not pour antifreeze out in the yard or into a storm sewer, stream, lake, or river. Also, do not mix it with used oil. Your first step should be to find out if the store that sells the antifreeze will take back the used product. You might also contact a local service station or an automotive or radiator repair shop to find out if they can dispose of or recycle the waste.

Your next option is to contact the nearest recycling operation. If that doesn't work, try your local wastewater treatment plant. Some wastewater treatment and disposal plants that used to accept antifreeze don't accept it any longer. So check with your local plant to make sure.

A new antifreeze on the market uses propylene glycol, which toxicology studies show to be three to four times *less toxic* than the ethylene glycol traditionally used in antifreeze. But it is not entirely nontoxic, so take the same precautions with it.

Fuels. Uncontaminated gasoline can be used up in engines. But if the gasoline is contaminated, you should contact the Cooperative Extension Service or hazardous waste agency to determine a proper disposal method.

Gasoline can become contaminated when used as a solvent for cleaning tools. Therefore, consider cleaning tools with kerosene, diesel fuel, or other solvents because these products can often be mixed with motor oil and then recycled. (Check with your recycling center first.)

Do not leave fuel stored in small containers for a long time—such as over the winter. The fuel decays over time.

Batteries. As mentioned earlier, old batteries should not be abandoned and left to corrode. Also, do not dispose of lead-acid batteries at a landfill; it's illegal in some states.

Lead-acid batteries can be recycled. You should be able to trade in your old battery at the store where you bought it or at the store where you are purchasing your new battery. Otherwise, you may be able to have batteries recycled at such places as service stations, auto parts stores, auto parts warehouses, discount stores, and junkyards. Contact your Extension office for recycling locations.

Tires. Tires take up a lot of space in landfills, attract insects (such as mosquitoes), and can result in devastating fires. In some states, whole scrap tires are no longer allowed in landfills.

Farmers are allowed to accumulate no more than 20 tires on their property, and these must be from agricultural activities. Tire piles should be kept dry or shredded or chopped so they cannot hold water.

The most common way to get rid of old tires is to turn them in to the retailer when purchasing new ones. Most retailers will then make sure the tires are recycled or remanufactured into retreads. Tires can also be shredded for use in paving or recreational surface materials. Contact your state environmental agency for more information.

Cleaners, solvents, and paints

Cleaners and solvents. Seal used cleaners and solvents in a jar until the particles settle out. Then strain the substance left in the bottom of the jar. That way, you can reuse the cleaner or solvent. Add an absorbent such as cat litter to the remaining residue and let it dry completely. Before you do this, however, make sure you know where you can dispose of the dried residue. For ideas, contact a garbage collection service, a hazardous waste collection program, or a local or state environmental control agency.

Paints. It is ideal if you can use up paint in a manner consistent with label instructions. If you are unable to use it all, donate it to friends, relatives, churches, recreation departments, community service organizations, or theatrical groups.

If this is not an option, check with recycling centers or hazardous waste collection sites or contact the state environmental agency for disposal ideas. Your last resort is evaporation. Evaporate *water-based* paints in a secure, outdoor area away from flames, children, and animals. Water-based paints can also be solidified using sand, sawdust, cat litter, or dirt as an absorbent material. Take the solid residue and dispose of it in a landfill.

Do *not* dry out oil-based paint because the fumes are hazardous. Also, do not put oil-based paints in the trash. Use them up or take them to a hazardous waste collection site.

Wood preservatives. Do not solidify, burn, or bury leftover wood preservative. Also, never burn any wood that has been treated with wood preservative. The best option is to keep wood preservatives in a secure container and wait until a household hazardous waste collection day is held in your area.

Guidelines

There are too many chemicals, compounds, and substances on a farm to cover them all in this book, but the following are some general guidelines when using any product.

- Always read the label and follow all usage and disposal instructions.
- Buy only the amount you need.
- Try to use up the leftover portion, but only if needed for the job.
- If you have some leftover product, give it to neighbors, friends, or community groups who need it—but only if the product is in its original container.
- Store drums that contain hazardous waste on pallets in a secure, dry, well-ventilated area. This will make it easier to spot leaks and will discourage rust and corrosion.
- Never bury waste or dump waste in a ditch or field. You also shouldn't burn waste, although sometimes the product label allows burning under certain conditions.
- Find out whether your community has hazardous waste collection days. If it doesn't, talk to neighbors about proposing a collection program.
- For information on how to start a recycling or collection program, contact the nearest Cooperative Extension Service office.

Prepared with Dan Kraybill, technical assistance engineer, Illinois Hazardous Waste Research and Information Center.

For more information

U.S. Environmental Protection Agency

Drinking water branch offices

REGION 1
Boston, MA
(617)565-3610

REGION 2
New York, NY
(212)637-3886

REGION 3
Philadelphia, PA
(215)566-2315

REGION 4
Atlanta, GA
(404)562-9329

REGION 5
Chicago, IL
(312)353-2147

REGION 6
Dallas, TX
(214)665-7115

REGION 7
Kansas City, KS
(913)551-7023

REGION 8
Denver, CO
(303)312-6627

REGION 9
San Francisco, CA
(415)744-1851

REGION 10
Seattle, WA
(206)553-1224

Liaisons to the USDA Natural Resources Conservation Service

REGION 1
Boston, MA
(617)565-1554

REGION 2
New York, NY
(212)637-3700

REGION 3
Philadelphia, PA
(215)597-3425

REGION 4
Atlanta, GA
(404)347-2126

REGION 5
Chicago, IL
(312)353-7979

REGION 6
Dallas, TX
(214)665-8081

REGION 7
Kansas City, KS
(913)551-7422

REGION 8
Denver, CO
(303)312-6070

REGION 9
San Francisco, CA
(415)744-1983

REGION 10
Seattle, WA
(503)414-3014

USDA Cooperative Extension Service

State watershed contacts

ALABAMA
Auburn University
Auburn
(334)844-3973

ALASKA
University of Alaska
Anchorage
(907)279-6575

ARIZONA
Maricopa Agricultural Center
Maricopa
(520)568-2273

ARKANSAS
University of Arkansas
Little Rock
(501)671-2168

CALIFORNIA
University of California
Riverside
(909)787-4327

COLORADO
Colorado State University
Fort Collins
(970)491-6328

CONNECTICUT
University of Connecticut
Storrs
(860)486-5428

DELAWARE
University of Delaware
Newark
(302)831-2531

FLORIDA
University of Florida
Gainesville
(352)392-1951

GEORGIA
University of Georgia
Athens
(706)542-9072

HAWAII
University of Hawaii
Honolulu
(808)956-8397

IDAHO
University of Idaho
Moscow
(208)885-7025

ILLINOIS
University of Illinois
at Urbana-Champaign
Urbana
(217)333-9410

INDIANA
Purdue University
West Lafayette
(317)494-8049

IOWA
Iowa State University
Ames
(515)294-1923

KANSAS
Kansas State University
Manhattan
(913)532-5813

KENTUCKY
University of Kentucky
Lexington
(606)257-4633

LOUISIANA
Louisiana Cooperative
Extension Service
Baton Rouge
(504)388-6998

MAINE
University of Maine
Orono
(207)581-3241

MARYLAND
University of Maryland
College Park
(301)405-1306

MASSACHUSETTS
University of
Massachusetts
Amhurst
(413)545-0143

MICHIGAN
Extension Service
East Lansing
(517)353-9222

MINNESOTA
University of Minnesota
St. Paul
(612)625-4756

MISSISSIPPI
Mississippi Energy
Extension Center
Mississippi State
University
Starkville
(601)325-3152

MISSOURI
University of Missouri
Columbia
(573)882-0085

MONTANA
Montana State University
Bozeman
(406)994-5683

NEBRASKA
University of Nebraska
Water Center
Lincoln
(402)472-3305

NEVADA
Nevada Cooperative
Extension
Las Vegas
(702)795-0767

NEW HAMPSHIRE
University of New Hampshire
Durham
(603)862-1067

NEW JERSEY
Rutgers Cooperative
Extension
New Brunswick
(908)932-8264

NEW MEXICO
New Mexico State University
Las Cruces
(505)646-1131

NEW YORK
Cornell University
Ithaca
(607)255-3131

NORTH CAROLINA
North Carolina State
University
Raleigh
(919)515-6767

NORTH DAKOTA
North Dakota State
University
Fargo
(701)231-7236

OHIO
Ohio State University
Columbus
(614)292-6007

OKLAHOMA
Oklahoma State
University
Stillwater
(405)744-8414

OREGON
Oregon State University
Corvallis
(541)737-6295

PENNSYLVANIA
Pennsylvania State
University
University Park
(814)863-0291

RHODE ISLAND
University of Rhode
Island
Kingston
(401)874-2903

SOUTH CAROLINA
Clemson University
Clemson
(864)656-3384

SOUTH DAKOTA
South Dakota State
University
Brookings
(605)688-5144

TENNESSEE
University of Tennessee
Knoxville
(423)974-7306

TEXAS
Texas Agricultural
Extension Service
College Station
(409)845-5366

UTAH
Utah State University
Logan
(801)797-2786

VERMONT
University of Vermont
Montpelier
(802)223-2389

VIRGINIA
Virginia Polytech University
Blacksburg
(540)231-5995

WASHINGTON
Washington State Univer-
sity
Pullman
(509)335-2914

WEST VIRGINIA
West Virginia University
Morgantown
(304)293-2219

WISCONSIN
University of Wisconsin
Madison
(608)262-1916

WYOMING
University of Wyoming
Laramie
(307)766-5479

USDA Natural Resources Conservation Service

State offices

ALABAMA
Auburn
(334)887-4574

ALASKA
Anchorage
(907)271-2424

ARIZONA
Phoenix
(602)280-8787

ARKANSAS
Little Rock
(501)324-6618

CALIFORNIA
Davis
(916)757-8255

COLORADO
Lakewood
(303)236-2886

CONNECTICUT
Storrs
(860)487-4017

DELAWARE
Dover
(302)678-4180

FLORIDA
Gainesville
(352)338-9506

GEORGIA
Athens
(706)546-2272

HAWAII
Honolulu
(808)541-3415

IDAHO
Boise
(208)378-5702

ILLINOIS
Champaign
(217)398-5379

INDIANA
Indianapolis
(317)290-3220

IOWA
Des Moines
(515)284-4371

KANSAS
Salina
(913)823-4547

KENTUCKY
Lexington
(606)224-7357

LOUISIANA
Alexandria
(318)473-7755

MAINE
Orono
(207)866-7249

MARYLAND
Annapolis
(410)757-0861

MASSACHUSETTS
Amherst
(413)253-4362

MICHIGAN
Lansing
(517)335-6967

MINNESOTA
St. Paul
(612)290-3670

MISSISSIPPI
Jackson
(601)965-4337

MISSOURI
Columbia
(573)876-0912

MONTANA
Bozeman
(406)587-6855

NEBRASKA
Lincoln
(402)437-4037

NEVADA
Reno
(702)784-5208

NEW HAMPSHIRE
Durham
(603)868-7581

NEW JERSEY
Somerset
(908)246-4110

NEW MEXICO
Albuquerque
(505)761-4448

NEW YORK
Syracuse
(315)477-6504

NORTH CAROLINA
Raleigh
(919)873-2133

NORTH DAKOTA
Bismarck
(701)250-4431

OHIO
Columbus
(614)469-6932

OKLAHOMA
Stillwater
(405)742-1278

OREGON
Portland
(503)414-3204

TENNESSEE
Nashville
(615)736-5873

WASHINGTON
Spokane
(509)353-2348

PENNSYLVANIA
Harrisburg
(717)782-3446

TEXAS
Temple
(817)774-1360

WEST VIRGINIA
Morgantown
(304)291-4152

RHODE ISLAND
Warwick
(401)828-8816

UTAH
Salt Lake City
(801)524-5025

WISCONSIN
Janesville
(608)755-2187

SOUTH CAROLINA
Columbia
(803)253-3314

VERMONT
Winooski
(802)951-6796

WYOMING
Casper
(307)261-6464

SOUTH DAKOTA
Huron
(605)352-1200

VIRGINIA
Richmond
(804)287-1663

Other sources of information

Conservation Technology Information Center (CTIC)

1220 Potter Drive, Room 170
West Lafayette, IN 47906
(765)494-9555
FAX: (765)494-5969
E-mail: ctic@ctic.purdue.edu
Website: http://www.ctic.purdue.edu/CTIC.html

Operates Monday through Friday, 7 a.m. to 4 p.m., Central Time.
Provides information about tillage practices and watershed management to the general public.

National Pesticide Telecommunications Network

Agricultural Chemistry Extension
Oregon State University
333 Weniger Hall
Corvallis, OR 97331-6502
(800)858-PEST
FAX: (541)737-0761

Operates Monday through Friday, 8:30 a.m. to 6:30 p.m., Central Time.
Provides information about pesticides to the general public and to the medical, veterinary, and professional communities.

Rinse pad designs

For more information about rinse pad designs, contact the following sources. If you cannot reach any of these sources, try contacting your area Extension agent or local land grant university.

MidWest Plan Service
122 Davidson Hall
Iowa State University
Ames, IA 50011-3080
(515)294-4337

David Kammel
University of Wisconsin
Biological Systems Engineering
Department
460 Henry Mall
Madison, WI 53706-1561
(608)262-9776

American Crop Protection Association
1156 15th Street NW
Suite 400
Washington, DC 20005
(202)296-1585

Agricultural Retailers Association
11701 Borman Drive
St. Louis, MO 63146
(314)567-6655

Safe Drinking Water Hotline

(800)426-4791
Operates Monday through Friday, 8 a.m. to 4:30 p.m., Central Time. Provides information on drinking-water contaminants, including possible health effects and contamination sources. Also makes referrals for water-testing laboratories in your area.

Scouting equipment

The following items can help you collect data fast and accurately. The well-prepared field scout should have access to these tools at all times.

Beat cloth
Clip board
County maps
Discarded film canisters
Forceps
Hand counter
10X hand lens
Hand trowel
Isopropyl alcohol
KAAD preservative
Measuring tape or wheel (50 feet)
Paper bags

Pencils
Pill boxes
Plastic bags
Pocket knife
Salt tablets
Sampling frame
Shovel
Survey forms
Sweep-net—15-inch-diameter
Vials
Wide mouth jars
Writing materials

Some of the specialized specimen-collecting tools listed on page 301 are available from the following companies.

VWR Scientific Products
800 E. Fabyan Parkway
Batavia, IL 60510
(800)234-5227
FAX: (630)879-6718

BioQuip Products
17803 LaSalle Avenue
Gardena, CA 90248
(310)324-0620
FAX: (310)324-7931

Carolina Biological Supply Co.
2700 York Road
Burlington, NC 27215
(910)584-0381
FAX: (910)584-3399

Edmund Scientific Co.
101 E. Gloucester Pike
Barrington, NJ 08007
FAX: (609)573-6295
Education Department:
(609)573-6270

Great Lakes IPM
10220 Church Road, NE
Vestaburg, MI 48891
(517)268-5693
FAX: (413)549-3930

Nasco-Fort Atkinson
901 Janesville Ave.
P.O. Box 901
Fort Atkinson, WI 53538-0901
(414)563-2446
(800)558-9595
FAX: (414)563-8296
(Nasco also offers soil conservation equipment, such as levels, tripods, and surveyor's capes.)

Ward's Natural Science
Establishment, Inc.
(East coast facility)
P.O. Box 92912
Rochester, NY 14692
(716)359-2502
FAX: (716)334-6174
Toll free number: (800)962-2660,
Monday through Friday, 7 a.m. to
6:30 p.m., Central Time
24-hour FAX ordering:
(800)635-8439

Related publications

MidWest Plan Service

The Midwest Plan Service (MWPS) is an organization of Extension and research agricultural engineers from the 12 states of the north central region, plus representatives of the USDA. The purpose of MWPS publications is to solve agricultural problems common to the region using fundamental engineering principles. The following publications provide additional information on topics discussed in this book.

Private Water Systems (MWPS-14), 72 pages $7.00

Livestock Waste Facilities (MWPS-18), 112 pages $8.00

Onsite Domestic Sewage Disposal (MWPS-24), 40 pages $6.00

Farm Buildings Wiring (MWPS-28), 68 pages $10.00

Designing Facilities for Pesticide and Fertilizer
   Containment (MWPS-37), 120 pages $15.00

Conservation Tillage Systems and Management
   (MWPS-45), 144 pages $15.00

To obtain copies, write to MWPS, 122 Davidson Hall, Iowa State University, Ames, IA 50011-3080; call (800)562-3618 or (515)294-4337 or fax (515)294-9589. Make checks payable to *MWPS*. In Illinois, write to MWPS, University of Illinois, Agricultural Engineering Department, 1304 West Pennsylvania Avenue, Urbana IL 61801; call (217)333-7964 or fax (217)244-0323. Make checks payable to the *University of Illinois*.

Also, be sure to add the following shipping and handling costs (these figures apply whether you order from the Iowa or Illinois office):

For orders under $15 .... add $3.50

For orders from $15 to $24.99 .... add $4.50

For orders from $25.00 to $74.99 .... add $5.50

For orders from $75.00 to $199.99 .... add $9.00

For orders over $200.00 .... call for information

University of Illinois publications

The Design, Application, and Maintenance of Contouring
and Contour Stripcropping, 102 pages $6.00

The Design, Construction, and Maintenance of
Grass Waterways, 66 pages $5.30

Designing, Implementing, and Controlling Mulch-till Systems, 272 pages . . $15.00

Designing, Implementing, and Controlling No-till Systems, 240 pages $14.00

Field Crop Scouting Manual, 280 pages $30.00

Illinois Agronomy Handbook (published every two years), 240 pages $10.00

The Land & Water series . . . . $.80 each

1. From Dust Bowl to Mud Bowl: The Erosion Problem, 6 pages

2. T by 2000: Illinois Erosion-Control Goals, 6 pages

3. Raindrops and Bombs: The Erosion Process, 4 pages

4. A Plan for the Land: Erosion-Control Alternatives, 6 pages

5. What Price Conservation? The Economics of Soil Conservation (out of print)

6. Returning to Grass-Roots: Hay and Pasture Establishment, 6 pages

7. The Land Under Cover: Hay and Pasture Management, 6 pages

8. Hay That Pays: Hay Marketing, 6 pages

9. The Residue Dimension: Managing Residue for Conservation and Profit, 20 pages

10. Maximum Control in Minimum Till: Economical Weed, Insect, and Disease Control in Reduced Tillage, 8 pages

11. Ridging: The Pros and Cons of Ridge Till, 4 pages

12. Pesticides and Groundwater: Pesticides as Potential Pollutants, 4 pages

13. Water Quality and the Hydrologic Cycle: How Water Movement Affects Water Quality, 4 pages

14. Planning Your Well: Guidelines for Safe, Dependable Drinking Water, 12 pages (available March 1998)

15. Septic Systems: Operation and Maintenance of On-Site Sewage Disposal Systems, 8 pages (available June 1998)

17. Safe Drinking Water: Testing and Treating Home Drinking Water, 20 pages (available March 1998)

18. Community Water: How Local Communities Can Protect Their Groundwater, 16 pages

19. Bottled Water: Crystal Clear Choice or Cloudy Dilemma?, 12 pages

To order by VISA or MasterCard, call (800)345-6087 or fax (217)333-0005. Make checks payable to the University of Illinois and mail orders to: Information Technology and Communication Services, Taft House, 1401 South Maryland Drive, Urbana, IL 61801. Be sure to add the following shipping and handling charges:

For orders under $25 . . . . add $2.50

For orders from $25 to $99.99 . . . . add $4.00

For orders from $100 to $199.99 . . . . add $6.00

For orders over $200 . . . . add $6.00 plus $2.00 for each additional $100

Index

Index

NOTE: Page numbers in italics refer to figures.
Tables and tabular sidebars are identified by (table) after the page number.

action threshold. *See* economic (action) threshold
adjuvants, 231
alfalfa
  common insect pests of, 67, 204 (table), 209 (table)
  insect-resistant varieties of, 209 (table)
  manure application on, 179
  as pasture plants, 66
  rotation of, 212 (table)
alfalfa weevils, 204 (table), 209 (table)
algae growth, prevention of, 129, 165
allelopathy, definition of, 47, 52
ammonium acetate exchangeable K test, 135
ammonium nitrate, 142, 147
anhydrous ammonia, 142
antifreeze, disposal of, 291
aphids, 209 (table)
armyworms, 201 (table), 212 (table), 245
atrazine, 223, 231, 232, 276-280

Bacillus thuringiensis (Bt), 206, 250
bait stations, for insects, 195, 215
banding (band application), 243,264
batteries, disposal of, 291-292
bean leaf beetles, 203 (table), 208 (table)
beat (ground) cloths, 192
beneficial insects, preservation of, 218-222, *220-221*
benomyl (fungicide), 251
biennial sweet clover, 242
big-eyed bugs, *220*
bird habitat, preservation of, 156
black cutworms, 189, 195, 197, 202 (table), 212 (table)
black nightshade, 229
Blackwater River (Missouri), 127
blow-outs, definition of, 120, 122
blue alfalfa aphids, 209 (table)
bovine leptospirosis, prevention of, 156
brassicas, as pasture plants, 61, 61 (table)
Bray P-1 test, 135, 165
broad-base terraces, 101, *102*
broadcasting
  of fertilizers, 143, 147
  of herbicides, 243
  of pesticides, 264
broadleaf weeds, impact on yield, 225, 227 (table)

buffer strips, 89, 99, 128, 156
butt systems, 94, 94

calibration
  of pesticide sprayers, 264-267
  of manure application equipment, 182-184, 184 (table)
Campylobacter jejeuni, 162 (table)
cedar trees, as streambank revetments, *124*, 124-125
chaff, distribution of, 7
chaff spreaders, 7, *7*
channelization, of rivers and streams, 123, 127-128, 277-278
checks, of waterways, 80, 81, *81*
chemicals, disposal of, 290-293. *See also* safety, for handling pesticides
Chinese praying mantis, *220*
chisel plowing (chisel plows)
  avoidance of, 11-12
  residue preservation with, 36-37, *37*, 39
chlorophyll meters, 135
chutes, 106, *106*
cleaners and solvents, disposal of, 292
closed handling systems, for pesticides, 272-273
Coast Guard, correction signals from, 149
cocklebur, 227 (table), 232
codling moth *(Laspeyresia pomonella), 200*
Colorado potato beetle *(Leptinofarsa decemlineata), 200*
combination tools, residue preservation with, 38
commercial radio stations, correction signals from, 149
common damsel bugs, *220*
common green lacewings, *220*
common milkweed, 238
composting, of manure, 165-166
Conservation Reserve Program, 89
Conservation Technology Information Center (CTIC), 13, 300
conservation tillage. *See* mulch-till farming; no-till farming
constructed wetlands, 89-90
contour farming
  benefits of, 76, 91
  buffer strips in, 99
  field borders for, 93, 97

contour farming (cont.)
  key lines for, *92*, 92-93, 95, *96*
  maximum slope lengths for, 91-92, 91
    (table), 95, 95 (table)
  standard techniques for, *93*, 93-94, *94*
  stripcropping in, 95-98, *96, 97*
control basins. *See* water and sediment control
  basins
convergent lady beetles, *220*
Cooperative Extension Service, USDA, 54, 59,
  66, 67, 126, 175, 176, 199, 201, 206,
  218, 279, 289, 290, 291, 293, 297-298
corn
  common insect pests of, *200*, 201-
    202 (table)
  insect-resistant varieties of, 207 (table)
  no-till farming of, 13, *14, 15*
  recommendations for nitrogen on,
    134 (table)
  residue levels of, *31*
  rotation of, 212 (table)
  scouting weeds in, 228
  as volunteer (weed), 226 (table)
corn billbugs, 212 (table)
corn leaf aphids, 201 (table)
corn rootworms, 51, 189, 196-197, 201
  (table), 207 (table), 210, 212 (table)
cornstalk testing, for nitrogen, 134-135
coulter-chisel plows, residue preservation
  with, 37
coulters, residue preservation with, 39-40, *40*
cover crops. *See also* surface cover
  benefits of, 18, 46, 49, 210-211, 245
  planting of, 46-49
  residue from, 49
  types of, 46-48
  weed control by, 47, 49, 245-246
crabgrass, 236
creeks. *See* rivers and streams
critical area plantings, 87-88
crop rotation
  benefits of, 50-52
  in contour stripcropping, 95, 211
  insect control by, 51, 210-211, 212-213
    (table)
  types of, 50
  weed control and, 51, 232, 238-242
  yield improvements with, 50
crop-oil concentrates, 231
crops
  aggressive weed competition from, 236-237
  fertilization of, 137-138, 145-146
  impact of manure application on, 186
  insect-related injury to, 190-191, *191*, 192
  insect-resistant varieties of, 205-206,
    207-209 (table)

nutrient needs of, 179
  setting yield goals for, 130-131
Cryptosporidium parvum, 161, 162 (table)
cultivation. *See* field cultivators
cutworms. *See* black cutworms
cyanazine, 276

denitrification, 85, 145, 186
Departments of Agriculture, state, 283, 289
direct injection, 270-272
disease control
  by crop rotation, 51
  by fall tillage, 11
disk-chisel plows, residue preservation
  with, 37
disks (disking)
  application of manure with, 185
  residue preservation with, 38
  types of, 38
ditches, setback zones around, 279
diversions
  construction of, 113
  maintenance of, 113
  placement of, 92, 95, 108
  planning of, 112-113
  purpose of, 112
  of feedlot runoff, 163-164
  to protect waterways, 80, *80*
drag-hose injection, of manure, 186
drainage systems
  benefits of, 119
  subsurface, 120-121
  surface, 121
drainage tiles, 80, 85, 89, 101, *101*, 120,
  279-280
drinking troughs, 160
drinking water
  contamination of, 3, 161
  for livestock, 158-159, 160

early spring nitrate-N test, 133
earthworms, 251, 252 (table)
economic injury level (EIL), for pests, 198,
  200, 248-250
economic (action) threshold (ET)
  for insects, 198-201, *200*, 201-204
    (table), 216, 219
  for weeds, 224-226
electric fencing, 67, 157
electronic (pesticide) spray control
  systems, 267
electrostatic particle sprayer, 274
Environmental Protection Agency (EPA),
  U.S., 2, 280, 296
equilibrium position (EP), of insects, *200*

erosion
  declining rates of, 2, 5
  estimation of rate of, 34-35
  impact of contour farming on, 76, 91
  impact of crop rotation on, 51
  impact of cultivation on, 243
  by livestock, 156
  pollution from, 2-3
  types of, 9-10
European corn borers, 199, 202 (table), 206, 207 (table), 250

fall application
  of manure, 186-187
  of nitrogen, 145
fall panicum, 238-240
fall tillage, avoidance of, 11-12
Farm Buildings Wiring (MidWest Plan Service), 159
farm equipment
  disposal of hazardous wastes from, 290-292
  prevention of soil compaction with, 74-76
  residue distribution with, 6-8
  residue preservation with, 36-41, 36 (table)
  for spreading manure, 182-183, 184 (table)
farm ponds. *See also* holding ponds
  benefits of, 114, 117-118
  installation of, 114-115
  as livestock water source, 158
  maintenance of, 116
  planning (design) of, 115
  setback zones around, 116, 279
Farm Service Agency, 279
fencing (of livestock)
  benefits of, 70, 116, 118, 156-157
  options for, 67, 157-158
  in paddocks, 65, 157
fertilizer. *See also* nutrients
  in grassed waterways, 83
  in pastures, 67
  philosophies for use of, 137-138
  replacement by cover crops, 46
  residue preservation with attachments for, 41
  selection of, 141-144
field borders
  insect invasions of, *194*
  use of, 93, 97, 103
field corn. *See* corn
Field Crop Scouting Manual (University of Illinois), 190, 201, 229

field cultivators
  and herbicide use, 242, 243-244
  residue preservation with, 38, 39
  types of, 244
filters. *See* vegetative filter strips
fish habitat, preservation of, 156
forage. *See* grazing; pasture plants
foxtail, 226 (table), 236, *239*
fuels, disposal of, 291
fungicides, impact on earthworms, 251

genetic engineering, 205-206
giant foxtail, 226 (table), *239*
giant ragweed, 227 (table)
Giardia lamblia, 161, 162 (table)
global positioning system (GPS)
  accuracy of, 149
  cost of, 151-152
  environmental impact of, 150-151
  fertilizer application with, 148-152, 153
  herbicide application with, 150
  primary uses of, 150
  processing of information by, *148*, 149
  soil testing with, 131, 132, 150, 153
  yield monitoring with, 17, 130, 150, 153-154
grade. *See* grade control structures; slopes
grade control structures
  benefits of, 105
  in grassed waterways, 80
  installation of, 107-108
  maintenance of, 108
  types of, 105-106
grape colaspis, 212 (table), 213 (table)
grassed waterways. *See* waterways, grassed
grassed-back-slope terraces, 102, *102*
grasses
  application of manure on, 186
  as cover crop, 46-47
  critical area plantings of, 87
  general forage characteristics of, 57 (table)
  as pasture plants, 54-56, 55 (table), 59, 59 (table), 60, 60 (table), 61, 61 (table)
  periodic burning of, 88
  response to soil drainage characteristics, 56 (table)
grasses
  in vegetative filter strips, 86-87
  as weeds, impact on yield, 225, 226 (table)
grasshoppers, 202 (table), 203 (table), 216
grazing
  annual plants for, 58-61

grazing (cont.)
  avoidance in timberland, 70
  in critical area plantings, 88
  pasture renovation for, 66-67
  perennial plants for, 53-57
  rotational, 62-65, *63*, 67
green cloverworm *(Plathypena scabra)*, *191*,
    200
grid sampling, 153, 154
ground beetles, *220*
ground speed, measurement of, 268-269
groundwater
  as livestock water source, 158
  pesticide leaching into, 27, *257*
  protection of, 159
gullies
  creation of, 10
  prevention of, 105
gully erosion, 10
gutters, 163

hairy vetch, as cover crop, 48
harvest
  distribution of residue at, 6-8
  estimation of residue cover after, 18-22,
    19 (table)
  scouting weeds before, 229
  of trees, 71-72
haulback tank mixes, disposal of, 285
hazardous wastes, disposal of, 281-284, 285-
    286, 287-289, 290-293
hemp dogbane, 11, 238
Hepatitis non-A: waterborne, 162 (table)
herbicides. *See also* weed control
  adjuvant use with, 231
  application in contour stripcropping, 97
  changes in use of, 223
  and cultivation, 242, 243-244
  impact on earthworms, 251
  in no-till farming, 238-242
  reducing rates of, 230-232, 233-234,
    235 (table)
  resistance to, 230
  runoff potential of, 26, 258 (table)
  selection of, 260-261
  split applications of, 232
Hessian flies, 208 (table), 213 (table)
highly erodible land (HEL), plant selection
  for, 53
holding ponds, 166, 169-171, *170*

Illinois
  container recycling program in, 283
  environmental concerns in, 248

fertilizing with delayed planting schedules
    in, 140
  herbicide use in, 223
  insect control in, 196, 210
  insecticide use in, 189
  maximum distances between sod strips in,
    99 (table)
  maximum slope lengths for contouring in,
    91 (table), 95 (table)
  no-till farming in, *14*, 16-17
  organic matter retention in, *44*
  pesticide container disposal in, 283, 284
  seed mixes for grassed waterways in, 82,
    82 (table)
  vegetative filter strip regulations in, 175
incorporation, of fertilizers, 147
Indiana
  insect control in, 196-197, 210
  insecticide use in, 189
  no-till farming in, *14*
injection. *See also* direct injection
  of fertilizers, 147
  of manure, 185-186
insect control. *See also* insecticides
  by beneficial insects, 218-222, *220-221*
  by crop rotation, 51, 210-211, 212-
    213 (table)
  economic thresholds for, 198-201, *200*, 201-
    204 (table)
  by fall tillage, 11
  with insect-resistant crop varieties, 205-206,
    207-209 (table)
  in pasture renovation, 67
  by scouting fields, 190-195, 196-197,
    301-302
  by spot treatment, 214-217, 219
insect traps, 195, 215, *215*
insecticides. *See also* insect control
  changes in use of, 189
  impact on earthworms, 251, 252 (table)
  minimizing application of, 218-219
  runoff potential of, 258-259 (table)
  toxicity of, 249 (table), 251, 252 (table)
intercropping, 211. *See also* stripcropping
intermittent streams, 276, 278
Iowa
  container recycling program in, 283
  environmental concerns in, 248
Iowa
  insecticide use in, 189
  nitrogen testing in, 133, 134
  no-till farming in, *14*, 42
Iowa State University, 134, 135, 199, 243, 248
irrigation, application of manure
    with, 185

Japanese beetles, 197, 202 (table), 203 (table)
jet-spray system, 281-282, *282*
jimsonweed, 227 (table)
John Deere, Inc., 148
johnsongrass, 236, 240
jug-rinsing system, 282

key lines, for contour farming, *92*, 92-93, 95, *96*
kickers, definition of, 80

ladino clover, as cover crop, 48
lady beetles, *220, 221*
lakes and reservoirs. *See also* farm ponds
    nonpoint pollution of, 2, 3, *3*
    setback zones around, 278
lambsquarters, 227 (table), 231, 232, 236
land improvement contractors, hiring of, 81, 104
Laspeyresia pomonella (codling moth), *200*
leaching, prevention of, 186
leafhoppers, 67. *See also* potato leafhoppers
legumes
    as cover crop, 47, 48
    critical area plantings of, 87
    in crop rotation, 50, 210
    general forage characteristics of, 57 (table)
    nitrogen contribution from, 139, 139 (table)
    as pasture plants, 53, 55 (table), 56, 56 (table), 57 (table), 59, 59 (table), 60, 60 (table)
    response to soil drainage characteristics, 56 (table)
Leptinofarsa decemlineata (Colorado potato beetle), *200*
line-point method (estimation of residue cover), 18, 22, 28-30, *29*
liquid fertilizers, as an adjuvant, 231
liquid manure, nutrient content of, 178-179, 181 (table)
livestock. *See also* grazing
    fencing of, 67, 70, 116, 118, 156-159
    management of waste of, 155-187
    microorganisms in waste of, 161, 162 (table)
    selecting pasture species for nutrient requirements of, 53, *54*
    water sources for, 158-159, 160
Livestock Waste Facilities (MidWest Plan Service), 163, 171, 180

macropores, definition of, 26, 42
manure
    application of, 169-170, 178-181, 182-183, 184 (table), 185-187
    clogging of drainage systems by, 120
    collecting and storing runoff contaminated with, 166, 167-171
    composting of, 165-166
    nitrogen contribution from, 139-140
    nutrient content of, 139-140, 178-179, 180 (table), 181 (table)
    pathogens in, 161, 162 (table)
    storage of, 172-174
    timing of application of, 186-187
marestail (horseweed), 238
mastitis, prevention of, 156
maximum contaminant level (MCL), 231
methylated seed oils, 231
Mexican bean beetles, 208 (table)
Michigan
    composting in, 165-166
    nitrogen testing in, 133
Michigan State University, 165-166
microorganisms
    benefits of, 43
    impact of crop rotation on, 52
    in livestock waste, 161, 162 (table)
    survival of, 43
MidWest Plan Service, 158, 159, 163, 171, 301, 303
Milwaukee, drinking water contamination in, 161
Minnesota, organic matter retention in, *44*
minute pirate bugs, *220*
Missouri
    channelization in, 127
    cover crops in, 46
    no-till farming in, *14*
morningglory, 227 (table), 232
Morrow Plots, organic matter retention in, *44*
motor oil, disposal of, 290
mulching
    of water and sediment control basin banks, 111
    of critical area plantings, 88
    of grade control structure banks, 108
    of grassed waterways, 83
mulch-till farming, definition of, 36

narrow-base terraces, 102, *102*
National Pesticide Telecommunications
  Network, 300
Natural Resources Conservation Service
  (NRCS), USDA, 28, 35, 78, 86, 91-92, 95,
  99, 104, 108, 109, 110, 112, 126, 175,
  176, 254, 261, 278, 279, 296, 299-300
Nebraska
  environmental concerns in, 248
  no-till farming in, *14*
  selecting pesticides in, 260-261
  yield goals in, 130
nitrate, residual, 140
nitrate-N
  contamination of surface water by, 119
  movement of, 141-142
nitrification
  description of, 141, *141*
  inhibitors of, 142-143, 186
nitrogen (N)
  alternative sources of, 139-140
  application of, 88, 142-144, 145-146, 147,
    150, 154
  capture with constructed wetlands, 89
  capture with filter strips, 85, 86 (table)
  contamination of surface water by, 119, 129
  cost of, 129
  in cover crops, 46, 48
  GPS mapping of, 150
  impact of crop rotation on, 52
  impact on vegetative filter design, 176
  losses during land application of manure,
    187 (table)
  philosophy for use of, 137
  recommendations for adjusting for legumes,
    139, 139 (table)
  recommendations for adjusting for manure,
    139-140
  selection of fertilizers for, 141-144
  soil testing for, 132-135
  from timberland, 68
  yield goals and, 130-131, 139
nonpoint pollution
  causes of, 2-3
  definition of, 2
northern corn rootworms, 51, 210, 212 (table).
  See also corn rootworms
Norwalk virus, 162 (table)
no-till farming
  benefits of, 1, 2, 16-17
  and distribution of crop residue, 6-8
  increasing use of, 13, *14-15*
  of pasture slopes, 66
  soil tilth (health) improvements with, 42-
    43, *44*, 45 (table)

weed control in, 238-242
  yield improvements with, 16-17
nutrients. *See also* fertilizer
  for grassed waterways, 83
  inventory of, 178-180, 180 (table),
    181 (table)
  management of, 129-154
  monitoring levels of, 132-136

oats
  aggressive weed competition from, 236
  as cover crop, 245-246
ochre, accumulations of, 121
Ohio
  cover crops in, 46
  environmental concerns in, 248
  erosion rates and fencing in, 156
  no-till farming in, *14*
  vegetative filter strips in, 86, 86 (table)
Ohio State University, 51, 233
oil filters, disposal of, 291
organic matter
  benefits of, 43, 45 (table), 52
  effect of tillage on, 43, *44*
  impact of crop rotation on, 52
  and prevention of soil compaction, 75
organic wastes, nitrogen contribution from, 140
overtopping, definition of, 104
overwintering, definition of, 21

P-1 test, 135, 165
paddocks
  definition of, 62
  fencing of, *65*, 157
  number of, 64
  size and stocking rate of, 64, *65*
paint, disposal of, 292
parallel-tile-outlet (PTO) terraces, 101
paraquat, 256
parasites (insects), 218
pasture plants
  annual, 58-61
  boot and bud dates of, 54-56, 55 (table),
    58-59, 59 (table), 60 (table)
pasture plants
  general characteristics of, 57 (table)
  livestock requirements of, 53, 54 (table)
  perennial, 53-57
  response to soil drainage, 56, 56 (table)
pastures, renovation of, 66-67
pathogens, in livestock waste, 161,
  162 (table)
pea aphids, 209 (table)
percent surface cover method (estimation of
  residue cover), 18-25

perennial streams, 276, 278
persistence, of pesticides, 256
pest control. *See* disease control; insect control; insecticides; pesticides; weed control
pesticide rinse water, disposal of, 282, 285-286, *286*
pesticides
    application near farm ponds, 116
    custom application of, 1, 274-275
    direct injection of, 270-272
    disposal of containers for, 281-284
    disposal of excesses of, 285-286
    persistence of, 256
    rinse pads for safe handling of, 286, *287*, 287-289, *288*, 301
    runoff potential of, 255-256, *257*, 258-259 (table)
    safe handling of, 263-289
    selection of, 247-261
    setback zones for, 276-280
    soil adsorption (K_{oc}) of, 255-256, 258-259 (table)
    sprayer calibration for, 264-267
    toxicity of, 248-250, 249 (table), 251, 252 (table)
    water solubility of, 256, 258-259 (table), 263
pheromone traps, 195
phosphate, 136
phosphorus (P)
    application of, 147, 180
    desirable levels of, 66, 165
    environmental impact of, 129
    levels in manure, 180 (table), 181 (table)
    GPS mapping of, 150, 153
    impact of crop rotation on, 52
    philosophy for use of, 137-138
    reductions with filter strips, 86 (table)
    testing for, 132, 135
photovoltaic (solar electric) power, 159
picket dams, for semi-solid manure storage, 172
pigweed, 227 (table), 236
pipes, 106, *107*
planting equipment, residue preservation with, 39-41. *See also* farm equipment
plastic sheet method (of manure application calibration), 182-183
Plathypena scabra (green cloverworm), *191, 200*
plow pan, reducing the formation of, 75
plowing. *See* farm equipment; field cultivators; tillage

pollutants, *See* erosion: fertilizers; manure; herbicides; insecticides; pesticides
pollution. *See* nonpoint pollution
polysaccharides, production of, 43
ponds. *See* farm ponds
postemergence herbicides, 231-232, 238, 240, 242
potassium (K)
    desirable levels of, 66
    GPS mapping of, 150
    philosophy for use of, 137-138
    testing for, 132, 135
potato leafhoppers, 204 (table), 208 (table), 209 (table)
precision farming. *See* global positioning system (GPS)
predators (insect), 218
predatory mites, *221*
prescription farming. *See* global positioning system (GPS)
pre-sidedress nitrogen test, 133-134
pressure-rinsing system, 281-282
Private Water Systems (MidWest Plan Service), 158
Purdue University, 144 (table), 196-197

ragweed, 227 (table), 232
rainwater (rainfall). *See also* splash erosion
    diversion of, 163
    erosion from, 9, 34
    impact on holding pond design, 170
    impact on vegetative filter design, 176
recycling
    of batteries, 292
    of oil, 290
    of pesticide containers, 283
red clover
    as cover crop, 48
    as pasture plants, 66, 67
reservoirs. *See* lakes and reservoirs
residue
    from cover crops, 49
residue
    distribution of, 6-8
    equipment adjustments for preservation of, 36-41, 36 (table)
    measurement (estimation) of coverage by, 18-22, 19 (table), 23-25 (table), 28-30, *29*
    organic matter impacted by, 43, *44*, 45 (table)
    problems caused by, 6
    reduction of runoff by, 26-27, 73, 254
    soil temperature impacted by, 43
    types of, 19 (table), *31-33*
    water availability impacted by, 42

Revised Universal Soil Loss Equation
   (RUSLE), 34
rill erosion, 9
rinse pads, 286, *287*, 287-289, *288*, 301
rippers (subsoilers)
   prevention of soil compaction with, 76
   residue preservation with, 38, 39
rivers and streams
   channelization of, 123, 127-128, 277-278
   nonpoint pollution of, *2*, 2-3
   pollutants in, 160
   setback zones around, 277-278
   stabilization of crossings of, 159
roof gutters and downspouts, 163
roofed semi-solid manure storage, 172-173
rotary hoes, 244
rotation
   of crops, 50-52, 95, 210-211,
      212-213 (table), 232, 238-242
   of grazing, 62-65, *63*, 67
Rotavirus, 162 (table)
rove beetles, *221*
row cleaners, residue preservation with, *40*,
   40-41
row cultivators. *See* field cultivators
ruminants. *See* livestock
runoff
   calculating pesticide's potential for,
      255-256, *257*, 258-259 (table)
   calculating soil's potential for, 253-254
   capture of, 42, 85, 167-171
   diversions of, 163-164
   erosion from, 9-10, 46, 73
   impact on vegetative filter design, 176
   pesticide amounts in, 26-27
rye, as cover crop, 46-47, 245

Safe Drinking Water Hotline, 301
safety
   for distribution of residue, 8
   for handling pesticides, 263-289
Salmonella sp., 162 (table)
satellites. *See* global positioning system (GPS)
scouting fields
   equipment for, 301-302
   for insect control, 190-195, *194*, 196-197
   for weed control, 224-229, 234
sedimentation
   description of, 10
   of drainage systems, 120-121
   prevention of, 68, 85
seed mixes
   for grassed waterways, 82, 82 (table)
   for vegetative filter strips, 176

semi-solid manure, storage of, 172-173
setback zones, for pesticides, 276-280
settling tanks and basins, 166, 167-169, *168*
seven spotted lady beetles, *221*
sex pheromone traps, 195
shade trees, benefits of, 68
shattercane, 226 (table), 236, 240
sheet erosion, 9
Shigella sp., 162 (table)
sidedressing, of nitrogen, 145-146
siltation, pollution from, 2-3
site-specific application. *See* global positioning
   system (GPS)
slopes. *See also* grade control structures
   application of manure on, 185
   contour farming on, 76, 91-94, 91
      (table), 95, 95 (table)
   key lines on, *92*, 92-93, *96*
   protection of, 66
   relationship to soil erodibility, 34
   terracing of, 85, 92, 95, *100*, 100-
      104, *102*
   tillage on, 37
   vegetative filter strips on, 85
small mammal habitat, preservation
   of, 156
smartweed, 227 (table), 232
sod webworms, 212 (table)
soil
   compaction of (*See* soil compaction)
   density of, 12
   erosion of (*See* erosion)
   fertilization of, 137-138
   health of (*See* soil tilth)
   infiltration rate of, 42, 74, 85, 176
   organic matter in (*See* organic matter)
   runoff potential of, 253-254
   temperature of, 43
soil adsorption (K_{oc}), of pesticides, 255-256
   257, 258-259 (table)
soil compaction
   causes of, 253-254
soil compaction
   disadvantages of, 74
   evidence of, 12
   measurement of, 12, 77
   prevention of, 11-12, 74-76, 254
soil cone penetrometer, 12, 77
soil drainage. *See also* drainage systems
   of compacted soil, 74
   selecting pasture species based on, 56,
      56 (table)
   selecting pesticides based on, 253-254
soil erodibility factor, 34, 151
soil maps, 130, 150

soil moisture
    of compacted soil, 74
    impact of cover crops on, 47, 48, 49
soil pH
    for pasture renovation, 66
    testing for, 132, 136
soil testing, 132-136, 150, 153-154
soil tilth (health), improvement of,
    42-43, *44*, 45 (table)
solar electric (photovoltaic) power, 159
solid manure
    nutrient content of, 179, 180 (table)
    storage of, *173*, 173-174, *174*
solvents and cleaners, disposal of, 292
Southern Illinois University, 281
soybeans
    aggressive weed competition from, 236
    common insect predators of, *200*,
        203 (table)
    defoliation by insects of, 190, *191*
    insect-resistant varieties of, 208 (table)
    no-till farming of, 13, *14, 15*
    residue levels of, *32*
    rotation of, 212-213 (table)
    scouting insects on, 192, 193
    scouting weeds in, 228
spider mites, 199, 203 (table), 208 (table),
    216-217
spined soldier bugs, *221*
splash erosion, 9
spot treatment
    insect control by, 214-217, 219
    weed control by, 231
spotted alfalfa aphids, 209 (table)
spotted lady beetles, *221*
spring application
    of manure, 186
    of nitrogen, 145-146
stalk borers, 214
stink bugs, 203 (table)
straw choppers (straw spreaders), 6-7, *7*, 8
streambank erosion, control of, 118,
    122-126
streams. *See* rivers and streams
stripcropping, 95-98, *97*, 211
subscription correction signals, 149
subsoilers. *See* rippers (subsoilers)
subsurface drainage systems, 120-121
summer application, of manure, 186
surface application, of manure, 185
surface cover. *See* cover crops; pasture
    plants; residue
surface drainage systems, 121
surface water
    definition of, 2

GPS-related reduction in
    contamination of,150-151
    impact of crop rotation on, 50
    as livestock water source, 158
    nonpoint pollution of, 2
    pesticide risks to, 249 (table), 250
    setback zones around, 276-280
surfactants, 231
sweep nets, 193, *193*
syrphid flies, *221*

terraces
    alternatives to, 109-111
    benefits of, 100
    definition of, 100
    installation of, 104
    maintenance of, 104
    placement of, 85, 92, 95, 103-
        104, 163
    and setback zone placement, 280
    types of, 100-102, *102*
Texas, fencing of farm ponds in, 118
tile surface-water inlets, setback zones
    around, 279-280
tiles, drainage, 80, 85, 89, 101, *101*,
    119-121, 279-280
tillage. *See also* mulch-till farming;
    no-till farming
    angle of, 39
    application of manure with, 185
    avoidance of, 11-12, 49
    costs of, 11
    residue preservation with, 36-39
    and soil compaction, 76
    speed and depth of, 39
timberland
    benefits of, 68
    grazing in, 70
    soil protection from, 68-70, *69*
tires, disposal of, 292
traps, for insects, 195, 215
trees
    benefits of, 68
    critical area plantings of, 87
    damage to subsurface drainage systems from
        roots of, 121
    harvesting of, 71-72
    soil protection from, 68-70, *69*
trichogramma wasps, *221*
triple-rinse procedure, 281
turnstrips, 94, *94*
twice-stabbed lady beetles, *221*
twospotted lady beetles, *221*
twospotted spider mites, 216-217

underground outlets, for gradient terraces, 101, *101*
Universal Soil Loss Equation (USLE), 34
University of Illinois, 11, 89, 119, 144 (table), 145, 151, 190, 197, 231, 243, 272
University of Minnesota, 50
University of Nebraska, 135, 199, 248, 260
urea, 142, 147
urea ammonium nitrate (UAN) solutions, 142
urease inhibitors, 143-144, 144 (table), 147

variable rate technology. *See* global positioning system (GPS)
vegetative filter strips
  benefits of, 85, 156-157, 175
  for handling feedlot runoff, 175-177
  installation of, 171, 175-177
  maintenance of, 87, 176-177
  placement of, 85, 175
  planning (design) of, 86-87, 175-176
  wetlands as, 89-90
  width of, 86, 86 (table)
velvetleaf, 227 (table), 231, 238, *239*
Virginia Polytechnic Institute and State University, 160
volatilization
  of nitrogen, 147
  of pesticides, *257*, 263
  prevention of, 186
volunteer corn, 226 (table)

water. *See also* drinking water; groundwater; runoff; surface water
  availability of, 42
  control of flow of, 73-128
  evaporation of, 42
  for livestock, 158-159
water and sediment control basins
  benefits of, 109
  construction of, 111
  maintenance of, 111
  planning (design) of, 109-111, *110*
water solubility, of pesticides, 256, 258-259 (table), 263
water-retention structures. *See* farm ponds
watershed, definition of, 115
waterways, grassed
  benefits of, 78
  installation of, 78-83
  maintenance of, 83-84
  placement of, 108, 164
  setback zones around, 279
  shape and size of, 78-81, *79*
  as terrace outlets, 100, *100*

weed control. *See also* herbicides
  by aggressive crop competition, 236-237
  by cover crops, 47, 245-246
  by crop rotation, 51, 232
  by fall tillage, 11
  in grassed waterways, 83
  in no-till farming, 238-242
  by scouting fields, 224-229, 234, 301-302
  by spot treatment, 231
weed maps, 224, 229
WeedSOFT (University of Nebraska), 260-261
weirs, 105, *105*
western corn rootworms, 189, 196-197, 210, 212-213 (table)
wetlands, constructed, 89-90
Wetlands Reserve Program, 89
wheat
  as cover crop, 245
  insect-resistant varieties of, 208 (table)
  residue levels of, *33*
  rotation of, 212-213 (table)
white grubs, 192, 212 (table)
willows (willow posts), to control streambank erosion, 118, 122-126, *124*, 128
winter application, of manure, 187
wirestem muhly, 240
wireworms, 192, 202 (table), 212 (table), 214-215
Wisconsin, nitrogen testing in, 133, 134, 134 (table)
wood preservatives, disposal of, 293

yellow woollybear (*Diacrisia virginica*), *200*
yield
  GPS monitoring of, 17, 130-131, 150, 153-154
  impact of crop diversity on, 211
  impact of crop rotation on, 50
  impact of weeds on, 225-229, 226 (table), 227 (table)
  setting goals for, 130-131
yield maps, 130-131, 154

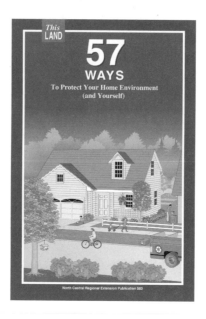

For the home:

57 Ways to Protect Your Home Environment (and Yourself)

- Create a beautiful and diverse landscape.
- Cut back or eliminate pesticide use in the home, yard, and garden.
- Recycle and dispose of household waste, yard waste, and hazardous chemicals.
- Reduce the risk of indoor contaminants, such as dust, radon, lead, asbestos, and formaldehyde.
- Save money by conserving energy and water.

57 Ways to Protect Your Home Environment (and Yourself) (NCR 583)
310 pages
Over 100 photos and illustrations
Only $8.00

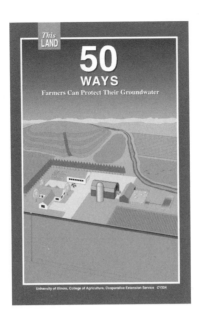

For the farm:

50 Ways Farmers Can Protect Their Groundwater

- Cut back on pesticides without giving up yields or profitability.
- Manage nitrogen applications with an eye on your groundwater.
- Protect your well from fertilizers and pesticides.
- Store and dispose of farm chemicals safely.
- Keep your family's drinking water safe.

50 Ways Farmers Can Protect Their Groundwater (NCR 522)
190 pages
Over 60 illustrations and photos
Only $5.00

How to order

To order copies of *50 Ways Farmers Can Protect Their Groundwater* and *57 Ways to Protect Your Home Environment (and Yourself)*, or additional copies of *60 Ways Farmers Can Protect Surface Water*, call: 800-345-6087
University of Illinois Extension, Urbana, Illinois

Save money by ordering the complete set of three books (SET600) for only $19.00.

Bulk discounts are available. Visa and MasterCard accepted.